30-SECOND POLITICS

30-SECOND POLITICS
Political Advertising in the Eighties

Montague Kern

New York
Westport, Connecticut
London

Library of Congress Cataloging-in-Publication Data

Kern, Montague, 1942–
    30–second politics : political advertising in the eighties /
Montague Kern.
    p. cm.
  Bibliography: p
    ISBN 0–275–93194–3 (alk. paper)—ISBN 0–275–93195–1
(pbk. : alk. paper)
    1. Television in politics—United States. 2. Advertising,
Political—United States. 3. United States—Politics and
government—1981– I. Title. II. Title: Thirty second politics.
HE8700.76.U6K47   1989
324.7'3'0973—dc19   88–34250

Library of Congress Catalog Card Number: 88–34250
ISBN: 0–275–93194–3
    0–275–93195–1 (pbk.)

First published in 1989

Praeger Publishers, One Madison Avenue, New York, NY 10010
An imprint of Greenwood Publishing Group, Inc.

Printed in the United States of America

The paper used in this book complies with the Permanent
Paper Standard issued by the National Information Standards
Organization (Z39.48-1984).

10 9 8 7 6 5 4 3 2

For Charlie,
my husband

Contents

Illustrations

Acknowledgments

Four and a half years in the making, this book would not have been possible without the assistance of many individuals: sources, colleagues, friends, editors, and students.

Peter Braestrup of *Wilson Quarterly* arranged for me to examine the media research literature at the Woodrow Wilson International Center for Scholars in the winter and spring of 1984. Jon Vondracek and Wilson Dizard made it possible for me to prepare a study of the research literature on political advertising and election news for the Georgetown Center for Strategic and International Studies Commission on National Elections during the summer of 1984. Tatyana Mishel was my research assistant on the commission study and worked with me as I launched an independent book project in September 1984. In December 1984, and again during the 1985 spring semester under the sponsorship of Kurt and Gladys Lang, co-chairs of the Department of Communications at the University of Washington, Tatyana participated in research trips to North Carolina, Georgia, and California and contributed to the development of a coding design for the 1984 ad sample. In 1987 film producer Lisa Strasbourg offered insights during my work on the *Campaigns and Elections* film *1986 Political Advertising Classics*. *Campaigns and Elections* also sponsors an annual conference in Washington on the electoral process from which valuable insights were gleaned.

The D.C. Community Humanities Council, an affiliate of the National Endowment for the Humanities, awarded me a major grant for the 1984–85 academic year to develop a school curriculum on media-societal interaction. This support was invaluable, as it enabled me, like the Republicans that year, to see the "future in the eyes of our youth"—eyes that are increasingly glued to the television set. The result was a renewed commitment to understand video aspects of the electoral process that will increasingly be present at the creation of all of our lives. I am grateful for this funding, which provided me with the support necessary to persevere with the book project.

Various colleagues and friends have kindly offered critiques of chapters of this book that were presented at various academic gatherings: Lynda Lee Kaid of the University of Oklahoma; Robert Savage of the University of Arkansas; Jarol Manheim of George Washington University; David Paletz of Duke University; Marion Just of Wellesley College; Mike Caspar of Carleton College; Larry Sabato of the University of Virginia; Joel Swerdlow of the Annenberg Washington Program; Noell Markwell of the International Society for Political Psychology; and David Beiler and Robert Deutsch, who are both consultants and authors. Anonymous readers of various drafts of the manuscript also offered useful guidance.

Other colleagues and friends have contributed ideas at various stages in my thinking about the mass media and politics: Doris A. Graber, University of Illinois at Chicago Circle; William C. Adams and Stephanie Larsen, George Washington University; Michael Robinson of Georgetown University; Patti Gillespie and Leonard Shyles of the University of Maryland; Hamid Mowlana of the American University School of International Service; Jannette L. Dates, Howard University; Anne Johnston Wadsworth, University of North Carolina; Kurt Ritter, Texas A&M University; Jeff McCall, Depauw University; and Mary Lou Galician, Arizona State University.

I would also like to thank three individuals from the American University School of Communication: Sanford Ungar, Dean, referee of numerous and invariably stimulating panels on mass media and elections; Louis Wolfson, the journalist and author of *The Untapped Power of the Press: Explaining Government to the People* (Praeger, 1985), whose concern for quality political reporting is unremitting; and Simi Edelstein, the student who served as my research assistant in 1987. Pat Shakow, a member of the editorial board of the *Washington Post,* also offered invaluable support during one stage in the evolution of my thinking about political advertising. Judith Whittlesey, press secretary to Joan Mondale, was also gracious with her assistance.

Furthermore, I want to say that without the cooperation of the numerous sources who shared their analysis of a wide range of political campaigns, either in interviews with me, or at various academic and professional conferences in the Washington area between 1984 and 1988, it would not have been possible to write this book. A complete list of such interviews and sources is in Appendix A.

I would like to mention here, however, with particular appreciation, a few of the political consultants who generously shared their time with me: Ed Blakely, Bob Beckel, Roger Ailes, Betsy and Ian Weinschel, Lou Kitchen, Doug Watts, Paul Sipple, John Franzen, Frank Greer, Michael Fenenbock, Richard Leone, Dan Payne, Frank Luntz, Dennis Woods, Randy Moorehead, Paul Curcio, Karl Struble, Bill Pope, Tim Ryles, Claiburn Darden, William Zimmerman, Stuart Mollrich, Michael Berman, Mike Gage, Jules Radcliff, Gary Pearce, Joe Grimsley, Gordon Durnil, Jeff Browne, Greg Fleetwood, Dick Dresner, Jay Townsend, and the late Dick Sykes. In this book it has not been possible to do justice to all of the ideas expressed to the author by this body of creative individuals. Nor, given the constraints of time and resources, has it been possible to interview all of the consultants who would make a worthy contribution to analysis of the subject. Clearly, the efforts of researchers to understand the role of media in the campaign process have just begun.

For their interest during the final year of this project, I also wish to thank several of my colleagues at Towson State University with whom I have had the chance to interact profitably: Ronald A. Matlon, Peter Lev, Richard Vatz, Phyllis Bosley, John MacKerron, Jim Kim, Brenda Logue, and Charles Flippen, from the Department of Speech and Mass Communication; and political scientists Michael Grossman and Martha Joynt Kumar. I also wish to especially thank the Towson State University Faculty Research Committee, which in the fall of 1988 generously awarded me a grant to extend my research to the 1988 presidential election, which emerged as a logical outcome to the trends described in this book. Findings for 1988, which extend well beyond those which it was possible to include in this study, will be the subject of a future publication.

Susan Pazourek, former editor at Praeger Publishers, provided support for the project at a critical juncture. For their expert assistance, Praeger editors James Himber and Frank Welsch, as well as copy editor Krystyna Budd, are also to be commended.

Alfred Wellons helped direct me to individuals with whom I could speak concerning Jim Hunt's 1984 Senate race. Help with the taping of the 1984 ads and news came from: Bill and Lois Van Hoy of Asheboro, North Carolina; Larry Leuszler of Stone Mountain and Atlanta, Georgia; Alton A. and Elizabeth Lindsey of West Lafayette, Indiana; and Frank Levering and Wanda Urbanska of Los Angeles, California and Orchard Gap, Virginia. Wilton J. Lindsey prepared the first draft of the figures and tables. Invaluable bibliographic and other assistance came from Al Christensen and David Freeman.

Sandra and John Dewey, of Washington, D.C., and my parents, kindly offered the shelter of their homes for unadulterated thought during critical periods. To all of my extended family, including Carol Lindsey, I am grateful for many favors great and small, most of which derive from a common tenacity and kindly spirit. My sons, Chris, Alex, and Deane Kern were present as the sun both rose and set on this project, and were frequent contributors to it. Chris also helped with the research in Atlanta, Georgia. Last, but not least, my husband, Charles E. Kern II, was extremely generous with his time and talent as this project evolved. Whether it was reviewing the data from the 1984 and 1986 ad samples, keeping the printer functioning, helping with bibliographic material, or providing the final, incisive editorial comment, his presence was felt throughout. It is to him that this book is dedicated.

This book is clearly a collective effort. All of its flaws, however, are my own.

30-SECOND POLITICS

1

Introduction: Has Political Advertising Changed since 1972?

In North Carolina a pregnant woman appears on the television screen, pats her very large abdomen, and announces that *she* cares about human life and here's one vote—no, *two*—for the congressional challenger who agrees with her, unlike the incumbent who has voted in favor of federal funds for abortion. In central Indiana a congressman, slipping in the polls, airs an ad that uses harsh sounds and the color black and focuses on the amount of political action committee (PAC) money his opponent has received from big utility companies, posing the question of whose interests he might serve.

These ads and thousands of others like them were created for 1984 congressional candidates from different parties and regions of the country. They illustrate two facts of political life in the 1980s that are the subject of this book. One is the widespread use of negative appeals. A second is that while issues are mentioned in the ads, conveying information is not their sole purpose.

There are three components in televised political advertising used in today's competitive elections: an *entertainment* device designed to arouse and hold the viewer's attention: a *message,* frequently about character as well as an issue in a process that might be dovetailing; and an *attempt to provoke a reaction,* surprise, excitement, recognition, affect, or an action message.

On the positive side, image making in the 1980s is highly personal, centered on intergenerational bonding and a focus on home as it is or ought to be, whether the cloud-swept mountains of your state or the front porch with the bright orange pumpkin and shocks of corn your mother set out to commemorate the harvest. Ads appeal to what commercial advertisers call experience, which is associated with affect: It is hope and reassurance directed to young people, many of whom have experienced the effects of dislocation and divorce, and to the old, who, as the 1984 Reagan ads proclaim, can see the future in the "bright eyes of our young." Intergenerational bonding focuses around the men, however, as women candidates are more hesitant to emphasize the caring side of their character for fear of appearing weak. The ironic result is that although women are disproportionately responsible for meeting daily family needs, men reap the political benefit by winning the female as well as the male vote.

Ads are believed by many consultants to be most effective if the issue and the character side of their overall message are complementary, or dovetail. Thus, family members frequently present the candidate's position on the issues. Who better than the son can testify to the fact that Dad is tightfisted, the necessary character side of the tax issue? Who better than the daughter or candidate's mother can more authentically testify that he would never cut Social Security? Image and issue messages commingle and reinforce each other for maximum impact.

Personal issues are thus squarely at the heart of politics, and increasingly personal ways are being found to present the candidate as a leader who will address them. Thus, many candidates operated in 1986 on the analysis circulated by the Democratic National Committee, that a Republican issue such as crime was really about parenting. In the 1980s fatherhood staged a comeback not only on the Bill Cosby Show but as a key ingredient in candidate messages, whether in the 1984 advertising of Ronald Reagan or Jesse Helms, described in this analysis, or in the 1988 ads of George Bush and Michael Dukakis, who had learned the lessons of 1984. Framing a message so as to relate to voters' personal lives, whether it involves a teary-eyed reference to one's father in a presidential nomination acceptance speech or an appearance at a day-care center, is essential to the language of politics in the 1980s.[1]

THE MYTHIC WORLD AS IT IS OR OUGHT TO BE

Political advertising has well been described as drawing on political culture, and a body of research literature has begun to focus on myths. Political advertising utilizes a variety of entertainment themes and techniques drawn not only from national myths relating to political institutions or small-town life but also from popular culture as expressed on television. Consultants have come to believe that it must do as well as commercial advertising in holding and motivating the viewer. Just as what are described in this book as *hard-sell* negative ads utilize suspense genres, including "scary" music and sounds to shake patterns of belief and tap existing uncertainties, *soft-sell* positive and negative ads rely heavily on humor and storytelling devices, even to the extent of including heroic myths and animal fables.

Thus, in California in 1986 we saw Senator Alan Cranston appear in timeless, mythical advertising whose camera angles depicted the candidate from the vantage point of a child, and in 1984 in western North Carolina we heard the cautionary tale of 11th District incumbent Democratic congressman Jim Clarke's frog. The frog, according to Lou Kitchen, media consultant to Republican challenger Billy Hendon, was casting a "spell" on the race. Hendon was charging Clarke with being a liberal and supporting Walter Mondale's tax plan. According to Kitchen, nothing worked, despite the "coattails" of the popular president, as the numbers kept moving back and forth, within a range of a few percentage points:

It was his frog, the frog he had coming on television every night, staring people in the face, going garumph, garumph, and saying "Jamie Clarke is as liberal as I am beautiful." Finally, we decided to have our candidate hold a news conference, and we planted a question with a reporter: "Mr. Hendon," he inquired, "what do you think of Jamie Clarke's frog?" "Sir," replied Billy, "Jamie Clarke can have his frog, but I've got Ronald Reagan."

That got headlines all over the district: CLARKE SUPPORTED BY FROG, RONALD REAGAN BACKS HENDON. That news conference broke the frog's spell. We finally pulled ahead and won.[2]

If a frog fable tells us anything, it is that supplying voters with information about candidate positions on issues is only one component in the advertising Triad of the 1980s. While it may be an important one, it is also sandwiched between other elements that include humor, myth, storytelling, doomsday music, and suspense motifs, all of which may obscure the fact that a message about a political candidate is involved until well after the viewer has been drawn fully into the "experience" of the ad.

The "experience" is one which, if it relates to myth or fable, will involve a moral lesson and thereby, in the case of myth, possible individual "empowerment." Heroes in myths, and candidates such as Ronald Reagan and Jesse Helms, whose efforts are examined in this research, run as mythic heroes, lending significance to the voters' lives through their courage and willingness to sacrifice. By exercising initiative, and placing their lives at risk, they achieve results, representing all who identify with them in the narrative. But, as Jerome Bruner has pointed out, the power of myth is that it "lives on the feather line between fantasy and reality. It must be neither too good nor too bad to be true, nor must it be too true." The source of authority of a mythic story is usually anonymous, and its power derives from the fact that if it is not true, it is "true to life." In other words, it presents a moral lesson. Its power is pedagogic, like that of the frog—or, more broadly, like today's political advertising as a whole, whose purpose is persuasive.[3]

If the frog points to the pedagogic role of myth and fable, it also points to another trend in political advertising, the disappearing candidate as "politician." It is a major conclusion of this book that in 1984 other groups that aggregate voter interests joined political party identification in the institutional advertising fade-out of the 1980s. Positive appeals may use general national symbols, the Statue of Liberty, or the mythic halls within which the congressman walks. But the appeal is to the lone individual, and identifiable interest groups were relegated to negative rather than positive advertising, save in the advertising of Democratic presidential candidate Walter Mondale, whose race, examined in Chapter 4, served more as a negative than a positive example for later candidates and their consultants.[4]

In the individualistic and entertainment-oriented environment within which messages are now formulated, it is no wonder that both character-based and single-issue campaigning have become an increasing focus of concern. Indeed, with the triumph by 1976 of the commercial 30-second spot, the cost of airing the longer ads, which were a staple of advertising in 1972 and earlier, became prohibitive below the presidential and heavily funded statewide levels. But it was clear from the Reagan campaign, which used the lengthier format in both 1980 and the 1984 advertising examined in this book, that even the longer ads, which in the 1970s relied heavily on the news documentary format, have absorbed the techniques of commercial advertising.[5]

Chapters 6 through 9, which draw on case studies of political advertising strategies on the presidential, senatorial, and House of Representatives levels, point to another dilemma raised by today's ads: the difficulty of explaining "new" or complex ideas. Successful commercial advertising relies on simple, repeated ideas. Why should it be otherwise in a political message that must compete for attention with commercial ones?

THE RESEARCH AGENDA

Research for this book began in the summer of 1984 with two questions: How important has televised political advertising become in the total network informational mix viewed by the U.S. voter in the mid-1980s? What impact does it have on the campaign process? Over a decade had passed since the question was first asked by Thomas Patterson and Robert McClure in *The Unseeing Eye* (1976). They examined the political ads and news that appeared on the air during the 1972 presidential election and concluded that ads were primarily oriented to communicating substantive candidate issue positions: further, that ads rather than news were for U.S. voters the primary source of information about election issues. Indeed, in comparison with news, the primary impact of ads was to educate voters about campaign issues. The authors reached this conclusion by tallying the total time devoted to issues in presidential ads and news during the final weeks of the election and then querying the media consultants about their objectives.[6]

The consultants said the purpose of their ads was to inform voters about candidate positions on the issues. The fact that 40 percent of the ads were longer, frequently news documentary–style ads, 5 to 30 minutes in length, confirmed this. The authors concluded that overall the ads provided voters with information about campaign issues four times as often as television news. Indeed, their primary impact was informational.

What, then, of the 1980s? Has the nature and significance of advertising changed? From the public perspective, how does advertising stack up as a source of issues information in comparison with news? Is it still possible to argue that its central impact is informational? Finally, how does political advertising fit into overall campaign strategy? What feedback and testing systems exist relating to its use?

Generally, the research literature on political advertising has concerned the presidential level, and Patterson and McClure's conclusion that ads had little effect, influencing "roughly three percent of the total electorate" in 1972, a year when there was a 23 percent spread between presidential candidates Richard Nixon and George McGovern, has engendered little follow-up research on advertising effects using a national sample. Political scientists, who leave political advertising variables out of their large-scale survey research designs, may nevertheless use such data as measures of presidential candidate popularity at the beginning and end of a general election campaign, to argue that ads had *no* effect on campaigns and are a waste of money. Indeed, "mediality" theorists argue that the significance of advertising is minimal. Television news alone has an impact on elections.[7]

Research relating to the sole effect of news on the public agenda, however, ignores human intervention in the form of public relations or "propaganda" campaigns. As Jarol B. Manheim and Robert B. Albritton have established for such efforts undertaken on behalf of foreign governments, these can produce significant results. Federal candidates and their consultants operate on this assumption. Thus, in competitive races the candidates spend two-thirds of their campaign dollar on political ads and related consultant fees, finding changes in public perceptions about themselves and their opponents following ad campaigns, which, as we shall see, are now coordinated with efforts to influence the news.[8]

Ads Have an Impact

Recent research findings indicate why ads have an impact and why researchers should pay more attention to the nature and use of political advertising. A good deal of literature has confirmed that viewers learn about issues from ads. Donald Cundy conducted quasi-experimental research that indicates that ads can influence viewer perceptions of candidates. His research underscores the significance of early candidate image-making efforts, which "are likely to act as an inertia factor, lessening the impact of subsequent propaganda efforts." Although he disagrees with Patterson and McClure on the special significance of presidential advertising, his finding about the importance of candidate imagery confirms their view that early advertising is important before voters have made up their minds. Research by Michael Pfau and Michael Burgoon indicates that "inoculation" messages, which raise a candidate's liabilities early in the campaign, "deflect the persuasiveness of subsequent political attacks." But so long as the "inoculation" message precedes attack, it can also work later in a campaign.[9]

Research has long focused on the significance of advertising for late-deciding voters. Ads are clearly important for late-deciding or uninterested voters. Patrick Devlin, summarizing the literature in this area, has noted that ads "are crucial [to that] 10 to 20 percent of the electorate [who normally] are reached only through television in the last stages of the campaign." [10]

Voter motivation is an important ingredient of response to advertising, as various studies have indicated. Recently, Michael Mansfield and Katherine Hale determined that people will see different aspects of a candidate in spots depending on their personalities. The person watching with the single motive of "current events surveillance" responds differently to ads from those watching television more for entertainment or social reasons. Campaign specialists function on the basis of their research, which suggests that highly partisan individuals are best reached by direct-mail or limited-circulation print media advertising, whereas television ads are most effective with the large body of the U.S. electorate who are *not* partisan and are thus *persuadable*. Cundy reviewed the literature and argues that the sheer "pervasiveness" of spots can overcome selective perception factors. Some commercial advertising research, examined in Chapter 3, involves right-brain, left-brain theory. [11]

If recent research indicates that contemporary political advertising has an impact that includes but is much broader than that of informing the public about candidate positions on the issues, content research based on ads supplied by campaigns also suggests that the purpose of advertising has changed since 1972. It is concerned as much with conveying impressions about candidate character as with providing information about issues. Richard Joslyn has argued that there are four types of ads, with issue statements that are largely sloganistic relating to only two of them: *prospective* and *restrospective* policy satisfaction appeals, as opposed to *election as ritual* and his largest category, *benevolent leader* appeals. More recently, research from Senate campaigns has begun to suggest that issues may in fact be selected and conveyed in ads primarily for the purpose of building candidate character, or image. [12]

Further, now-classic theory of media use argues that there are four types of ads associated with four stages in a campaign: first, *name identification* spots, which are shown early in the campaign; second, *argument* spots, which present candidate positions on issues; third, *attack* spots, which focus on the opponent; and fourth, *positive* visionary appeals, which are used at the end of a campaign to give voters a reason to vote for the candidate. [13]

Such findings indicate that a study of a sample of ads taken from the air a decade after Patterson and McClure's 1972 research would unearth major changes in the nature and use of ads and in the perceptions of their effects. One way to focus on change since 1972 would be to replicate Patterson and McClure's approach, starting with taping the ads and news that appeared on the air during the final period of one election, 1984. I could similarly follow an analysis of the ads with interviews with those responsible for airing them. One thing that could not be attempted in this research, however, was the selection of a panel of voters in the four market areas around the country who could give their views concerning the ads' impact on them. This research, however, did make heavy use of campaign poll results from campaigns on various levels. Lengthy, one-hour to two-hour interviews were conducted with persons involved in nearly all the federal campaigns whose ads were picked in the 1984 ad sample.[14]

Taping Ads and News, Followed by Interviews. Ads in four states aired between 6:00 P.M. and 9:00 P.M. were videotaped during the final ten days of the 1984 election. This was followed by travel to those states immediately after the election, and subsequently to other states as well, to talk with the campaign managers, other campaign figures, media consultants, and in some cases the candidates who shared responsibility for media strategy as well. In all, over 450 media-consultant philosophical statements were examined between 1984 and 1987, either through such interviews or from public lectures conducted in the Washington, D.C., area. Television news station directors were also queried in two states—North Carolina and Indiana—concerning their news coverage in the 1984 ad and news sample. A close analysis of the nature and use of issues first in news and then in ads ran parallel with the ongoing interview process, in relation to social science theory.[15]

One conclusion quickly emerged. It was that although issues were included in the ads, they were just one element in much of the advertising that appeared on the air in the 1984 election. The decision was therefore made to examine visual and aural symbols as well in relation to theory about their nature and effects. Would it be possible to analyze the difference between ads that are broadly termed positive and negative in the original evaluative and affect-laden meaning of that term, focusing not only on issues but also on examination of rhetorical styles relating to the use of sound and visual symbols?

Could one catalogue the aural and visual symbols employed to build or break what Richard Fenno has described as the essential bonds of trust that bind candidate and voter? The question seemed particularly appropriate in a year awash with Reagan "feel-good" advertising, produced by a commercial team that not only pulled out all the musical stops but also quite literally shot film through Vaseline-smeared camera lenses for long-ago-and-far-away nostalgic effects. The question would become doubly relevant by 1989 following an election in which, not just one, but both parties' presidential nominees utilized Madison Avenue and commercially oriented consultants. Appeals to basic human emotions are not confined, however, to consultants who describe themselves as belonging to what media consultant Roger Ailes, who spearheaded Republican presidential candidate George Bush's 1988 election, calls the "feel good-school." For Ailes, who has built his reputation about his ability to respond quickly to a situation, messages must be crystal-clear because "you have to move the needle a long way in a short time." Still, the themes of his advertising campaigns are frequently emotional ones, such as crime in the case of the famous 1988 Willie Horton ad used to attack Democratic presidential candidate Michael Dukakis. According to Ailes, "the candidate who makes the public most secure will win.'' Visual and aural usage would need to be examined for affect, and in relation to issues in what I would find are three varied schools of media consulting.[16]

Finally, for this research the 1984 ads collected from the air and systematically examined for content were compared, albeit less systematically, with a sample of 569 ads produced for the major 1986 statewide and congressional races to determine whether the techniques of 1984 were carried further.

This book, in sum, compares political advertising at a key turning point in the 1980s with that of the 1972 presidential election when Patterson and McClure concluded that the impact of ads was primarily informational and that what they called "mindless," "emotional" 30-second advertising played a minor role.

Multilevel, Multimarket Research. The authors of *The Unseeing Eye* had concentrated on the presidential election and selected a single market area that received the national network news. Multiple broadcasting markets were chosen for the 1984 sample that serves as the core of the present study in order to examine both the presidential race and a broad range of advertising campaigns and to facilitate a parallel consideration of local news, which, with the help of new satellite technologies, was beginning to compete with the national news.

For this study, which sought to focus more broadly than its predecessor on the use of advertising on all levels, a similar decision was made to focus on political advertising during the final period of the 1984 election. But since questions should be raised concerning ad campaigns on all levels, it was decided that four areas (Los Angeles; Atlanta, Georgia; Greensboro, Winston-Salem, and High Point, North Carolina; and Indianapolis and Lafayette, Indiana) should be selected for diversity. Together, these districts represent diversity relating both to balance of competitive and noncompetitive districts, geography, and such demographic factors as urbanization and educational levels.[17]

The content analysis was of the news and advertising that appeared on the air in these areas between 6:00 P.M. and 9:00 P.M. during the final ten days of the 1984 election. The final period of a race is a time of intensified voter interest and corresponding efforts to influence the election through advertising and favorable news coverage. During the 1980s, however, in contrast with 1972, there was an intensification of such phenomena with candidate "fly-arounds" to major media markets. In this research the effort would be to test whether media blitz strategies involving the coordination of news and political advertising under one central direction according to single-message, advertising principles involved only the celebrated Ronald Reagan presidential effort, or were media blitz techniques used on other levels as well.[18]

In this book, I do not attempt to examine all elements of strategy in relation to the 1984 Ronald Reagan re-election effort, although reference is frequently made to path-breaking details of his political ads which were included in the 1984 sample. Attention is paid to the lessons of less well-known campaigns; such as that of his opponent, Walter Mondale; the North Carolina Senate candidates, Democrat Jim Hunt and Republican Jesse Helms; and a number of Congressional races.

It has nevertheless become quite clear that Ronald Reagan's 1984 media blitz strategies, which involved the coordination of news and advertising strategies according to what are essentially single-message, advertising principles, will become the standard against which future political campaigns will be judged on all levels. This is because the 1988 general election campaign of George Bush was able to replicate its success. The failure of the Dukakis campaign, which followed a much more open strategy—of allowing the candidate to make "news"—only serves to focus the crucial question of the degree of use and effectiveness of prior campaign efforts to influence news media coverage of elections.

How frequently were media blitz strategies used in political campaigns in the eighties, and how effective were they in influencing news coverage? The purpose of an abortion ad, such as the one with which I introduced this chapter, might be to obtain news coverage that would facilitate fund-raising, or a news conference might be scheduled to combat a televised frog. But in focusing on the significance of electronic political advertising in the 1980s, it is necessary to examine a campaign's overall effort to influence the press through such strategies as presenting a unified "theme of the day" or "theme of the week." Is advertising successfully being used in a fashion that influences news coverage?

Chapter 3, "Issues in Televised Ads and News," focuses on the amount of news coverage as compared to ads on various levels, and on the significance of issue expression in televised news as compared with advertising. It also focuses for the first time on the *nature* of the issues that appear in both ads and news on the basis of a sample taken from the air. This makes it possible to examine the validity of what might be conceptualized as *thousand-flower* as opposed to *single-issue* theories of issue expression. The former, drawn from the research literature, which has dealt with the presidential primary level, argues that ads "reflect" the major issues of a campaign, at least as they appear in newspapers. Single-issue theory, instead suggests that a central goal of a media campaign is that of developing a "fanatic common thread"—that is successfully turning the discussion in all aired messages to one's own limited number of campaign issues. As shown in Chapter 2, this is a major goal of many competitive campaigns. In Chapter 3, as in Chapter 6 on the presidential level, in Chapter 7 on the Senatorial level, and Chapter 9 on the House level, such questions are also examined by means of case studies drawn from the 1984 ad and news sample.

Do Ads Affect the News?

The final question is, how extensively can a campaign influence the total televised campaign agenda? Is it possible to turn to one's own issue not only the advertising but the news media agenda as well? Or does "mediality" theory developed from research on the presidential level apply on other levels as well? Is it, in short, the news media or the political campaign that determines which issues are discussed on the air and how they are framed? Are there differences between varied campaign levels? Is there a difference between local and national news coverage of campaign issues?

In the 1970s Patterson and McClure examined network news coverage. Since then local news programs, such as those examined in Chapter 3, have become more significant. Further, they will play an increasingly important role by the 1990s because local news programs have gained access to satellite news film programs. This, along with the overall impact of home videos and cable, is having an adverse effect on network news. Indeed, panels are being organized at such gatherings as those of the Broadcast Educators Association to enquire, "Is national news necessary?" In 1984 the Reagan campaign and numerous incumbent congressmen recognized this and fed information to local stations by satellite. By July 1988 a Republican team had invaded the Democratic convention town of Atlanta intent on feeding "their side of the story" to a growing body of local television news reporters.[19]

It is, of course, possible here only to begin to answer all of the questions that should be raised about news and advertising on different levels. Given the limited time frame of this study of the news, and the great number of news stations across the country, much more research will need to be conducted before any firm conclusions can be drawn.

However, the 1984 data indicate that the ads dominated the airtime devoted to news. On the presidential level, the ratio was still 4 to 1, as found by Patterson and McClure in 1972, indicating that not much had changed on that level. Yet on the senatorial level, the ad-news ratio was much higher, 6 to 1. On the level of the House of Representatives, despite the large number of races in which the use of ads is not relevant, they still dominated the televised campaign information agenda by 1½ to 1.

If only ads and news which contain specific information concerning the issues and status of a campaign are considered, however, it is clear that the dominance of ads is even greater. It is not possible to draw comparisons based on previous research on levels below the presidency. The overall conclusion emerges that ads are playing a role that is even more significant as a part of televised campaign information than was the case in the 1970s.[20]

The Growing Significance of Ads

In 1984 ad-driven information was more important to voters than it had ever been before. This is because in 1984 Americans were relying more heavily on television as a source of information than had been the case in 1972. While 97 percent of all homes had a television set, daily newspaper circulation had sharply declined from about one newspaper for every three persons in 1960 to one newspaper for every four persons in 1984. In 1984, of those who responded to a Roper organization poll, 64 percent said they got most of their news from television, and for the first time among persons with a college education television was ahead of newspapers as their preferred source of news by a significant margin, ten points.[21]

This growing reliance on ads during the final stage of a campaign occurred in a climate in which educators deplored the possibility that Americans' reading skills were beginning to atrophy for lack of use. They cited the fact that a growing percentage of U.S. high school graduates and adults were ignorant of such basic facts as when World War II occurred, who U.S. allies are, and where the Persian Gulf is located. Much of the analysis of this phenomenon has focused on the U.S. educational system. But one perspective, offered as usual by that prescient media consultant Tony Schwartz, suggests that the United States is an electronic "post-literate" society in which individuals can function perfectly well without significant amounts of reading and writing. Thus, for better or for worse, they are not reading and writing.[22]

Not only were Americans reading fewer newspapers; they were receiving less information first-hand through involvement in traditional party politics. Further, although the question of how much direct mail voters receive and react to is beyond the scope of this book, it is clear that the pieces they receive are increasingly impersonal and computerized. In the 1980s, for example, no middle-income voters received such typewritten invitations to party functions as the ones that were routinely cohosted by Eleanor Roosevelt and local party officials in honor of John F. Kennedy in 1960. In the 1980s the argument is frequently made that the time of "big name" party leaders and candidates is instead increasingly consumed raising money from the well-to-do to pay for such high-tech appurtenances as direct mail, computers, phone banks, and, most costly of all, television ads and their related consultants and polling technologies. The significance of political advertising operates on many levels.

What one finds is an increasingly video-oriented political environment. The proposition tested here, in comparing the mid-1980s to 1972, is whether this increasingly significant era of 30-second politics is also more focused than before on "intimate" communication, in short, on building and breaking the "ties that bind." To what extent has the formula of the American Telephone and Telegraph (AT&T) company ad "Reach Out, Reach Out and Touch Someone"—starring Grandma in California and Junior, who is off at college—become the language of electoral politics in the 1980s?

In 1972 the media aspect of a campaign could be conceptualized in terms of television news, which, as an "unseeing eye," failed to cover the issues. Fortuitously for the U.S. public, they were covered in the political commercials. But is the time not ripe for a new overarching concept? National news, which is on the list of endangered species, has many virtues. It has improved over the years, including much more well informed and analytical coverage, including that relating to electoral strategy, which can be quite important, but which is generally lumped in coding schemes into a simple bifurcate good and bad dichotomy: issues and horserace coverage. The amount of issues coverage is a significant measure. But what this analysis indicates, if it indicates anything at all, is that coverage of what a campaign does, and how it does it, is important. Nor is it clear at this point that society would be better off entirely with the cable programs and videocassette recordings and local news programs that today represent the major alternative to network news.

The concept that, in fact, best epitomizes the language of televised electoral politics in the 1980s is that of the televised 30-second *appeal,* which, in competitive races, draws on the world of commercial advertising. And, as in the AT&T ad, it may well involve "experience," or "affect," as in "Reach Out, Reach Out and Touch Someone." In fact, has not a *cri de coeur* drawn from the commercial world, *Touching Someone,* emerged as the best metaphor for the new mass media election that is broadly influenced by a merger of political skill with commercial advertising values?

Schools of Consulting

From the work of Patterson and McClure, and from other interviews conducted with consultants in 1972, it is clear that although the lines are blurry because the use of sound and symbols has always been important on the electronic media, in 1972 there were two dominant political advertising philosophies—those of an *emotional* school, which is more influenced by commercial advertising techniques producing what the authors called "mindless" ads, and an *informational* school, which is more focused on issues. The analysis developed here, based on interviews and statements of philosophy by over 40 media consultants with particular attention to the philosophies of "insurgents" who have recently become successful media consultants, tests this proposition: Is there *still* a clear distinction between an emotional and an informational school? Or have other distinctions become more important in the world of media consulting in the 1980s?

Overall, it will be seen that the 1980s have not been like the 1970s. More commercially developed and affect-laden theories have gained the ascendancy. Indeed, there are three major schools of media consulting, which might be termed emotional, new informational, and quick-response. Yet in their different ways, described in Chapter 2, they are all "emotionally" oriented.

Changes in Ad Strategy

In this book much detailed analysis is devoted to an examination of decision making in order to flesh out major as yet unexplored areas of research. These relate to "new" uses of media beyond those suggested in so-called classic theory. They also relate to such questions as *feedback,* or factors, in addition to poll results, that influence media decision making. In some cases, such as those examined in Chapter 9, it is clear that a candidate and his or her consultants can have different views on the nature and use of media. In others, it is clear that the lessons of one year can have a profound impact. [23]

As it turned out, 1984 was just such a year. Classic theory, as outlined by Diamond and Bates, experienced a profound setback, and it was clear that advertising, including negative advertising, would be used in new ways in subsequent elections on all levels.

In 1988 history was made on the presidential level as negative advertising was used early and often in the general election campaign by Republican George Bush. This strategy came as a surprise to some Democratic media consultants. It was definitely a surprise to Democratic candidate Michael Dukakis who still appeared to be influenced by the lessons of his 1982 gubernatorial race: that the press covers such advertising skeptically and critically and that negative campaigning thus backfires. This conventional wisdom of 1982 had already been exploded to the satisfaction of campaign consultants on all but the presidential level, however, in 1984 and 1986.

In fact, with the benefit of hindsight, it can be argued that the use of highly symbolic negative advertising focusing on single "emotional" issues, would be the next logical step in the presidential general election, as such advertising had been tested and found to be effective on all other levels in 1984 and 1986. By the end of the decade negative advertising was thus an integral part of the ad-driven mass media election.

Understanding "Feel-Good" and "Feel-Bad" Advertising

Following discussion with a number of 1984 campaign managers and consultants, it became clear that the content analysis of the 1984 broadcast ad sample must examine not only issues and visual and aural symbols but also the "feeling" to which an ad might appeal.

The political science literature speaks of bonds of trust that are at the core of the relationship between voter and politician, a relationship that Richard Fenno describes as built not only on assessments of candidate qualifications but also on bonds of "empathy" (or feeling) and identification. It has also long been known that symbols relate to the building of this trust relationship, which is based both on concepts and on *affect,* or appeals to the emotions. Charles E. Elder and Roger W. Cobb have given a modern interpretation in this area to a theoretical literature that is as old as Aristotle and as new as Murray Edelman and the growing body of scholars interested in information processing research. [24]

Researchers who in 1972 would have argued the sufficiency of issues and reason in voter evaluation of candidates were by 1988 suggesting that attitudes are much more complicated than that. Over the years, as Roger Tourangeau, a psychologist at the National Opinion Research Center, has argued, the pollsters' view of what comprises the politically significant "attitude" has become steadily more complex, reflecting changes in the research literature. In practical

terms, pollsters once considered attitudes to be a series of pro or con senti-
ments. Now they are being forced to regard attitudes as structures in long-term
memory: amalgams of interconnected concepts, feelings, beliefs, and images.[25]

In visual communication research, there is a major problem of understanding
how aural and visual devices are used in nonrational appeals. Varda Langholz
Leymore, an anthropologist who focused on advertising theory, has noted that
television advertising

is much more turbulent than static advertising for one obvious reason. Television images
are complex representations which simultaneously draw upon several sign systems—the
verbal, the visual, the auditory and the locomotive. The regularized points at which
these independent systems are allowed to intersect with each other, and the constraints
imposed on the manner in which their elements are juxtaposed and superimposed one
upon the other, are still largely unknown.[26]

Little is understood about communication on a medium that involves the
complex interplay of verbal, aural, and visual messages. Since Varda Langholz
Leymore made this comment in 1975, communications researchers have focused on the selectivity of the camera in film and television production. Herbert
Zettl has focused on how the camera can create an event or the feeling of a
particular event by manipulating emotions and moods electronically. Other research has also focused on movement, color, editing, music and sound, light-
ing, and other techniques that "can produce emotions or feelings." Lynda Lee
Kaid, Dorothy Davidson, and Anne Johnston Wadsworth have been focusing
on candidate "videostyle," which incorporates much of this research and has
drawn important distinctions between incumbent and challenger styles. Some
of this research, relating particularly to camera framing, composition and angles, and candidate eye contact, has been applied to an analysis of presidential
election debates. Semiotic theory has begun to focus on theoretically "emotional" dimensions of signs or symbols.[27]

The analysis of sound and symbols—but not camera work, which perhaps in
later research will help flesh out the findings reported in Chapters 4 and 5—
represents the result of a systematic, but not scientifically representative, panel
of content coders. The focus is on an examination of patterns in the sounds and
symbols, notably those relating to varied types of music, people, and place,
which appear in the 1984 sample of campaign advertising taken from the air.
The attempt is, further, to develop a typology based on symbols and sounds,
and in the case of one category of issues, of positive and negative feelings to
which ads appeal. The findings presented in these chapters are examined in
relation to commercial advertising theory and social research relating to emotional appeals aired on television.

The initial categories of emotional appeals developed in Chapters 4 and 5
grew out of discussions with campaign consultants about *one* affective purpose
of advertising in the 1980s and about some of the symbols used in association

with such effects. There are, of course, *other* purposes of political advertising, as our growing understanding of the complexity of attitudes—which include, for example, concepts as well as feelings—and certainly as the previous research would suggest should be the case. The affective side of politics, as Chapter 2 indicates, has become a common subject of discussion in the media consulting community. The effort made here is to isolate concrete dimensions of a term such as *feel-good advertising.*

It is self-evident that such a term describes something. But what? What is the purpose of this advertising, and what are its components? The overarching proposition examined here is whether such advertising was unique to Ronald Reagan's 1984 political media. The further question is raised, is there not just ''feel-good'' but ''feel-bad'' advertising?

Overall, the proposition tested in these content chapters, which involve a close examination of the 1984 and 1986 ad samples, followed by ad strategies in races on three federal levels, is a simple one: Is it possible that *affect-laden appeals are quite common in political advertisting, particularly in competitive races?*

Measuring Response to Ads

Researchers, including Patterson and McClure, have been faced with the problem of developing reliable ways to measure responses to ads. One problem has been that language in either its written or spoken form can be an inaccurate vehicle for the expression of real attitudes. Further, the context within which ads are aired is important. This context receives careful attention in commercial advertising research, whether it relates to viewer inattention or how the ad will relate to other ads and television programs that appear on the air. This is rarely the case in political advertising research, but this may change as more scholars focus on the significance of visual communication.[28]

In general, whereas most academic research has been seriously underfunded and is therefore experimental, in the political world, there is a commitment to political advertising research. There the trend in effects research is to nonverbal forms of communication. ''Electronic response'' mechanisms such as those used by some commercial advertisers and the team of social scientists that monitored viewer reactions to Ronald Reagan's facial displays in 1984 (whose categories are reported in Chapter 4) have become more refined. They were used by Republican presidential candidates in their 1988 televised debates. John Fiedler, who directed media and communications research for the 1984 Reagan reelection effort, in which such technologies were used, had by 1987 founded one of the several firms that marketed the wares used by Vice-President George Bush and other campaigners. Fiedler described his system as enabling

a speaker, if he's got a healthy ego, to close a lot of the loop between himself and the people he's talking to. It's an overall emotional reaction, not terribly cognitive, not terribly rational, to what people are seeing and hearing.[29]

According to Greg Markus, of the University of Michigan's Center for Political Studies, such technologies "give candidates an idea of what kinds of phrases, intonations and body language convey a favorable impression." This research, wittingly or not, is tending to confirm the analysis of academic researchers who have been focusing on such variables as viewer reactions to televised facial expressions, examined in Chapter 4.[30]

CHANGES IN THE AD ENVIRONMENT

Advertising takes place in an electronic world in which news and entertainment values commingle. It is an environment in which truth coexists not only with fantasy but with deception as well.

In the spring of 1987 one perceptive observer noted that

we live with the anguish of recognizing that television can bring us face to face with truth, but is often a mesmerizing deception. . . . It can beam a lie broadside to millions of homes (McCarthy waving his "list of traitors" in front of the camera, Nixon denying knowledge of the Watergate break-in); but it can also incisively expose the truth (Joseph Welch confronting McCarthy, the carnage of Vietnam battlefields that seemed to belie the official "body count").[31]

It is, indeed, difficult in America's video-dominated environment to separate truth, the result of documentary probing, from images created for public relations purposes that have been tailored to produce an effect.

Advertising in this news–public relations environment caters to public attitudes that, unlike those of 1972, are characterized by a great deal of mistrust not only of political institutions but also of candidate messages.[32]

Further, voter turnout reached an all-time low in the presidential elections of 1984. In the midterm elections of 1986 barely one-third of the nation's 178.3 million eligible voters cast ballots, a decline of more than four percentage points from 1982 and the lowest midterm election rate since the wartime election of 1942. Standard explanations for the decline in voting include socioeconomic factors and a rise in the number of young voters who have not settled down and fail to master voter registration procedures. According to political scientist Richard Boyd, they comprise one-fourth of the total nonvoting population. There are mysteries, however. In the past, well-educated voters have been consistent voters. Recently, the proportion of educated voters who regularly cast a ballot has declined. Research in this area has not included factors that might relate to communication.[33]

A number of media-related questions should be asked. Why is there less voting among educated voters? Why are younger voters not motivated enough to master voter registration procedures? Does lack of "settledness" fully explain the political abstinence of young Americans? One fact emerges clearly and is reported in Chapter 8 on the congressional race in the Indiana district that includes Purdue University. First, college-age students could be relied on *not* to vote even in one of the nation's major university centers—even when self-interest relating to student benefits was at stake. Still, it must be stressed, no direct connection has been drawn between a decline in voting and political advertising.

Whatever the long-range impact of highly individualistic advertising, and the evidence has not been developed to prove any thesis in this area, including those relating to voter turnout, consultants recognize that today's political advertising operates in an environment of skepticism of political institutions and decline in voter turnout.

The analysis turns first to changes in philosophy relating to political advertising, drawing on over 40 consultant statements between 1984 and 1988.

NOTES

1. Sydney Greenburg, memo to Democratic party leaders, unpublished and undated, spring 1986.

2. Interview with Lou Kitchen, southern regional director, Reagan-Bush 1984, Atlanta, March 20, 1985.

3. Jerome Bruner is quoted in William F. Lewis, "Telling America's Story: Narrative Form and the Reagan Presidency," *Quarterly Journal of Speech* 73 (1987): 280–302. Lewis offers a first-rate analysis of narrative and myth in the speech style of Ronald Reagan.

4. Richard Joslyn, *Mass Media and Elections* (Reading, Mass.: Addison-Wesley, 1984), pp. 35–54, on the disappearance of partisan appeals from political ads.

5. On the demise of the longer political commercials and the fact that this coincided with the demise, for economic reasons, of affordable longer commercial ads in 1976, see Joseph Napolitan, "Media Costs and Effects in Political Campaigns," *Annals, American Academy of Political and Social Science* 427 (September, 1976): 119.

6. Thomas Patterson and Robert McClure, *The Unseeing Eye* (New York: Putnam's, 1976).

7. Agenda-setting literature, including that relating to elections, suggests that news, including television, is solely responsible for changes in public attitudes. See the 1984 election postmortem on the impact of presidential advertising by Diamond and Bates, *Public Opinion,* November 1984.

8. Jarol B. Manheim and Robert B. Albritton, "Changing National Images: International Public Relations and Media Agenda Setting," *American Political Science Review* 78, no. 3 (September 1984): 641–56.

The general estimate is that in races in which television is relevant, media costs comprise 60 to 80 percent of the campaign's total expenditures. See F. Christopher Arterton, *Financing the Presidential Campaigns: An Examination of the FECA on the Conduct of Presidential Campaigns* (Cambridge, Mass.: Campaign Finance Study Group, John F. Kennedy School of Government, Harvard University, 1982). See also the German Marshall Fund, No. 11, April 1984.

Testimony from media consultants to congressional hearings prior to the 1984 election suggested that media costs in major markets double every four years. Task Force on

Elections, Committee on House Administration. U.S. House of Representatives, 98th Congress, *Campaign Finance Reform* (Washington, D.C.: GPO, 1984).

9. Donald T. Cundy, "Political Commercials and Candidate Image: The Effect Can Be Substantial," in *New Perspectives on Political Advertising*, ed. Lynda Lee Kaid, Dan Nimmo, and Keith R. Sanders (Carbondale: Southern Illinois University Press, 1986), pp. 210–35. Michael Pfau and Michael Burgoon, "Inoculation in Political Campaign Communication," *Human Communication Research* 15, no. 1 (Fall 1988): pp. 91–111.

10. L. Patrick Devlin, "An Analysis of Political Television Commercials, 1952–1984," in *New Perspectives*, p. 22.

11. Donald T. Cundy, "Political Commercials and Candidate Image: The Effect Can be Substantial," in *New Perspectives*, pp. 210–235. Michael Mansfield and Katherine Hale, "Uses and Perceptions of Political Television: An Application of Q-Technique," in *New Perspectives*, pp. 268–293. For right-brain, left-brain theories see Chapter 3.

12. Richard Joslyn, "Political Advertising and the Meaning of Elections," in *New Perspectives*, pp. 139–84.

13. For an elaboration of "classic" theory, see Ed Diamond and Stephen Bates, *The Spot: The Rise of Political Advertising on Television* (Cambridge, Mass.: MIT Press), 1988 (revised edition), pp. 302–345.

14. For the campaigns with ads picked up in the 1984 ad sample, see Appendix B. For interviews that were conducted relating to the 1984 ad sample, see Appendix A.

15. Ibid.

16. Richard Fenno, *Homestyle: House Members in Their Districts* (Boston: Little, Brown, 1978). Roger Ailes is quoted in Stephen Battaglio, "Roger Ailes: Taking the Gloves Off for George Bush," *Campaign Industry News* 2, No. 5 (August 1988); pp. 22–23.

17. Los Angeles was chosen because of its strategic importance in presidential politics and the fact that major local news stations were producing their own coverage of national news that would include the presidential race. There was also interest in the contrast between proposition campaigns on the California ballot and candidate advertising that appeared there and in other areas. There was little expectation that congressional advertising would appear in this analysis because the huge market is not cost-effective on that level.

Atlanta, Georgia, was a smaller but comparable urban environment, selected because it is the heart of a region that is now pivotal to both parties' presidential aspirations and because it would provide a test of whether local and congressional advertising would be used in a major city.

The Greensboro–Winston-Salem–High Point (Triad) region in North Carolina was picked because it would include the Hunt-Helms U.S. Senate race, which had both advertising and political impact far beyond North Carolina, and because it included three congressional seats that are among the most competitive in the nation.

Indianapolis and Lafayette, Indiana (separate market areas in television's Area of Dominant Influence (ADI) coding but treated as one for some purposes in this study), were selected because they were comparable with the North Carolina markets in size and therefore a relatively equal amount of advertising could be expected. Differences could be related to campaign strategies in an area that was competitive, as opposed to one that was much less so. There were three competitive districts in the North Carolina sample compared to only one in the Indiana sample. The two widely separate areas would also ensure inclusion in the sample of group-related appeals whether in the more conservative and religiously expressive political culture of the South or the more labor and party oriented political culture of Indiana.

In terms of their ADI, a standard market definition that includes all counties in which the home market station received a preponderance of viewing, the television markets selected for this study show wide variation. Los Angeles contains 4.4 million ADI television households, plus an additional 1.1 million in which the home market stations are viewed to a significant extent, for a total of 5.5 million households in the survey area. This is the second-largest ADI market in the country with 5.13 percent of all U.S. TV households. Atlanta contains 1.1 million ADI households, a total of 2.9 million in the survey area, fifteenth in the country, and 1.34 percent of all households.

In regard to the smaller areas, Indianapolis contains .8 million ADI households and there are 2.3 million in the survey area. It ranks twenty-third nationally with .92 percent of all U.S. households. Greensboro, Winston-Salem, and High Point, North Carolina has .5 million ADI households and 1.5 million in the survey area; the area is fiftieth in the nation and comprises .56 percent of the whole country. Finally, Lafayette, Indiana, contains 44,900 ADI households and 330,600 in the survey area and is 191st nationally and comprises .05 percent of the nation.

The comparability of the Indiana and North Carolina samples emerges from the fact that when the two Indiana stations, Indianapolis and Lafayette, are added together in the sample, the average is fifty-seventh in the nation, which is comparable to the two Piedmont Triad stations' fiftieth percentile rating. *Broadcasting-Cablecasting Yearbook, 1986* (Washington, D.C.: Broadcast Publications, 1986).

18. For one analysis of the 1984 Reagan campaign see Martin Schram, *The Great American Video Game: Presidential Politics in the Television Age* (New York: William Morrow, 1987). I am also further examining the 1984 Reagan ads and those of 1988 presidential candidates Michael Dukakis and George Bush in an ongoing research project.

19. Broadcast Educators Association Convention, Las Vegas, Nevada, May 1988.

20. See Chapter 3.

21. Overall, 64 percent of those who responded to this poll said that they got most of their news "about what's going on in the world today" from television, 40 percent from newspapers, 14 from radio, and 8 from other sources. This was the widest margin over newspapers since the polling began. Self-perception, of course, does not describe actual behavior. But changes in Americans' pattern of buying newspapers and television sets also supported the view that major changes were taking place in this area. Daily newspaper circulation in the United States rose from 58.9 million in 1960 to 62.1 million in 1970 and 63.1 million in 1984. This was far out of proportion to population growth. Per capita newspaper circulation sharply declined from about one newspaper per every three persons in 1960 to one newspaper to every four persons in 1984. Over the same time, the number of households with TV sets rose from 48.8 million in 1960 to 58.5 million in 1970 to 83.8 million in 1984, or about 97 percent of all U.S. households. See *Public Attitudes toward Television and Other Media in a Time of Change,* fourteenth report in a series by the Roper Organization (New York: Television Information Office, n.d.); and *Statistical Abstract of the United States, 1986* (Washington, D.C.: U.S. Department of Commerce, Bureau of the Census, 1986).

22. See Barbara Vobejda,"Many Americans Lost When It Comes to Geography:

Nation's Young Adults Ranked Last in an International Comparison of Knowledge,''
Washington Post, July 28, 1988, p. 4.

Ted Koppel cited the figure of 60 million Americans who are functional illiterates
and who therefore use television not as "the medium of choice, but as the medium of
necessity" in a recent lecture, "The Last Word" published in *Reports* (July-August
1987): 46. Tony Schwartz's quote is from Tom Shales, "The Media Merlin," *Washington Post,* February 17, 1983.

23. Diamond and Bates, op cit.

24. For classic theory, see Charles D. Elder and Roger W. Cobb, *The Political Uses
of Symbols* (New York: Longman, 1983); Murray Edelman, *The Symbolic Uses of Politics* (Urbana: University of Illinois Press, 1964); Doris A. Graber, *Processing the News:
How People Tame the Information Tide* (New York: Longman, 1984).

25. Roger Tourangeau is quoted in Rich Jaroslovsky, "What's on Your Mind, America?" *Psychology Today* (July–August 1988), p. 56.

26. Varda Langholz Leymore, *Hidden Myth: Structure and Symbolism in Advertising*
(London: Heineman, 1975), p. 59. See also Dan Nimmo and Arthur J. Felsberg,
"Hidden Myths in Televised Political Advertising: An Illustration," in *New Perspec-
tives.*

27. Herbert Zettl, *Television Production Handbook* (3rd ed.) (Belmont, Calif.:
Wadsworth, 1976); Anne Johnston Wadsworth and Lynda Lee Kaid, "Incumbent and
Challenger Styles in Presidential Advertising," paper presented at the International
Communication Association Convention, Montreal May 1987; and Lynda Lee Kaid and
Dorothy Davidson, "Elements of Videostyle: Candidate Presentation through Television
Advertising," in *New Perspectives,* pp. 184–210.

On camera work and debates see R.K. Tiemens, "Some Relationships of Camera
Angle to Communicator Credibility," *Journal of Broadcasting* 14 (1978): 483–90; L.K.
Davis "Camera Eye-Contact by the Candidates in the Presidential Debates of 1976,"
Journalism Quarterly 55 (1978): 431–37, 455; and Susan A. Hellweg and S.L. Phillips,
"A Visual Analysis of the 1980 Houston Republican Presidential Primary Debate,"
paper presented at the International Communication Association Convention, Minneap-
olis, May 1981.

For an introduction to semiotic theory relating to commercial advertisements see Judith
Williamson, *Decoding Advertisements: Ideology and Meaning in Advertising* (New York,
Marion Boyars, 1984).

28. For a critique of research that has relied on viewer analysis of whether they have
been influenced by television ads and other "effectiveness" measures, see Roger C.
Aden, "Televised Political Advertising: A Review of the Literature on 'Spots,' " paper
presented at the International Communication Association Convention, New Orleans,
1988. Aden focuses on the major problem of advertising effectiveness research: the
dilemma of giving up either internal or external validity in selecting experimental versus
real-life research designs.

29. Lloyd Grove, "Candidates Experiment with Instant Feedback: Voters Linked to
Computer Watch TV Debate," *Washington Post,* November 13, 1987, p. 3.

30. See Chapter 4. Wadsworth and Kaid have concluded from a review of the still
largely theoretical literature that the "nonverbal dimensions of [a] candidate's style are
also very important." This includes the belief that viewers value "ungovernable" nonverbal aspects of communication highly and that "nonverbal communication may be
even more important than verbal communication in the interpretation of some messages

when the two are in conflict." Wadsworth and Kaid, "Incumbent and Challenger Styles."

31. Florence Newman Trefethen,"Truth and Fabrication/Image and Reality," *The Lamp of Truth, The Dragon of Deceit,* Bryn Mawr, Alumnae Bulletin (Spring 1987), p.1.

32. Doris Graber, *Processing the News: How People Tame the Information Tide* (New York and London: Longman, 1984).

33. In the 1960 national election 68.8 million people, or 62.8 percent of the eligible voters, cast a ballot for Kennedy or Nixon. In the 1972 election 77.7 million people, or 55.2 percent of eligible voters, voted for Nixon or McGovern. In 1984 92.6 million—but only 53.1 percent of the eligible voters—made the choice between Reagan or Mondale. See Table 14, p. 243, *Statistical Abstract of United States,* (107th ed.) (Washington, D.C.: Bureau of the Census, Department of Commerce, 1987). The congressional figures are cited in "1986 Elections: A Show of Voter Indifference," *Congressional Quarterly,* March 14,1987, pp. 484–86.

Richard W. Boyd focuses on the problem of the youth vote in "Decline of Voter Turnout: Structural Explanations," *American Politics Quarterly* 9 (April 1981).

Other explanations for the decline in turnout, also based on large-scale survey data that include no media exposure variables, have focused on socioeconomic status, education, and measures of "political efficacy." See Ivor Crewe, "Electoral Participation," in *Democracy at the Polls,* ed. David Butler, Howard R. Penniman, and Austin Ranney (Washington, D.C.: American Enterprise Institute, 1981); and Richard A. Brody, "The Puzzle of Poltical Participation," in *The New American Political System,* ed. Anthony King (Washington, D.C.: American Enterprise Institute, 1978).

2

Schools of Consulting: The Responsive Chord Revisited

In the mid-1980s, the commercial advertising language of sounds and symbols intended to stimulate recall and/or an affect-laden reaction on the part of the viewer was also the one that political consultants believed best facilitated the "learning" of their message. In this the world of political advertising absorbed its commercial counterpart and became as one. A common thread was that simple print—facts, unadorned by visual and aural persuasion—could not compete with evocative imagery. The key was experience, or how does purchasing the product make me feel, as in the Toyota ad: "Oohh, what a feeling! Toyota."[1]

This is a major conclusion of this study of 669 political ads made in 1984 and 1986 on behalf of political candidates on all federal levels. Examination of these ads for language and for visual and aural motifs was followed by interviews with many of the political consultants who were responsible for the ads. In all, over 40 media consultant philosophical statements were examined between 1984 and 1987, either through interviews relating to specific ads or from public lectures conducted in the Washington, D.C., area. (See Appendixes A and B.)

The result reported here is an elite study of the philosophies that underlie strategic thinking in the area of political advertising. As such it meets such methodological criteria for elite studies as that suggested by Jarol Manheim: that the major participants in decision making may be interviewed in an open-ended fashion, but conclusions must be checked through more than one source. Conclusions concerning media philosophies in the mid-1980s are examined in relation to academic research, commercial advertising theory, and similar research conducted in 1972, a benchmark year against which current media theory can be evaluated.[2]

In general, belief in the use of techniques comparable to those of commercial advertising prevailed both among the well-established political consultants, or "majors," who handled the largest market share of statewide and congressional and presidential races in the 1980s, and among the "insurgents," who each election cycle join the majors following a successful year, moving into positions of primary responsibility for the advertising side of multimillion-dollar Senate and presidential campaigns. In the 1980s the successful insurgents combined well-honed strategic political skills with a stylistic approach that drew heavily on commercial advertising.[3]

MAJORS AND INSURGENTS

As the 1980s began, on the Republican side the majors included the agencies of Roger Ailes, Bailey-Deardourf, Robert Goodman, and, perhaps to a lesser degree, Don Ringe and Ian and Betsy Weinschel. Insurgents came from the 1984 Reagan commercial team, including Phil Dusenbery, who continued to be primarily a products advertiser, and Doug Watts. They also included Michael Murphy and Alex Castellanos, who helped elect Jesse Helms; Moore, Hoch and Hughes; Jan Bryant's Research/Strategy/Management; Sandler-Innocenzi; commercial stylist Chris Motolla; and Paul Sipple, who broke away from Bailey-Deardourf in 1987. Among the majors on the Democratic side were the firms of Robert Squier, David Sawyer, David Garth, Zimmerman and Galanty, and Dresner-Sykes. Successful insurgents of the 1980s included David Doak and Robert Shrum, Frank Greer, John Martila, Jill Buckley, Joe Slade White and Karl Struble, and Dan Payne, all of whom combined political skills with a commercial advertising orientation. Ken Swope more clearly represented a specifically commercial advertising background.

A commercial orientation was not only bipartisan, for it prevailed in all three of the major philosophical camps of political advertising in the 1980s, blurring the lines between them. The *emotional* school resembled commercial advertising most closely and relied most heavily on visual and aural effects. The *new informational* school relied heavily on such techniques, while viewing itself as more language based, in the sense of devoting more attention to clarifying candidate issue positions. The *quick-response* school was the least oriented to entertainment techniques and high-quality visuals and took particular advantage of a "factual" format that drew heavily on news. Everyone's objective was to break through the clutter of commercial advertising and news and entertainment programming and communicate a message, which, as with commercial advertising, would score highly with the audience on measures of recall, persuasiveness, clarity, and identification or empathy.

DOVETAILING AND COORDINATED AD AND NEWS EFFORTS

Although differing on questions of technique, most major media consultants in the 1980s focus on both sides of the advertising message—issues and candidate character—in a fashion that is frequently believed to be most effective if visual and linguistic messages *dovetail,* or reinforce each other. An example of dovetailing is the use of an overweight Tip O'Neill to accompany the message that Democrats waste money and raise taxes. Or, to combat this image, 1986 senatorial candidate Tom Daschle might appear in an ad driving to work in a beat-up car. A whole taxonomy of visual symbols that illustrate the penny-pinching side of the tax and government spending issues has emerged in the 1980s. Issues are frequently developed on all levels with an eye to reinforcing candidate images. This conclusion in fact reinforces other research that has reached a similar conclusion.[4]

Further, the major media consultants coordinate news as well as advertising strategies in a fashion that was unthinkable in the early 1970s. (This will be examined in subsequent chapters on specific races.) A common strain is the emergence in the 1980s of regular use of "projective" polling techniques in well-heeled campaigns. During a campaign's planning phase, as "benchmark" polls test candidate and opponent assets and liabilities in the areas of character and issues, projective techniques are used to introduce issues that would shift opinion if voters knew about them. An issue such as "license branches," for example, which was used effectively in statewide Indiana races in 1984 and 1986, might not appear in any preexisting list of voter concerns; but when explained, it might rank significantly on measures of affect or intensity and therefore be introduced into the campaign.[5]

Although there is great deal of discussion of emotional messages and advertising, little biophysical research comparable to that undertaken in the commercial advertising community, and more recently in academic research, is in common use in political campaigns. In some Republican campaigns, however, and in the testing of audience reaction to Ronald Reagan's speeches and the 1988 presidential campaign of George Bush by a polling team such as that of Richard Wirthlin and Bob Teeter, buttons and dials are used to test immediate nonverbal responses to televised candidate presentations. Other independent firms that specialize in such research for commercial clients are also beginning to move into the political advertising field on behalf of congressional and statewide clients.[6]

One further major conclusion emerges: It is that negative advertising was perceived to work, and that campaigns must be prepared to use it. This represents a major shift from opinion held in 1972, when the major consultants publicly doubted the effectiveness of negative advertising that focused not only on issues but also on the opponent's character. By 1986 a number of pollsters engaged in the effort to determine advertising effectiveness on behalf of media consultants and their clients argued that the messages that stirred the deepest reaction, and that therefore were most likely to "move the electorate," were negative ones.

WHY NEGATIVE ADVERTISING IS EFFECTIVE

One reason given for the effectiveness of negative advertising was increased public distrust of politicians and large work-related institutions. This view has been expressed for a number of years by California pollsters, who reiterated it in interviews conducted for this study. By 1986, however, such Democratic pollsters as Bill Hamilton, Paul Maislin, Peter Hart, Doug Schoen, and Paul Melman, and a Republican pollster, Robert Teeter, expressed similar views, if they gave varied reasons for what they described as a rise in public cynicism. For Democrat Maislin, rising levels of cynicism reflected the fact that politicians were not listening to the electorate. Republican pollster Robert Teeter agreed that cynicism had gone up, but he viewed this as reflecting a long-term suspicion of politicians, which he contrasted with a "greater trust" that came into politics with the Reagan presidency.[7]

Maislin, who worked as a pollster on Paul Simon's hard-fought but ultimately successful 1984 challenge to Illinois senator Charles Percy, believed that negative advertising was quite popular, particularly among younger voters

reared on television and skeptical of ads generally and of political ads in particular. They welcome ads that give negative information about an opponent's voting record or conduct in office. There used to be a saying in our business that you could never find anyone who would tell you they liked a negative ad. This year, for the first time, we're finding people who are saying, "Hey, that's interesting." It's the positive stuff they're more cynical about.[8]

In short, in relation to the measure used by advertisers to gauge the effectiveness of a message—*persuasiveness*—negative messages were believed to rate highly because of existing predispositions. The same was believed to be true in the area of *recall*. Democratic pollster Paul Melman echoed a body of social science research findings, including those of Doris Graber, with his conclusion that negative information was better remembered than its positive counterpart. He commented:

We know from years of research psychology that people process negative information more deeply than positive information. When we ask people about negative ads they'll say they don't like them . . . [however] the point is that they absorb the information.[9]

For Frank Luntz, of the Richard Wirthlin Group, negative advertising is remembered better because it stands out. This is because the United States is a "compromise" political culture, with final decisions representing a consensus viewpoint. Sharp-edged statements, such as those enunciated in negative advertising, are therefore more noteworthy.[10]

THE INFORMATIONAL BECOMES THE NEW INFORMATIONAL SCHOOL

A series of interviews with majors in the early 1970s can be contrasted with the views of majors and insurgents in the 1980s to facilitate understanding of changes in advertising. Thus, in 1972 Democrat Robert Squier, then representing the informational school, addressed the importance of the documentary format which drew on film and television news documentaries, and was in pervasive use on both sides of the political aisle. This format, he said, as did Charles Guggenheim, another major active in the 1970s, met the primary purpose of advertising, which was to provide viewers with information about candidates and the issues. Similar views were expressed by the major consultants of both parties during the presidential races of that year, comprising what might be described as an informational school of media consulting. This is the school whose work is examined in Thomas Patterson and Robert McClure's study of the 1972 election, *The Unseeing Eye.*[11]

In 1972 Squier also expressed the view that advertising must fit within a world dominated by news, and he expressed his disbelief in the effectiveness of negative advertising such as that used in the 1970 Texas primary in which Lloyd Bentsen defeated Senator Ralph Yarborough in a campaign that featured the airing of riot clips from the 1968 Democratic convention in Chicago along with the at-least visual implication that Yarborough was in some way responsible. Robert Goodman, who then, as now, represents the emotional school, had a different view in 1972. "Elections aren't won or lost on the basis of hard news, but on the way people feel and the ability of a campaign organization to get a candidate's supporters to the polls.[12]

In 1986 Squier and Goodman were even more prominent in their field, but Squier now defended emotional negative advertising as effective. Thus, the "new" informational school. And in media-consulting circles he was known for his "barbed ads," which could force the debate conducted in both news and advertising onto his issues—a criterion that was becoming a standard of self-evaluation for media consultants. Unlike a leading competitor, David Sawyer, who lost ground in 1984 as a result of a weak showing in both the Jim Hunt North Carolina senatorial contest and the Walter Mondale presidential campaign, Squier was believed capable of developing a fanatic common thread—which could subsume all questions to one simple message.[13]

An example that is frequently cited was the successful 1986 campaign of Democratic representative Richard Shelby against Republican Senator Jeremiah Denton. It was a negative campaign, and, as in the case of Jesse Helms in North Carolina two years before, it began early. According to New York consultant Doug Schoen, who did the polling for the race, it was developed around a message that emerged from early projective polling that focused not only on character and issue perceptions already in the minds of the electorate but also on reactions to suggested messages. The negative message about Senator Denton's character focused on class (use of public funds to pay "country club dues") which added up to an image of "aloofness" or failure to care about his constituents. This character failure, which could be expressed well visually, dovetailed with the campaign's central policy issue: the incumbent's votes against Social Security.[14]

Squier won all six of his Senate and House races in 1986, consolidating his status as the single leading Democratic major. In 1988 he and his partner, Carter Eskew, worked for ten Senate and gubernatorial candidates, a full fourth of the Democrats running statewide who hired media consultants. He was also hired along with several other consultants by one of the national network news programs during the presidential primaries and made frequent televised appearances. In 1988, in the context of cutting down on journalistic coverage, political consultants served as paid network consultants to explain an increasingly professionalized campaign process to the U.S. public. The consensus emerges from this research that in the 1980s it has also been a task of the media consultant to serve as a leading source of information and "spin" for reporters on behalf of their clients. A conflict of interest is in the making that will probably be resolved only as more academic research focuses on the role of media in the campaign process and as reporters are better trained in the "new" politics and the news media continue to improve their polling operations.[15]

Michael Murphy, who had polled and developed media for the 1984 Jesse Helms campaign in North Carolina before moving into "mainstream" Republican consulting in 1986 with two important senatorial races, admired Squier's ability to control the television agenda in the Shelby race by developing negative themes early in January–February and then following up from September to election day in November. This strategy does not involve extensive debate on specific issues. Rather, as Murphy suggested, the process involves a non-debate: "Every time you say 'batter up' they would say, 'the sky is blue' and 'what about Social Security' . . . , which is one way to kill a Republican." Murphy used a similar strategy, dovetailing character and issues, in such Republican Senate races as those of Jesse Helms in 1984 (examined in Chapter 7) and Georgia senator Mac Mattingly in 1986.[16]

Emerging from the 1986 trench warfare, Squier was an elder statesman among Democratic majors who had come to believe in the regrettable need for negative advertising. He had defeated his old rival, Robert Goodman of the emotional school, in the Alabama Shelby-Denton race albeit by a narrow 50–49 percent. Goodman lamented the passing of the fact that "clobbering" one's opponent had moved from the final six weeks of the campaign ["you had all that time to build up a head of steam about your candidacy—show how wonderful he was"]. Now, he said, in some cases "people started running negative ads right after election day and never stopped." This meant that it was necessary for him to create twice as many ads per statewide campaign—50 to 60 in 1986 compared to 25 to 30 six years before.[17]

According to Murphy, who should be identified with the quick-response school, and whose work is "data" or "poll driven," the purpose of media is cognitive:

getting people to know something, for example, "Wyche Fowler is an absentee." You do a wave of media, 20 percent of the people know it; you do another wave of media, 50 percent. With up to 75 percent of the people knowing it, then you move on. You have penetrated. Polls tell you what attacks have carried, how far, when it's time to switch: in other words how you're doing.[18]

Goodman's view on this subject: "Data driven, hell. Don't bother us with the facts. Let's get to the feelings, let's get to the essence."[19]

Still, despite such apparent differences, mid-1980s political consultants of all three philosophical schools were convinced of the value of what were being described as emotional appeals to reach voters of all ages. Special reference is frequently made to the prized baby-boom market of individuals now in their early 40s. Baby-boomers are of interest to commercial advertisers because of their affluence, and to politicians because political advertising research has suggested that ads are particularly effective with undecided voters and baby-boomers are an important group of likely voters who are relatively unaligned—and one which Pat Caddell estimated would comprise 60 percent of the electorate in 1988. Raised on television and, arguably, geographically homogenized by it, many believe that television is the best way to reach them.[20]

Commercial advertising scholars and practitioners agreed in the 1980s that advertising should appeal to what was variously and sometimes interchangeably called the emotions or experience. From the perspective of vocal commercial practitioners in election year 1984, the view was frequently stated that the best route to engaging potential buyers such as the baby-boomers was by seeking to "evoke" the "experience" of owning a product. In this the key focus, according to Richard Kiernan, an executive vice-president of Gray Advertising, Inc., is "aspirational"—"how does it make me feel. . . . If you say the words no one will listen." According to Burt Manning of J. Walter Thompson, "If you use words, it can be patronizing. You must imply that you know [what people want]. But if you state it, even if it's true, it can be an embarrassment." This is because "there's a wariness. Fifteen years ago, people knew where they were [in relation to institutions]. . . . People who are now in the establishment [as compared with 1966 when there was respect for "the family doctor"] have almost none of the old beliefs." In an age of changing values and feelings about institutions, the key is the use of visual or audible cues which evoke a more personal experience with which the viewer can identify.[21]

Appeals vary, not only in relation to different personality types and the quality of the medium through which advertising is targeted but also, in experimental research, in relation to individuals believed to be dominated either by right-brain or left-brain styles of perception. Thus, the Chicago advertising firm of Foote, Cone and Belding developed a grid, derived from this split-brain theory that designates the left side of the human brain as analytical and the right as creative. Products that consumers tend to analyze logically before purchasing them—such as life insurance—are placed in the left-hand portion. The right side is for products that people tend to buy based more on feelings, looks, taste, touch, smell, or sound. Strategy on the "thinking" side involves "learn, feel, do" while the affective side requires "feel, learn, do."[22]

The important point is that although the lead-in may vary in relation to the product being sold and even, in some experimental research, perceptions of the personality type of the buyer, in both cases the attempt is to engage viewer "feelings" in a total appeal that involves a "do" side—which is intended to provoke a reaction, whether it be recall of the message, developing a "liking" or "dislike" for a product or candidate, or, finally, to vote for or against a product or candidate.

After 1984 there was increased discussion of affect-laden or emotional appeals that seek to engage the viewer's "thinking" function only late in the ad, well after attention has been caught by means of entertainment and affect-related appeals. The explanation offered by New York commercial advertiser Peter Markey for the effectiveness of Ronald Reagan's advertising effort—that the viewer was well "into" the ad before the "thinking" function was engaged, a process that grew out of the commercial advertising orientation of the president's advertising team—had a profound influence on the political media-consulting community. The process was termed emotional. Understanding the theory of emotional appeals is thus a key to understanding media strategies in well-funded races on all levels in 1986.[23]

ENGAGING THE VIEWER: TWO CONCEPTS

Two concepts are helpful in understanding theories of affect in advertising. One is the concept *referential* advertising. Although she does not use the term *referential,* the concept is well described by critical semiotic theorist Judith Williamson. The basic premise of advertising, she argues, is that of transferring meaning from one affect-laden symbol, such as a child, place, or object, to a product. Interviewed in Washington in 1987, Adam Goodman of the emotional school described the concept of referential advertising drawn from the commercial world as central to his work. The idea is to use symbols toward which the viewer holds positive feelings and "associate these with the product in the marketing process." Goodman described this as the "politics of love." Referential advertising is that which uses a symbol already believed to have "affective" meaning for the viewer in a fashion that transfers or refers that meaning to the candidate or the opponent.[24]

A second concept is *wheel of emotions,* which focuses on how people organize their feelings and how advertising can best tap into this. Developed in 1984 by products advertiser Stuart J. Agres, research director of a New York advertising firm, Lowe-Marschalk, the wheel concept refocuses a long-term advertising theory, indeed one as old as "get 'em sick, then get 'em well," which means, according to one advertising scholar, "buy me and you will overcome the anxieties I have just reminded you about." Structural anthropologist Varda Leymore, whose work is enjoying a resurgence of interest, has focused this concept around commercials tapping into life's underlying tensions—life and death, animal and man—and resolving them with a product. Sociologist Richard M. Merelman has taken this idea a step further to argue that the resolution in the form of a product may very well represent *life itself.*[25]

A number of scholars are building on the central focus of Leymore on my-

Figure 2.1
The Wheel of Emotions

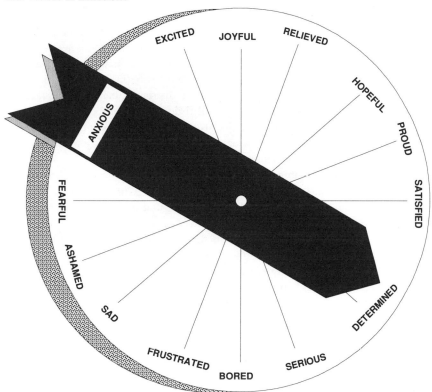

Source: Developed by Stuart J. Agres, Lowe-Marschalk, Inc., New York, NY, 1984.

thology as a means through which a product—or, they argue, a candidate—is marketed. Ads appeal to values and feelings that may well be communicated through the language and symbols of mythology, drawn from both cultural and religious traditions. But advertising also utilizes other appeals that may be purely entertainment oriented. These include humor, various linguistic, aural, and visual devices, and symbols that some consultants interviewed for this research believe to be associated with various forms of positive and negative affective appeals. These will be examined in the chapters on positive and negative advertising.[26]

A practical formulation of affect-related commercial advertising theory that builds on the Leymore approach was developed in 1984 by Agres, of Lowe-Marschalk:

The best commercials incorporate emotional empathy and operate by cutting across the wheel [of emotions]. You create a heightened arousal level. When you generate this biological-psychological excitement, it yields better communication and learning. But you have to resolve that emotion by the end of the commercial—hopefully with the product.[27]

In 1985 Lowe-Marschalk produced a controversial but award-winning political ad on the federal deficit issue for W. R. Grace Company using wheel-of-emotions theory (see figure 2.1). Two somber Internal Revenue agents enter a nursery, lean over a newborn child, and hand it a bill for $50,000—its share of the deficit. The ad concludes with a close-up of the distraught baby and the tagline, "Write to Congress. If you don't think that'll do it, run for Congress." It was a success, Agres said later, because it started with anxiety, confusion, a sense of being overwhelmed. Then it cut across the wheel, providing a serious, determined means of resolving those feelings.[28]

The wheel concept combines the "get 'em sick, then get 'em well" idea that underlies conventional theories about how ads organize emotions with the simple referential idea of using symbols and sounds that already have meaning— whether cognitive or affective—in ads. Both ideas are relevant to political advertising philosophy as developed by all three schools, emotional, new informational and quick-response. Before focusing on the approaches of some of their key representatives, however, we will take a fresh look at the original bridge between the worlds of commercial and political advertising, New York media consultant Tony Schwartz, whose influence continued to inform political advertising theory in the 1980s.[29]

A BRIDGE: TONY SCHWARTZ

Two central points emerge from a reexamination of the ads of Tony Schwartz, the commercial advertiser who entered the political world in the 1960s arguing that communication by means of sights and sounds is more effective than concepts, rationales, or indeed the presentation of "real life." The first is that he was an innovator in both wheel-of-emotions and referential advertising—in the sense not just of seeking to tap preexisting feelings about a particular candidate but of seeking to *transfer* or *refer* positive and negative affect evoked by means of sight and sound from emotionally laden symbols to the candidate and his opponent. The idea that the sole purpose of this advertising is to surface preexisting feelings about a candidate is part of the story, but not the whole of it.[30]

Secondly, Schwartz argued in the 1980s that the central purpose of such advertising may well be to try to create order in a "boundless" world, that is one in which communication by means of the electronic medium has replaced institutional expression as a source of social sanctions. For Schwartz, if not for his followers, this means that advertising plays a vital role as the latter-day equivalent of the community.

Even for those many consultants who do not share his global view of political advertising, however, the impact of Schwartz's theories relating to sound and video was profound. One of his key conclusions was that the brain processes such information more rapidly than the spoken or learned word. Thus he might eliminate parts of words. "I've very carefully studied how the brain hears," he said in 1983, "and I can record with that in mind. We can hear four times as fast as we can talk. So the question is, what do you do with the other time?" For him, there is a difference between "learned recall" and "evoked recall." The difference is that the latter, evoked through sound and sight, "functions about a million times faster than the former."[31]

Schwartz pioneered in the use of the sights and sounds of childhood in advertising, primary human symbols in the process of "evoked recall," and ones that replaced reality—infected organs, for example as in his early anti-smoking ads. The old ads, according to Schwartz,

show[ed] how your lungs were affected or this or that. I took a different approach. [Instead] I showed kids playing in their parents' clothing. You know, the boy and girl dressing up in their parents' wedding clothes up in the attic, and then we have the announcer say, "Children learn by imitating their parents. [Pause]. Do *you* smoke cigarettes?"[32]

Visual and aural symbols from childhood seek to associate the message—stop smoking—with evoked feelings about childhood and parenting.

"Daisy Girl," Schwartz's most famous ad using sounds and symbols of childhood, has often been interpreted just as Schwartz has written about it, as simply evoking preexisting feelings of mistrust of Barry Goldwater, President Lyndon Johnson's opponent in the 1964 election, against whom it was directed. If considered verbally, it is true that no fingers were pointed at Goldwater; but the verbal side, in Schwartz's theory, is only a complement to the visual and aural side. A little girl picks petals from a daisy, counting one to ten. Then the count is reversed, and over an atomic explosion the familiar voice of President Johnson intones, "These are the stakes: to make a world in which all God's children can live, or go into the dark."[33]

Children and missiles are the referential symbols and sound used in a wheel-of-emotions approach that seeks to propel the viewer through surfaced feelings of anxiety to resolution in the form of presidential protection. The anxiety is not just about Goldwater; it is about war itself. The ad seeks to evoke negative affect associated with fear of nuclear war, prevalent in the early 1960s. Tension mounts surrounding such issues and the selection of an alternative to the incumbent. Finally, President Johnson emerges as "contrast," or *resolution* to the dilemmas raised in the ad, through the sound of a steady, known, presidential voice—one which took the country through a previous, emotionally difficult time, John F. Kennedy's assassination. Lyndon Johnson, in sum, represents "life itself."[34]

That the overall approach is a matter of more than historical relevance is indicated by a survey of consultants conducted by David Beiler in connection with the 1987 film *The Classics of Political Advertising*. From the 1980s perspective he concluded that the 1964 Lyndon Johnson advertising campaign was viewed as the most effective in recent presidential history.[35]

For Schwartz, interviewed in 1983, "Daisy Girl" tapped feelings of "shame" that in preelectronic cultures would have been imposed by the community. In such cultures "wherever people couldn't get away from their communications environment, a neighborhood, a town or a village," shame worked as a sanction. But, Schwartz argued,

once people began to flake away, shame didn't work; they could escape. But in recent years, the speed of communication has changed to 186,000 miles a second. So it means that you can reach anywhere in the country in less than a sixtieth of a second. Everyone, everywhere. Which makes shame one of the most powerful means of social control again.[36]

Few consultants express themselves quite that globally, but in the 1980s Schwartz has had successors who have sought to use the language of childhood to tap this feeling. One is Democratic consultant Gary Nordlinger, who combines new informational and quick-response methodologies and works largely on the congressional level. In 1984 he produced a response ad for his client, Congressman Alan B. Mollohan (D-West Virginia), which used the sounds of children playing to charge the opponent with false advertising:

"Airplane"

(Children at play, making engine sounds.)

Child: "Look at me, I'm an airplane."

Narrator: Little children play make believe, and that's okay, but when a grown-up man who's running for Congress says the same thing, that's not okay. Jim Altmeir's trying to make us believe that Congressman Mollohan voted to raise our taxes. But that's just not true.[37]

It was not just in candidate advertising that children were making their appearance in advertising in the 1980s. By 1984 childhood had already emerged as part of the language of political lobbying. Thus, an Edison Electric Institute ad, created by a Baltimore commercial advertising agency known for its emotional advertising, featured a child turning on a lightbulb. In this, the effort of Edison Electric Institute, a leading lobby for nuclear power, was to establish a positive presence with the Washington policy-making audience that watched *The McLaughlin Report,* which it sponsored.[38]

Advertising oriented to such commercially developed principles was in the ascendant in the days following the 1984 election, both among the majors who handle most of the high-priced contracts, and among the insurgents, who were seeking to move up into the ranks of the majors.

A number of insurgents worked out of the newly formed Harriman Communications Center, a Democratic party media center, and practiced on congressional races. Their focus was on innovative attack advertising and ads that sought new ways to draw a humorous and affect-laden connection between the candidate and the voter. In making its first generic ads in 1984 Harriman Center director John Franzen, who has since established an augmented independent business, sought "something that's arresting" to get people's attention. Franzen's orientation was closest to the emotional school and the attack ads that he created for the Democratic Congressional Campaign Committee that year focused on dissonant sound effects, such as clocks ticking increasingly loudly to raise the question of what the Republican incumbent had done "for you," and dripping faucets to raise the toxic wastes issues. The focus was highly visual and individualistic. One ad only asked people to vote in order to retain a "Democratic" Congress, and it was made at the request of a party official. It aired only in Guam.[39]

Asked after the 1984 election, for which he had personally created ads for the Democratic party and for successful congressional candidates, which new media consultant held the greatest promise on the Democratic side, Franzen spoke of Ken Swope, who had an extensive background in New York and Philadelphia in commercial advertising and television production, and who in 1984 had worked in association with the Harriman Center on behalf of congressional candidates and on behalf of George McGovern's presidential primary campaign. Swope moved on to become one of the Democratic consulting community's bright stars, in 1986 creating the well-regarded statewide media for Florida's unsuccessful Democratic Senate candidate, Steve Pajic, and moving on in 1988 to the position of presidential primary consultant first to Joe Biden, and then, with Dan Payne, to Michael Dukakis. It was a rapid rise.[40]

Franzen spotted Swope in 1984, arguing that his success would be based on the fact that he hailed from the products world, a fact Franzen associated with recognition that people *don't like politicians or their issue-related ads*. Swope contends that "political advertising has a bad reputation," with Americans "disliking it a lot" because of "video-newspaper," or "walk-me-talk-me" political advertising. "If you watch television, " he argues, "you will see that emotions are what is most important. In order of importance on television come pictures, music, then words." Humor is also a Swope trademark, and his work, including an ad featuring a little old lady scolding a congressman saying, "Shame on you, Congressman," has been widely copied. An example of the Swope style, which is of the commercial emotional school moving to a political appeal only long after the voter has been drawn deeply into the ad through entertainment devices and common experiences, is an ad he created in 1984 that connected Connecticut congressman Sam Gejdenson with all the remembered feelings associated with a fishing trip, away from all institutional structures and obligations.[41]

The congressman stood in a river listening to the sounds of the outdoors, being "taken" by a fish, and stating his support for the Clean Water Act. Most significantly, self-deprecating humor, used daily by Ronald Reagan and both the Hollywood world of Jack Benny and commercial advertising, assured viewers, impatient with politicians and political institutions, that the candidate is a guy who values the simple life, will not be sucked in by "Washington," and is, in sum, an ordinary person with whom they can positively identify.[42]

The ad that Franzen believed to be his own best 1984 ad was sculpted with reflections of the language of one of life's most deeply personal and emotional experiences—the wedding ceremony. This language was spoken by Democratic congressman Leon Panetta (D-California) who walked the bluffs at Big Sur with his wife. The words—evoking a common, still widely shared emotional experience—were spoken not only to her, but of his commitment to the district's land and people. In 1988 Swope worked with another leading Boston media consultant, Dan Payne, on the 1988 presidential primary campaign of Michael Dukakis. Payne was similarly known for ads which had brought his candidate, the cerebral Massachusetts governor, into the consciousness of the voters of his state as a guy who grew up in a "neighborhood," had worked in a family restaurant, and was, in short, an "ordinary" guy. Payne produced the lengthy ad that ran at the 1988 Democratic convention and included references to a governor who mowed his own lawn and was so penny-pinching he still retained his antiquated snow plow. Both Swope and Payne experienced anguish during the general election campaign however, as the overarching decision was made to make Dukakis look "presidential." It was left to George Bush to co-opt the "ordinary guy" image in shirt sleeves dandling babies on *his* knee.[43]

Media consultant Joe Slade White, also of the emotional school, follows in the clear tradition of Tony Schwartz. He rose rapidly, from Congressional and other statewide campaigns and a senatorial candidacy in 1986, to a presidential race in 1988. In Washington it was said that White's rise was limited only by his unwillingness to expand his operation beyond his home. The babysitter received the call that resulted in his taking over the 1986 Harriett Woods Senate race against Kit Bond in Missouri from Robert Squier after controversy arose over an emotional "crying farmer" ad the latter had made. Such advertising, incidentially, made clear how far the informational school, which Squier had represented in the early 1970s, had migrated into the ranks of the emotional school by 1986.

THE FIRST "WORDLESS" AD?

After replacing Squier in the Woods race, White produced and aired what may have been the first truly wordless ad. He had made it earlier in the year for successful Oregon Democratic gubernatorial candidate Neil Goldschmidt. The ad is a superb example of Schwartz's theories of sound and visual sculpture. The candidate is represented fully through visuals and music that conveys what can only be described as inexorability. Both draw the viewer into the momentum of a building experience. There is no narration. Three slogans appear, in white on a black screen: It's About Change. It's About Time. It's About Now.

The ad was one element in a two-part response to Bond after the "Crying Farmer" fiasco. The campaign believed Woods was hurt when Squier's three-part "Crying Farmer" ad series received unfavorable press attention and was withdrawn from the air. "Crying Farmer" was one of a three-part series that was intended to focus on the farm situation and then link Bond, who was on the board of one of the big insurance companies buying up farm land, with the farmers' plight. The problem, according to one media consultant who preferred not to be identified, was that

they put out one ad, which made the farmer cry, and then kicked Bond. . . . But the third of the three ads had no resolution. It showed Harriett Woods talking about how great farmers are after you had seen the farmer cry. It insinuated that she was responsible for this. And then they attacked Bond.

The problem, in short, was, not emotional advertising, but an ad series that failed to present the candidate as the "resolution," wheel-of-emotions fashion, to the affect-laden dilemmas raised by the ad. Another problem, described by the opposing candidate's campaign, was that the Woods consultants failed to deal well with the news media that bore down on the "crying farm family." The family had not been informed that the ad would be used and balked at its role in the affair. Under such conditions, the Republican charge that the ad was exploitative, which is the kiss of death for negative advertising, sank in.[44]

THE "POWER OF A LIFE"

There were a number of other "crying farmer" ads in 1986, which unlike Squier's entry on behalf of Harriett Woods, did not backfire. How did they differ from the Missouri crying farmer? One answer is that they used a more subtle, understated wheel-of-emotions style that focused on the very personal story of a single life with which the viewer could identify and, unlike the Squier ad, which involved a cameo appearance on the part of the candidate, kept the candidate out of the ad as much as possible. Further, they operated on the principle, adopted in the 1984 Reagan advertising and described by products advertising executive Peter Markey, of drawing the viewer far into an "experience" before the "thinking" function is engaged. In fact the candidate does not make an appearance at all.[45]

One such "crying farmer" ad was cut in 1986 for South Dakota senatorial candidate Tom Daschle by Karl Struble National Voter Contact, who from this race entered the majors. It stood out among all such ads. Some argued that this was because the crying farmer's wife, in her kitchen, was entirely credible. "She was a *real* farmer," commented Charles E. Cook, a Washington elections newsletter entrepreneur, who functions for the Washington press corps as a "Great Mentioner." Struble considers himself part of the "emotional, commercial advertising school" of the 1980s. His pre-1980s background was voter targeting, but he quite unabashedly describes himself as eagerly going home at night to watch product advertising for ideas. His 1986 ads for Daschle were clearly part of a school of advertising that focuses on "real lives." Adam Goodman, of the emotional school, said the Robert Goodman Agency first used such highly personal real-life ads in 1984 in the Senate races of Republican incumbents Rudy Boschwitz (Minnesota) and Thad Cochran (Mississippi). According to Goodman, "Real people are the best subjects of our spots. This involves 'the power of a life,' which is an incredible motivator." Such ads appeared frequently on all levels in 1986.[46]

It is worth examining the style of one of the ads created by Struble's National Voter Contact in 1986 in order to illustrate a point. Like the story of a number of other insurgents who have entered the Democratic media-consulting field in a major way, the ad illustrates why campaigns keep turning to less well known consultants with a products orientation for fresh ideas about fitting political ads into the world of commercial television messages.

Struble's "Opal" focused on the Social Security issue and was used by Tom Daschle to attack Republican senator Jim Abdnor of South Dakota. It proceeds in a highly personal fashion without making a list of Social Security bills or indeed attacking Abdnor directly. Instead, "Opal" epitomizes the soft, real-life approach, which in 1986 characterized not only positive "inoculation" ads designed to "put the incumbent on a mountain," in the words of Adam Goodman, but subtle attack ads as well.[47]

It draws the viewer into the experience of "being" an 80-plus woman for whom each move is important, as the camera closes in on her face in the kitchen to the sound of loving music that alerts the viewer who is not elderly to the fact that this could be your mother or aunt, or indeed you yourself someday. The first five to ten seconds do not mention politics. Instead, the focus is on the slow progress that Opal makes along her lifeline, as she walks to the mailbox to pick up her Social Security check. Only one person appears in the ad, and only one place, her home, in order to increase the emotional impact of one single common experience. The announcer's voice is soft, as no ill will is implied toward anyone. Rather, the threat that is implied, wheel-of-emotions style, is finally expressed more as regret that a vague entity—"someone in Washington"—is again trying to harm the elderly.

"Opal"

Audio	Video
Soft music.	Opal in kitchen.
Announcer: For 83-year-old Opal Fine,	Begins slowly

the walk to the mailbox for her Social Security check gets a little longer each month. It seems like almost every year someone in Washington tries to cut Social Security. And more than a few times they've convinced Jim Abdnor to go along. In fact, Jim Abdnor has voted more than 30 times against Social Security and Medicare. Fortunately, Opal and all seniors have a friend, Tom Daschle. He votes for Social Security. And always will.	walking down steps and sidewalk to mailbox.
	Camera continues panning from left against plain wall of house.
	Opens mailbox. Takes out letter with check.
Opal: Thanks, Tom.	Closeup of face, which lights up. Opal's first smile.

There is a venerable history of a limited number of issues including Social Security that, according to consultants, appear heavily in political advertising. One of them is Social Security, which according to the Wirthlin Group's Frank Luntz, Republicans have found "there is no answer for." Whether there is quantitative support for this view, which might be called single-issue or fanatic common thread theory, is examined in Chapter 3. If there turns out to be any validity in this idea, it is to be expected that there would also be a limited number of human and visual symbols that are used in attempts to tap a responsive chord as the character side of the issue—elderly people, and mailboxes, for example. Visual and aural "freshness" become crucial, in this case catching the slow gait and the verbal understatement of an aging woman. The power of a life, in short. The ad uses emotionally charged symbols and an understated wheel-of-emotions style, moving from uncertainty—which associates the opponent with "someone in Washington"—to resolution, summed up in a full-frontal bright smile at the end of a lifeline and few, but significant words: "Thanks Tom."

Neither the opponent nor the candidate appears in the ad, which, like much attack advertising, focuses on the perennial uncaring quality of the opponent as the character side of an unpopular issue in what I argue has become a key concept in political advertising, dovetailing.

"Opal" is an example of why recruits in the field of political advertising, whether in the offices of majors such as the Republican Robert Goodman Agency or in newly successful firms such as National Voter Contact, draw on the work of commercial advertisers. Karl Struble and Goodman share orientations toward the style of the emotional school. A major point, however, is that there is a blending of styles. Emotional advertising is a basic part of the campaign advertising arsenal even of those who might well be placed in the new informational school because they consider their work to be "language-based and is-sues oriented."[48]

CREATING A "FEELING" ABOUT A CANDIDATE

The success of advertising that focuses on creating a feeling about a candi-date is illustrated by the case of Frank Greer, a Democratic consultant who emerged from 1970s obscurity to be the head in 1986 of one of the top Dem-ocratic consulting firms in terms of statewide races and dollar volume. His status was assured by the fact that his firm won 11 out of 13 races in 1986, several of them highly competitive Senate races that brought the Senate back into Democratic hands. Greer is known for his use of jingles. Asked about this after the 1986 election, he commented:

We're real strong on message and language and we're real strong on issues. People make decisions also on how they feel about a candidate, however. The one thing music does, the way it's used in commercial advertising, the way it's used in movies, the way it's used everywhere, it creates a feeling about a candidate. I think you need to do that, as well as communicate a message about issues. . . . Visuals do that as well.[49]

Thus, in the North Dakota Senate race in 1986, where a recession in the farm and energy economies was a campaign issue, Greer's ads on behalf of the successful Democratic challenger, Kent Conrad, took a cue from Republican Ronald Reagan's rather than fellow Democrat Walter Mondale's approach—a cue that was expressed musically. Greer commented:

We didn't want to be depressing and down. . . . People want to be offered hope, and some sense that there is some future, some inspiration. So you'll notice that in the music for the opening of this spot: [music] "Here in North Dakota, there's a feeling for the land. And the spirit's in the people 'that's the best we can.' "[50]

The process in positive advertising of "making a candidate North Dakota," or associating him or her with feelings about a state, as in Greer's case, is at-tempted through music.[51]

Greer also believes in the power of affect-laden visual symbols. He described this in relation to an ad designed to help voters get to know 1986 Georgia Democratic senatorial candidate Wyche Fowler by his first name. Fowler had said that this is important in Georgia, but even his media consultant, Greer himself, was mispronouncing the candidate's first name. So the ad focused on one advertising goal, name identification; but according to Greer, voters read much more into it than that. The ad ran:

Audio	*Visuals*
Class: "With liberty and justice for all."	Classroom shot saluting flag.

One Kid: Okay, who can name the Democratic candidate for the United States Senate. Okay, Sandy.

Student raises hand.

Sandy: Senator Fowler.

Teacher: He's not Senator yet, Sandy.

Sandy: Congressman Fowler is running for Senator. And his first name is Wyche. Y-ch as in CHURCH. Wyche Fowler.

Other kid: Senator Wyche Fowler. [Pause to reflect] And *my* Dad said he's the best.

According to Greer, they took the ad to rural Macon and asked a focus group of undecided voters what the message was. Among the various answers:

Belief in parental discipline. Because that little girl says people should listen to her daddy when he talks. And that Wyche Fowler believes in school prayer, when he doesn't. How much people can read into symbolism. . . . People read a lot more into television spots than we give them credit for.[52]

Even more important as symbols, according to Greer, were spots made a year before the election focusing on Wyche Fowler at Fort Benning. These were designed for a state that is proud of its defense installations and promilitary, and in which Fowler therefore "faced a little problem with our record on defense." The Fowler campaign ran the Fort Benning ad in the primary the night Hamilton Jordan attacked his record on the MX and the contras. It focused on strength symbols with planes flying and paratroopers jumping, moving finally to the candidate saying, with lyrical music playing in the background, that he had learned how important strong, well-trained combat troops were "when I was training at Fort Benning."

Fowler concluded with an invocation of the name of Georgia's Senator Sam Nunn, with whom he said he voted in Congress for a strong national defense. Nunn was very positively perceived, and his endorsement was important. "You know," Greer concluded, "from that point on, we were considered stronger on defense than both [Republican incumbent Mac] Mattingly and Hamilton Jordan [Fowler's competitor in the Democratic primary]." A combination of military symbols, the evoked experience of military training, and the reflected glory of favorite Georgia son Sam Nunn, with his strong defense record, were enough to carry the day. They counted for more than a thousand attempts to offer details concerning his less than prodefense voting record.[53]

The new breed of 1980s consultants well understands television, a medium on which sound, visuals, and language intersect in a fashion as yet not fully understood by students who specialize in one or the other aspect of the medium. We have thus seen how, in the 1984–87 period, media philosophies varied from the emotional to the new informational side of the spectrum.

The quick-response school is represented in its strongest form by Michael Murphy, of Murphy-Castellanos, but its polling techniques by the spring of 1989 had been absorbed by all of the other schools, including the most "emotional" side of the advertising spectrum represented by Robert Goodman. The focus in this philosophy is on poll-driven ads, and its model is news rather than entertainment. Murphy's ads seek as much to answer the question "what's next?" as to tug on the heartstrings. Still, he believes, television news, which serves as the model for his ads, is "entertaining." And, further, despite his emphasis on quick responses, Murphy employs referential symbols and wheel-of-emotions style advertising, examples of which are examined in Chapter 7 on the Hunt-Helms Senate race.[54]

On the Republican side, this is also the case of work emerging through the firms of Roger Ailes and Bailey-Deardourf, which with the Robert Goodman Agency continue to be Republican majors. Ailes's work is examined in Chapter 9 on the 1984 race of Republican challenger Patrick Swindall of Atlanta, Georgia, who ran as a born-again Christian. Ironically four years later he was indicted for perjury before a grand jury in a drug money investigation. On the Republican side, which, given Democratic control of the House, involves more challenger than incumbent races, a whole school of humor and entertainment is growing up around such independents as Chris Motolla, Steve Sandler and Jim Innocenzi, and Ian and Betsey Weinschel. The latter husband-and-wife team came from commercial advertising 20 years before to become a major force in Republican advertising, frequently operating behind the scenes.[55]

Few consultants for major statewide races do not include referential advertising in their campaign arsenal. As indicated, such advertising seeks to transfer what is described as (although not scientifically proven to be) emotionally-laden meaning through visual and aural symbols. On the level of safe incumbent congressmen and low-budget campaigns, more traditional biographically oriented and candidate-centered advertising was still used in 1984, as evidenced in the chapter on congressional incumbents. Several quite successful, if not as wealthy, consultants specialize in this lower-budget advertising that might be labeled the work of the candidate-coat-over-the-shoulder traditional school. Much of its advertising could be included in a category that Richard Joslyn termed "benevolent leader" ads.[56]

Some consultants use primarily entertainment devices and little referential advertising. This can take the form of ads such as those made by Republicans Chris Motolla and Jim Innocenzi, which use suspense-story genres, parodies, comedies, and fairy tales. Still, the political advertising story of the mid-1980s was of a philosophical trend to the emotional, noninstitutionally related advertising that involved heavy use of sounds and symbols intended to stimulate learning of candidate messages. Heavy use was made of a wheel-of-emotions format, with close-up shots of real people with whose lives voters can identify, as attempts are made to draw an affect-laden connection between the viewer and the on-stage character.

The upshot of all this is a humanization of "nonpolitical" candidates, as indicated in the strategy chapters of this book, and in the chapters on positive and negative advertising. The campaign world of 1984 was also lacking positive nonnational institutional symbols. For as the content analysis of the 1984 ads taken from the air indicates, if, as Richard Joslyn established, the party disappeared from political advertising in the 1970s, in the mid-1980s symbols relating to other institutions (work or class-related interest groups, for example) were experiencing a fade-out, save in negative advertising. Thus, to the television viewer of 1972, who saw ads created by Charles Guggenheim, a leader in the documentary-oriented informational school, the familiar scene depicting George McGovern discoursing on his views on the Vietnam War in a working-class restaurant was a relic of the past. Less candidate-oriented and institutionally centered schools of consulting had emerged in the 1980s and were focusing, like their counterparts in commercial advertising, on highly personal common experiences. Further, as in the products advertising of the period, the appeal was to the lone individual.

We turn now to an overview of the 1984 ad content and to an examination of the significance of issues in advertising and news.

NOTES

1. The Toyota quote is from James Ogilvy, "The Experience Industry," *American Demographics* 8, no. 12 (December 1986):27–29, 59.

2. Jarol Manheim and Richard C. Rich, *Empirical Political Analysis: Research Methods in Political Science* (Englewood Cliffs, N.J.: Prentice Hall, 1981).

3. *Majors* are defined as consultants who have successfully moved into the area of statewide gubernatorial or senatorial and/or presidential races.

4. See R. Rudd, "Issues as Image in Political Campaign Commercials," *Western Journal of Speech Communication* 50, no. 2 (Winter 1986): 102–118.

5. Statements concerning the development of the license branch issue came from two different media consultants, Richard Dresner and Douglas Schoen, who respectively polled for and created ads for gubernatorial candidate Wayne Townsend (D-Indiana) in 1984 and Evan Bayh (D-Indiana) in 1986.

Author interview with Dresner Sykes and Townsend, New York, September 10, 1985; and Douglas Schoen lecture on the integration of polling and campaign messages at the *Campaigns and Elections* Conference, Washington, D.C., May 7, 1987.

6. Interview with Dennis Woods, Columbia Information Systems (CIS), April 29, 1988. Columbia Information Systems is a $6 million per year business whose clients are largely commercial. Its dial-based "perception analyzer" was used to evaluate viewer reaction to a 1988 Republican presidential primary debate. Its system has been adopted by the Wirthlin Group and along with the Teeter firm, it is moving into the business of evaluating audience response to ads for congressional and senatorial races.

7. Interviews with William Zimmerman, Los Angeles, California, June 25, 1985, and Michael Berman, Los Angeles, California, July 24, 1985. Hamilton, Schoen, and Teeter addressed these issues at the *Campaigns and Elections* Conference, Washington, D.C., May 7, 1987. Hart and Maislin were quoted in Paul Taylor, "Negative Advertising Becoming a Powerful Political Force: More Candidates Going for Jugular on TV," *Washington Post,* October 5, 1986, p. 1.

8. Maislin, as quoted in Taylor, "Negative Advertising."

9. Ibid.

10. Interview with Frank Luntz, of the Wirthlin Group, McLean, Virginia, April 4, 1988.

11. Lewis W. Wolfson, "The Men Behind the Men Behind the Candidates: Parts I and II," *Washington Post, Potomac Magazine,* February 13 and March 5, 1972; Thomas Patterson and Robert McClure, *The Unseeing Eye,* (New York: Putnam's, 1976).

12. For 1972, Robert Squier and Robert Goodman as interviewed extensively in Wolfson, *Men behind the Men.* Robert Squier's 1987 philosophy was developed in a lecture at the American University School of Communications, September 10, 1987.

13. Will Marshall, Democratic Leadership Council, Washington, D.C., July 6, 1987.

14. Doug Schoen, lecture on the integration of polling and campaign messages at the *Campaigns and Elections* Conference, Washington, D.C., May 7, 1987. Jerry Hagstrom and Robert Guskind, "Changing the Guard," *National Journal* (October 22, 1988): 2660–2667.

15. Robert Bechel and Robert Squier appeared frequently on network television news programs.

16. Michael Murphy, lecture on integrating polling and campaign messages at the *Campaigns and Elections* Conference, Washington, D.C., May 7, 1987.

17. Robert Goodman, "What Works in Political Television Advertising?" lecture at the *Campaigns and Elections* Conference, Washington, D.C., May 9, 1987.

18. Murphy lecture.

19. Goodman lecture.

20. Pat Caddell, "Baby Boomers Come of Age," *Wall Street Journal,* December 30, 1985. This is an adaptation of extended remarks ("Reassessing the Political Spectrum") that Caddell presented at a Cato Institute conference in the spring of 1985. Academic research has focused recently on the homogenizing impact of television. See also Ogilvy, "The Experience Industry," pp. 27–29, 59.

21. For one summary of leading theoreticians whose views are taught in commercial advertising and the central role that appeals to the emotions play in them, see Don E. Schultz, Dennis Martin, William P. Brown, *Strategic Advertising Campaigns* (Chicago, Ill.: Crain Books, 1984). Richard Kiernan and Burt Manning are quoted in the *Washington Post,* July 8, 1984.

22. The Foote, Cone, and Belding grid was published in "Modern Advertising: The subtle persuasion—Finding Out What Makes Us Tick," *Christian Science Monitor,* January 27, 1987, p. 16.

23. Peter Markey at the American Film Institute Conference, Washington, D.C., November, 1984.

24. Judith Williamson, *Decoding Advertisements: Ideology and Meaning in Advertising* (New York: Marion Boyars, 1984); Adam Goodman, interview in Washington, D.C., June 23, 1987.

25. Stuart G. Agres of Lowe-Marschalk quoted in the *Christian Science Monitor,* "Modern Advertising: The Subtle Persuasion—Finding Out What Makes Us Tick," January 27, 1987, p. 16; see also Stuart J. Agres, "The Marschalk Emotional Expression Deck," September 1984 (unpublished document). Varda Langholz Leymore *Hidden Myth: Structure and Symbolism in Advertising* (London: Heineman, 1975); Richard M. Merelman, *Making Something of Ourselves: On Culture and Politics in the United States* (Berkeley: University of California Press, 1984).

26. For recent research on myths, see Dan Nimmo and A. J. Felsberg, "Hidden Myths in Televised Political Advertising: An Illustration," in *New Perspectives on Political Advertising,* ed. Linda Lee Kaid, Dan Nimmo, and Keith R. Sanders (Carbondale: Southern Illinois University Press, 1986), pp. 248–67. See also Dan Nimmo, *Subliminal Politics: Myths and Mythmakers in America* (Englewood Cliffs, N.J.: Prentice Hall, 1980).

A close examination of the 1984 ad sample taken from the air is being completed in relation to sound and symbols mentioned by some consultants as having affective meaning in positive and negative advertising appeals.

27. Stuart Agres, *Christian Science Monitor,* p. 16.

28. Ibid.

29. For traditional "get 'em sick, then get 'em well" theory see Michael Schudson, *Advertising: The Uneasy Persuasion* (New York: Basic Books, 1984), p. 6.

30. L. Patrick Devlin, "An Analysis of Presidential Television Commercials, 1952–1984," in *New Perspectives,* p. 26. Devlin examines "Daisy Girl" in the light of Schwartz's view that the ad simply appeals to preexisting mistrust of Goldwater.

31. "The Media Merlin," Schwartz interview with Tom Shales, *Washington Post,* February 17, 1983.

32. Ibid.

33. Ibid.

34. Johnson's slow-paced drawl contrasts with the building tension.

35. *Political Advertising Classics.* Handbook, *Campaigns and Elections,* Washington, D.C., 1987.

36. Schwartz quoted in Shales, *Washington Post.*

37. Gary Nordlinger and Ed Blakely, forum on political advertising, American University School of Communications, November, 1984.

38. Background discussion with an official of Edison Electric, November 17, 1986.

39. Interview with John Franzen, Washington, D.C., March 5, 1985.

40. Ibid.

41. Ibid.; author telephone interview with Ken Swope, December 16, 1987. An example of a copy of the elder woman crying "shame on you" was used in a fashion that was believed to be quite successful in the Helms campaign. It concluded, "Jim Hunt just wants to get elected, too bad."

42. Franzen interview.

43. Ibid. Interview with Dan Payne, Boston, Mass., January 2, 1989.

44. Interview with Republican consultant Paul Sipple, December 11, 1987. Sipple in 1986 was with Bailey-Deardourf in charge of the Bond candidacy. He has since formed an independent firm and is ranked by Republican party officials among the most successful of the mid-1980s insurgents.

45. Markey, American Film Institute.

46. Interview with Charles E. Cook, Washington, D.C., June 24, 1987; Adam Goodman interview.

47. Adam Goodman interview.

48. Frank Greer used this language to describe his approach in a lecture he gave along with Don Ringe, "Devising a Media Strategy," at the *Campaigns and Elections* Conference, Washington, D.C., May 7, 1987.

49. Ibid.

50. Ibid.

51. Ibid.

52. Ibid.

53. Ibid.

54. Michael Murphy lecture, *Campaign and Elections* Conference. See Chapter 7.

55. See also Ian and Betsey Weinschel lecture, "Creative Media," *Campaigns and Elections* Conference, May 5, 1987; interview with Ian and Betsey Weinschel, Mt. Airy, Maryland, November 27, 1987.

56. See Richard Joslyn citation in Chapter 1.

3

Issues in Televised Ads and News

On the basis of research on the 1972 presidential election, Thomas Patterson and Robert McClure argued that the central impact of televised political advertising was to inform the public about the positions of the candidates on the issues. They concluded that by a ratio of 4 to 1, Americans received the majority of their information about candidate positions on the issues from ads rather than the news. Further, they determined that 42 percent of all commercials were primarily issue communications, while another 28 percent contained substantial issue material. They drew a distinction between the functions of two types of ads, image and issue ads, and argued that while the "image content is intended to draw an emotional reaction, the issue content is intended to make voters think." Given the high level of issue content and their view of its purpose, they concluded that the primary impact of political advertising was to make "people who were poorly informed by the news media more knowledgeable." [1]

In the years since 1972 not only has there been a significant shift in consultant views concerning the purpose of political advertising, but there have been important strides in content research. Much of it has followed Patterson and McClure and focused on the shortcomings of television news, particularly its tendency to focus greater attention on the "horserace," and less on the substance of political issues. A smaller, but significant, amount of research has focused on the content of political advertising. Particular attention has been devoted to developing categories of ads, with the greatest body of research devoted to attempts to define the difference between "issue" ads, whose primary purpose is that of conveying information about issues, and "image" commercials, which are focused on candidate character. [2]

There has, however, been no attempt to determine whether ads are more or less important in providing U.S. voters with information about issues in the mid-1980s than was the case in 1972. Nor has research focused on the ads that actually appear on the air. What type of issue content do they contain, developed by which party, for what type of candidate? How does their issue content compare to that of television news? The changes since 1972 in consultant philosophy examined in Chapter 2 make it especially appropriate to take another look at the nature and use of the ads that actually appear on the air.

The task in this chapter is to focus on several questions: How significant is televised advertising in defining the information that Americans receive about campaign issues? What types of issues appear in ads? Do the issues as articulated in political ads offer a clear statement of candidate positions? Is information presented in a fashion that gives reasons for or against a position one favors or opposes? Or are issues in ads articulated more as slogans whose learning would require little rational thought?

Further, do the issues that appear in the ads actually appearing on the air reflect a broad range of issues, according to what might be termed thousand-flower theory? Or do they instead reflect single-issue or fanatic common-thread theory, which suggests that the most effective strategy is a repetitive, offensive one, continually returning the agenda to a few issues?

Finally, how significant is advertising in influencing the total televised agenda of issues information appearing on the air? Is it possible to turn not only the advertising but the news agenda to one's own issues according to media blitz theories? Or does theory developed on the presidential level prior to the 1988 election, suggesting news media dominance of the total electronic agenda, apply on other levels as well?[3]

THEORY RELATING TO ISSUES IN ADS

Content research conducted since 1972 suggests that issues are indeed a significant component of ads, but it has become difficult to find ads whose sole purpose is that of conveying information about issues. Scholars have found that ads serve a number of purposes in addition to informing voters about candidate positions on issues. The purpose of ads that stress issues content can in fact be that of building an image of the candidate. W. Lance Bennett theorized concerning this proposition in 1972, and Robert Rudd found it to be operative in a gubernatorial campaign a decade later.[4]

Further, analysts were finding it difficult to find a pure *issues* ad, one whose sole function was informational, as early as 1976, the year the economics of the broadcast industry resulted in the triumph of the 30-second spot both in commercial and political advertising. Richard Joslyn examined a sample of 500 ads in 1976 and concluded that the largest of his ad categories mentioned issues, but their purpose was less to discuss policy positions than to convey a particular impression of a candidate that the policy statement was designed to leave with the voter. Leonard Shyles examined production and issue characteristics of 1980 presidential primary ads and concluded that the *candidate-to-camera talking head* (or introspective) ad without stimulating visual effects and music was the single vehicle whose purpose was clearly that of conveying information about candidate positions. By contrast, ads that include a variety of aural and visual production characteristics are *image* ads, those whose primary purpose is to focus attention on the candidate's character. A third type of ad, which he called a "hybrid," dealt with both character and issues.[5]

Kathleen Hall Jamieson argues that there is a *concept* spot that focuses on candidate records without benefit of aural and visual production devices, setting forward a series of factual statements that invite or stipulate a conclusion and then invite the viewer to make a judgment. A "neutral observer ad" may offer information about a candidate's record, compare it with what he says he will do for the voter, and then raise a leading question relating to what the voter thinks the candidate will do given the facts. There has been no study of frequency of use of such ads. Jamieson has argued that they were particularly significant in presidential elections during the period after Watergate, for example, in Jimmy Carter's 1976 presidential advertising. In his 1976 study Richard Joslyn determined that by far the most frequent spot was what he called the "benevolent leader" ad, which focuses on character, extolling to the public the candidate's services, which were motivated by the highest of personal qualities. On the basis of a 1960–84 ad sample he argues that ads serve a variety of purposes, including providing voters with an opportunity to evaluate past policy performance and to reward or punish incumbent parties and candidates. He terms this genre "retrospective" ads. But such ads frequently contain production characteristics—visual and aural effects—which would cause Shyles to place them in the category of hybrid ads. And, as Joslyn suggests, they rarely indicate specifically what the candidate "would have done differently or what he would propose to do in the future."[6]

Theory would thus suggest that issues might be expected to play an important role in the 1984 sample of ads, but it would be difficult to find ads whose *sole* purpose would be informational.

What, then, would theory suggest concerning the range of issues that appears in the ads? Would the ads be focused around many, or only a few, themes? No study relating to this question has been based on the actual content of ads taken off the air, or of ads that appeared on any level during a general election campaign. Leonard Shyles's examination of 1980 presidential primary ads led to the conclusion that they dealt with a "plethora of issues" that were "consonant with the political climate during the 1980 election year and underscore a concern with issues featured in the news media as prime concerns of the political system at the time."[7]

By contrast, consultant David Beiler, who studied hundreds of political ads from both primary and general election campaigns while making the *Campaigns and Elections* film *The Classics of Political Advertising,* reached the opposite conclusion. He argued that over half of the political ads he examined dealt with a few key issues, such as taxes or Social Security. In the literature two theories thus exist that remain to be tested for varied periods of election campaigns: thousand-flower theory, which suggests that a "plethora" of issues appear in ads reflecting general discussion in the news media, and single-issue or common thread theory, which assumes a more proactive role for campaigns.[8]

Finally, on the question of whether specific issues mentioned in the ads can overwhelm the news coverage, there has been little research that would lead to testable propositions. *Mediality* theory developed on the presidential level suggests that advertising strategists must fit their issues into a context dominated by national news reportage. The research findings presented here examine local as well as national news in market areas that differ in size and educational variables.

THE 1984 SAMPLE OF ADS AND NEWS

All of the ads and news from races on all levels appearing on the air between 6:00 P.M. and 9:00 P.M. in the final ten days of the 1984 election in four varied market areas in Indiana, California, North Carolina, and Georgia during the final ten days of the 1984 election were collected and examined.[9]

The 1984 sample consisted of 122 different ads, which appeared 301 times altogether, totaling over five hours (315 minutes) of airtime. Approximately half (45.9 percent) of this time was devoted to 289 aired 30-second spots and approximately half (47.6 percent) to five 30-minute ads that appeared on the presidential and senatorial levels. The remainder consisted of four 5-minute ads and three 10-second ads.

The sample indicated that the use of ads is greatest in the smaller, more competitive markets. Ads were used least, and primarily on the presidential level and in proposition campaigns, in Los Angeles, California, the nation's second largest media market. In Los Angeles, 47 minutes of campaign news overwhelmed 19 minutes of adtime. By contrast, in the Piedmont area of North Carolina, whose two stations covered in this sample together averaged a fiftieth percentile ADI rating, adtime overwhelmed newstime by a ratio of over four and a half to one. Almost three hours of adtime appeared, approximately half in 30-minute ads and slightly less in 30-second ads. On the senatorial level, where there were two varied races, one highly competitive race in North Carolina between Governor Jim Hunt and Senator Jesse Helms, and one noncompetitive shoo-in involving Senator Sam Nunn in Georgia, the ads overwhelmed news by a ratio of over six to one. In our mixed districts in Atlanta and Indiana, which respectively had average ADIs in the fifteenth and fifty-seventh percentile in the nation, ads played a lesser but still surprisingly significant role, totaling in both cases close to one hour of ad fare for the average viewer over the ten-day period, as compared with three-quarters of an hour of newstime devoted to all aspects of elections.[10]

Overall, approximately one-half the adtime was devoted to presidential ads, while lesser but still significant figures appeared on the lower levels: 20 percent senatorial; 9 percent congressional; 7 percent statewide, including gubernatorial races in Indiana and North Carolina, and close to 5 percent generic, party ads. In relation to news, adtime played its greatest role on the senatorial level, overwhelming news by a ratio of close to six to one. On the presidential level, interestingly enough, little had changed since 1972: The same ratio of 4 to 1 favoring ads over news was found in 1984. Surprisingly, on the congressional level, where one might expect to find little role for ads, given the fact that at least two of the market areas in the sample were large, expensive, and involved a number of noncompetitive House races, ads still overwhelmed news, totaling approximately 28 minutes of airtime to 18 minutes for news.[11]

Overall, a significant role was found for ads. Indeed, Americans obtain the overwhelming majority of their information about the elections from ads during the final period of a campaign. It thus seemed worthwhile to examine them in detail in relation to the sample of news that also appeared on the air.

ISSUES IN THE 30-SECOND SPOTS

The focus in the close analysis of the issues that appeared in the ads will be on the 104 30-second ads relating to candidate races, proposition campaigns, and generic (party) ads that appeared on the air. This is because there are dramatic stylistic differences between 30-second and 30-minute ads, because they could be expected to be found more commonly on the air over the longer course of a campaign, and because the pattern of their appearance was different from that of the longer ads. The latter could be seen in the ten-day period of the sample during only 5 viewing periods, as compared with 289 for the shorter spots.

In general, issues were mentioned in 89 percent of such ads, an amount greater than Patterson and McClure's 70 percent, and Hofstetter and Zukin's 85 percent for the 1972 election. But the issue references were usually vague. For purposes of examining the degree to which the ads would inform voters about what the candidate would do if elected, they were divided into two categories. The first, *platform* ads, contain either a commitment by a candidate to a position, or a rationale for taking a position or opposing that of the opponent. It was inspired by Richard Joslyn's research, which isolated ads containing prospective policy statements, that is, ones which include a statement of what the candidate will do if elected. But the category of platform ads is slightly broader because ads could be included in it if a rationale is suggested in the ad concerning *why* a position should be favored or opposed. In *slogan* ads, by contrast, no prospective policy statement is made, nor is there a why statement or answer. In developing the codings, the benefit of the doubt is given to the candidate. The coding platform ad, for example, would be given even in the case of an indefinite statement of intent, such as Dwight D. Eisenhower's famous 1952 campaign promise, "I will go to Korea."[12]

Confirming the view that the impact of the 1984 ads could not be informational in any rational sense, almost three-fourths of the ads in the sample, or

Figure 3.1
Platform and Slogan Ads on the Federal Level (in minutes aired, 30-second and 1-minute ads)

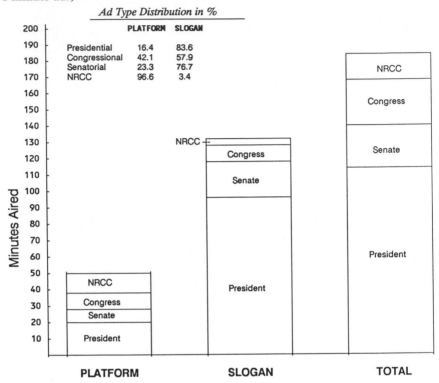

71.2 percent, proved to be slogan ads and 28.8 percent were platform ads. Only 16.5 percent of the 30-second spots were platform-oriented. (See Figure 3.1.)

There were significant differences, however, between the spots that appeared on the various federal levels. The presidential advertising was the most slogan oriented, with the advertising becoming more specific at the lower federal levels. The presidential advertising was 16.4 percent platform and 83.6 slogan oriented. The Senate advertising was 23.3 percent platform and 76.7 percent slogan advertising. The House of Representatives advertising was more evenly divided, with 42.1 percent platform and 57.9 percent slogan ads. Generic House advertising, developed by the National Republican Campaign Committee (NRCC) was even more heavily platform oriented, with 96.6 percent platform and 3.4 percent slogan ads.

Interestingly, there were differences relating to specific issues. (See Figure 3.2.) Advertising on the tax issue was more platform oriented than other advertising. Its heavy use on the House level contributed greatly to the high level of platform oriented ads that appeared there. If all House advertising by both

Figure 3.2

Issues in House of Representatives Democratic and Republican Candidate and Party Generic (NRCC) Ads (30-second ads, in minutes)

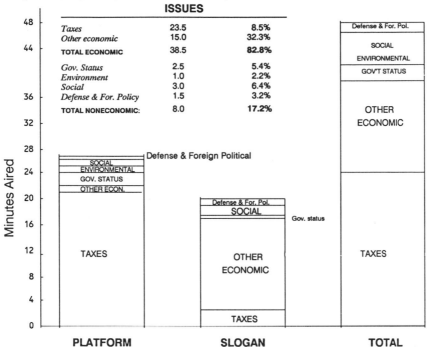

Note: Of the total of 26.5 argument ads in the Congressional tally, 21 (79.5%) relate to the tax issue.

candidates and the NRCC generic advertising is examined, it is clear not only that more platform than slogan ads were used in House campaigns, but that 50.5 percent (23.5 minutes) of all House adtime dealt with the tax issue. Half of all the tax issue ads were NRCC ads. Candidates produced more slogan statements relating to the issue of taxes than did the NRCC, but the ratio was still over two to one platform ads. Republican advertising contained a clear commitment not to raise taxes and the congressional issues agenda was dominated by this advertising.

Martin Franks of the Democratic Congressional Campaign Committee later charged that the NRCC advertising was illegal under Federal Election Commission rulings because it provided candidate assistance above and beyond the federal spending limits. Republicans argued that because it did not represent assistance to individual candidates, it should not be included in the Federal Election Commission limitation. The analysis of the issues included in the 1984 sample reported here indicates that NRCC ads represented a third of all the aired Republican ads. There was a difference between the issues included in them and those included in ads aired on behalf of Republican congressional candidates. Whereas the only issue included in the NRCC ads was taxes, only 37 percent of the congressional candidate ad airings included the tax issue. Still, this represents a significant area of issues congruence, and it is clear that the NRCC advertising reenforced the message of GOP candidates. One explanation, offered by a Republican consultant and examined in a subsequent chapter focusing on congressional incumbent-challenger issues that have emerged from this analysis, emphasizes the degree to which Republican congressional challengers were able to develop the character or image side of the tax message. The underlying theory is that dovetailing of character and issues messages is necessary because voters will not vote solely on the basis of a candidate's stand on an issue.[13]

NO SUPPORT FOR THOUSAND-FLOWER THEORY

In terms of what actually appeared on the air, the dominance of the tax issue indicates that far from finding support for thousand-flower theory of televised issues, those represented in the 1984 sample lend support to the idea of a race boiling down to a few single issues. The GOP successfully attempted to create a unified national issues theme so as to amplify the party message at all levels. By contrast with the GOP, the Democratic presidential ticket, headed by Walter Mondale, did not have the advantage either of unity or consistency. It was every candidate for himself, and Mondale's major themes, for example, were aired only by Mondale.

It was not just the congressional agenda that was dominated by tax advertising. Tax advertising was the vehicle through which the Republicans dominated the overall issues agenda on television. (See Figure 3.3.) Three-fourths (72.5 to 27.5 percent) of all the issues mentioned in the ads were Republican issues in Republican ads. The Republican version of the economy consumed 54.5 percent of all advertising airtime (100 out of the 183.5 minutes). Focusing only on economic issues, Republicans prevailed even more overwhelmingly. The statement of their side of the case consumed 81.3 percent of airtime compared to 17.7 percent for the Democrats. The tax issue consumed one-third of all the 30-second-spot time devoted to the Republican version of the economy. Few GOP ads focused on other federal issues.

From an examination of the issues included in ads for federal office in the 1984 sample, it is clear that Democrats achieved a major statement of their issues only on the question of the need to create jobs, with 10 minutes of airtime. But even here they were seriously outgunned by the Republicans' 18 minutes on the issue. Despite the importance of presidential advertising, Democratic presidential candidate Walter Mondale's major economic issue, the federal deficit, appeared infrequently in the 1984 sample: with 3.5 minutes of Democratic airtime to the Republicans' 3 minutes. Social policy issues were expressed largely in slogan ads (16 minutes out of the total of 20 minutes airtime). Over half of these were aired on the senatorial level. The social issues

Figure 3.3
Issues in Ads for Federal Office (argument and slogan)
30-second spots, in minutes*

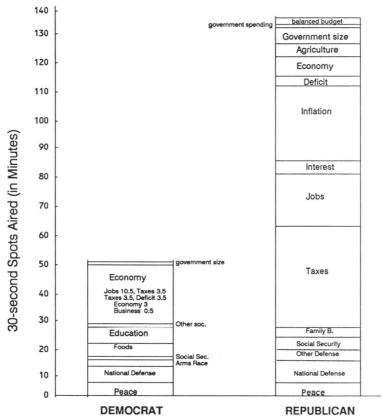

*Presidential, Senatorial, Congressional, and National Republican Congressional Committee (NRCC)
generic party spots

were highly personal: education (2.5 minutes), family or birth control (4.0 min-utes), and Social Security (4.0 minutes). On the presidential level, the only social issues included were education (3.5 minutes), which was dealt with vaguely, and food stamps, which involved greater specificity than most. The lack of comprehensive social policy debate in the domestic area was striking. There was no expression in advertising of questions relating to civil rights, housing, transportation, or medical care.

In subsequent chapters, the context in which these policy issues were raised is examined. On the presidential level, it became clear that issues were devel-oped in a fashion intended to build candidate character of image. Few foreign policy issues were elaborated. It is clear that little airtime was devoted to such issues as arms control, Central American policy, hostages, or defense spend-ing. To the extent that the public relied on the ads for information in such areas, they were little informed. To the extent that any of these ads affected votes, it was also clear that the relationship between voter and elected official involved scant focus on specific policy issues.

Overall, two points are clear from this analysis of the issues included in the 1984 sample of ads. First, their purpose was not informational in the sense of focusing on clear candidate positions. There were far more slogan ads than ads that stated a clear candidate position or rationale for favoring a position. The tax issue was an exception, a fact which has significant implications. Second, they reflected Republican domination of the airwaves with their version of the economic issues before the country. When numbers of issues mentioned in the ads are totaled, the issues that appeared on the airwaves most frequently were there because Republicans decided to create a single issue, or set of issues. Federal taxation was the issue that was promoted most heavily in Republican ads and that appeared on the air most frequently. Further, William Greener, communications director of the Republican National Committee, argued that voters' evaluation of taxes as the major issue in the 1984 election came after, not before, their advertising campaign, in which the same issue was raised on all levels—from the House to the presidential. He saw public acceptance of the tax issue as the major issue of the campaign as a measure of the campaign's effectiveness. In his view, it achieved this status on election day because it was promoted so heavily. "When people were asked, according to the exit polls, why they voted the way they did, for most the answer was 'because they [the Democrats] want to raise taxes.' When your attack message is believed to be your opponent's campaign slogan, you're truckin.' " In the 1984 ad sample, the issues which appeared on the air reflected more single-issue than thousand-flowers theory.[14]

In subsequent chapters on 1984 House races, the focus is on Republican advertising strategy that linked House Democratic candidates with Walter Mondale's plan to raise taxes. There are a number of factors in addition to advertising that affect candidate electoral success; and whatever its effectiveness in terms of actual numbers of candidates elected, this Republican advertising dominated the issues agenda in the televised ad sample. The ads actually appearing on the air during the final period of the campaign focused around a single issue and were there because of a strategic decision to pound a specific message home.

Interestingly enough, however, the single issue that figured prominently in this analysis is one that also involved a specific platform statement. The candidate stands for something quite specific whose benefits can easily be understood. In strategy chapters, the focus will be on how candidate qualities can be linked with it in a positive and negative fashion.[15]

ISSUES IN THE NEWS: PLAYING CATCHUP
TO ADVERTISING

As noted, voters who tuned in at the end of the 1984 election campaign obtained the overwhelming majority of their campaign information from political ads, rather than from television coverage. On all levels, the total was 315 minutes adtime to 174 minutes newstime, or a ratio of a little less than two to one favoring ads. If one excludes the newstime that was not devoted to candidate races but that dealt instead with such questions as polling procedures, voter turnout, or changes in the women's vote over time, then the ratio is higher. Overall, *on all levels relating to specific electoral contests from the local to the presidential level, ads dominated newstime by a ratio of three to one.*

Conventional wisdom concerning news and political advertising, born of extensive network news coverage of presidential elections, has offered the theory of mediality. The theory suggests that news is the most important phenomenon on the air, and it even defines the agenda of issues that appear in political ads. This study, based on the ads and news appearing on the air in four market areas during the final days of the 1984 election, instead offers confirmation on lower levels for media blitz principles, which suggest that it is possible to use advertising as part of a process, involving controlled (non-news conference) appearances in the press to set a news media agenda.

During the final stages of the 1984 election, advertising was the television viewer's primary source of information about political campaigns by a margin of three to one. It can also dominate the issues agenda. In this analysis the focus is on the national and local news coverage that appeared in the same market areas during the period of the 1984 sample. Was there a difference in levels and in market areas that varied on a factor such as audience education level? Particular attention is paid to television stations in North Carolina's Piedmont and West Lafayette, Indiana, which varied markedly in this area.

The nature of issue coverage in the 1984 news sample is first examined. Particular attention is then focused on television news coverage of congressional elections in an effort to answer the question of whether congressional advertising plays a role in setting the news agenda that is more important than that on the presidential level, if only because there is a greater amount of presidential news coverage. It has been suggested that there is greater news coverage of Senate than of House races because the former affect viewers statewide and are consequently of broader news interest. This gives Senate challengers an advantage which is not enjoyed by House aspirants because television market areas and congressional districts infrequently coincide.[16]

The news coverage of the two Senate races included in the 1984 sample is examined. These were the Helms-Hunt race in North Carolina and the campaign in which the popular Sam Nunn strolled to reelection in Georgia. They were selected for examination because they were at opposite ends of the competitiveness spectrum. Issues coverage that appeared on the air in House and local elections is then examined, the major differences emerge between local stations in two states, Indiana and North Carolina.

The news coverage in one area illustrates how ads not only can be the viewers' major source of issues information but can set the agenda for local news coverage as well. This occurred in one major market area, Atlanta, Georgia, where a well-placed last-minute negative ad provoked local television news coverage of a local race that otherwise netted few stories in the local news sample. This had important consequences for the candidate who lacked the resources to respond to the charge in similar fashion.

ISSUES IN THE FEDERAL NEWS

The 1984 sample of news coverage of issues in federal races indicates, simply, that for the final period of the election the focus was on the campaign strategies and the horserace, not issues, a fact which allowed the electronic media agenda to be set by candidates through staged media events. On the national level, as other research has suggested, Ronald Reagan excelled in this area.[17]

A total of 128 news stories were collected in the sample of ads and news which appeared on the air in the final days of the 1984 election: Half (68) related to federal elections. Of these, 50 concerned the presidential and vice-presidential races, and only 18 related to Senate and House races; 37 dealt with state, local, and proposition campaigns, and 23 dealt with noncampaign election issues. Approximately one-fourth of these stories (34) dealt with issues. (See Figure 3.4.)

Major national issues that were a primary focus of election advertising, including the economy, defense, and foreign policy, were scarcely mentioned in network and local news stories. A single news item dealt with the economy in terms of the tax issue. No news stories dealt with the environment or the size of government. In short, complex national issues were not a focus of the telecasts picked up from the air during the final days of the election. This meant that the campaigns could dominate the television issues agenda because television news programs were not focusing on issues.

California's issues-oriented news tally was highest, totalling 25 of the 30 minutes in the 1984 sample devoted to such stories. All of these stories appeared on the presidential level, but much of the coverage appeared in interviews with the major presidential and vice-presidential candidates, who valued California so highly that they blitzed in this state during the final days of the race. The interviews appeared on the increasingly important local news on such stations as KABC and KCBS in Los Angeles. In Atlanta, there were stories about a "nonpolitical" trip by First Lady Nancy Reagan to a day-care center, but no federal elections issues newstime. All of the campaign stories in Atlanta dealt either with the "horserace" or "other" aspects of the only two elections

Figure 3.4
Issues in Federal Election News: Time Aired by Race and State

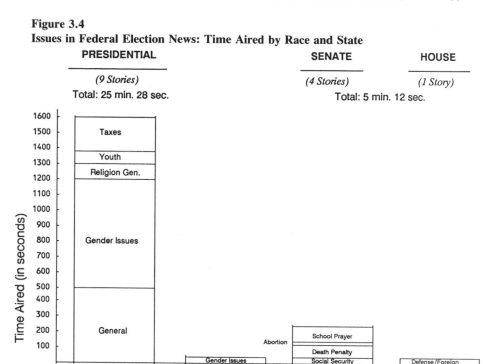

covered, the presidential race, to which three-fourths of the stories were devoted, and the hotly contested Levitas-Swindall congressional race in the fourth district.

The federal election picture was similar in the smaller markets. In Indiana the federal tally yielded only one story, totalling 28 seconds, which touched on issues. It was an October 31 story on Channel 6 in Indianapolis that was coded for "gender issues" because it included Ronald Reagan's view that Democratic vice-presidential candidate Geraldine Ferraro was selected because she was a woman. There were no stories on the North Carolina stations devoted to the issues that divided the Democratic and Republican presidential candidates. This pattern of issueless coverage of the final period of the race supports research that focuses on the value of visually oriented media events such as those staged by the Reagan campaign.

LOCAL ELECTIONS COVERAGE: THERE IS A "DIFFERENCE"

The greatest number of stories mentioning issues occurred on the nonfederal level and were almost entirely in the Indiana sample, which included Indianapolis and West Lafayette, which happens to include Purdue University with

Figure 3.5
Story Types in North Carolina and Indiana

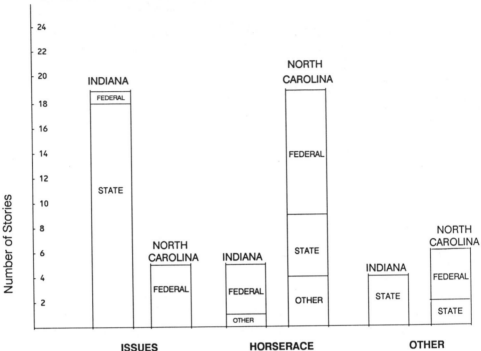

N = 53 Stories consuming 30 minutes of airtime.

its 33,000 students. (See Figure 3.5.) The coverage indicated that in this one market stories focusing on the issues dividing candidates were alive and well, even during the final period of the election. Of the total 19 state and local issues oriented stories in the blitz sample, 18 appeared on the air in the West Lafayette market. By contrast, the North Carolina stations, which were most comparable in terms of market size, included no stories about the issues and few about the status of state and local campaigns.[18]

Mike Piggott, news director of WFLI-TV Channel 18 West Lafayette, said the station's coverage was part of a 50-part series on the 1984 elections. During the final period of the election the focus was on state and local, not federal, campaigns. Interviews were conducted with candidates, most of whom were responsive to such requests (one exception was incumbent congressman John Myers, whose race is examined in Chapter 8). Piggott had become acquainted with many of them during his 15-year career in local radio news. A staff of ten reporters worked with him on the project, which had been organized after he was hired by the station with a mandate to improve the local coverage and thereby increase the competitiveness of the 6:00 P.M. news slot. Two Indianapolis stations, Channels 6 and 13, were the competition. His station could not succeed through "flashy" coverage because the Indianapolis stations could "afford all the bells and whistles," given the greater advertising revenue linked with their greater audience. Indianapolis's ADI rating (its market size compared with other stations in the United States, with number 1 ranking at the top) was 20 to West Lafayette's 193. In this instance, competition in the area of local news, which was not flashy but informative, not only served the community well by facilitating public knowledge of candidate positions, but it also served the West Lafayette station, which pulled well ahead of the Indianapolis stations during 1984. According to Piggott, the Arbitron ratings tell the story.

Arbitron Ratings for 6:00 P.M. News Slot

		July 1984	**February 1985**
W. Lafayette	Ch 18	25%	43%
Indianapolis	Ch 6	27%	16%
Indianapolis	Ch 13	17%	16%

In this effort, according to Piggott, the station had the advantage not only of a serious commitment to news but also of an educated audience, "ninety-eight percent of whom" had at least a high school diploma. Further, "local names and faces make bigger news in a smaller community."[19]

Channel 18 demonstrates what is possible given an experienced reporter directing a news effort and a commitment to local news. Few would argue such coverage is the norm in larger, less-educated news environments.

In North Carolina, where the audiences were larger and the educational level markedly lower (statewide 27.8 percent of adult North Carolinians had graduated from high school versus 41.7 percent statewide in Indiana), no stories mentioning local issues appeared in the blitz sample. David Summer of WXII Channel 12 in Winston-Salem, whose ADI ranking is 50 among all market areas, noted that his Pulitzer-owned station accepted no political advertising during the 7:00 P.M. national news. This put a lot of pressure on the 6:30 P.M. to 7:00 P.M. local news because candidates like to advertise during and surrounding the news programs, which attract what he calls an "upscale" audience more likely to vote than those who watch the "Dukes of Hazzard." The news is also an information vehicle, so people watch with an informational purpose, presumably giving an ad a chance of being more effective. He said, however, that "the weather is the most important part of the news for people in this area. A lot of money goes into the weathercast."[20]

The 1984 election coverage occurred in the context of a heavy investment of network resources and reportorial talent in the national news effort. By the end, however, the president's campaign had, for reasons which were not entirely the fault of the national networks, become stage managed, in a fashion which, a number of studies have indicated, facilitated presidential influence over the news agenda according to advertising principles. During the final period of the 1984 election, the most issue-oriented news coverage occurred to increase market share and presumably to meet a demand in a small Indiana market area with a high educational level.

Issue coverage in 30-second-spot advertising outran issue coverage in local and network newstime by five to one in the North Carolina and Georgia senatorial races. This was a higher level than the ratio of presidential issue-oriented adtime to presidential issue newstime, which ran a little over four to one (110 to 25 minutes). No news stories on issues appeared in the noncompetitive Senate race involving Georgia incumbent Sam Nunn; whereas, news that contained issue mentions comprised four and a half minutes in the competitive Hunt-Helms race, compared to 30 minutes of adtime.

NEWS COVERAGE OF HOUSE RACES

Theory suggests that news coverage of House races depends on the degree of congruence between congressional district and television market. In large media markets containing multiple districts there is little coverage of House races, and few television ads would therefore be expected. This situation favors incumbents, since challengers can rarely raise the money necessary to launch a television-based challenge, and will otherwise fail to reach a sufficient number of voters. Generally, findings from the 1984 sample research supports this theory. In two large television market areas, Los Angeles and Atlanta, there was little congressional news coverage. Nevertheless, in one, a congressional candidate was able to launch a television advertising campaign and fill the news void: Patrick Swindall in Atlanta.[21]

In the midsized markets in Indiana and North Carolina, a total of six congressional election news stories appeared, one of which was issue oriented and the rest either horse-race stories or stories devoted to other aspects of the election process. There has been little research in this area, but that which has been conducted would suggest that when relatively good overlap of market size and district boundaries exists, both ad and newstime will be "plentiful" or "extensive." In the cases included in the 1984 sample, the overlap was not particularly good, and the expectation in such cases was that there would be little of either: little news and little advertising. As it turned out, there was no congressional race news coverage in Indiana and but eight minutes and 13 seconds in North Carolina. Only one of the North Carolina congressional news stories mentioned issues. The congressional advertising thus heavily outstripped the newstime, both overall and in terms of issues information. The heaviest advertising appeared in competitive races, a fact that confirms previous research. Television viewers in markets of this size viewing the spots during the final days of the election obtained the greatest proportion of their information about issues dividing congressional candidates from the spots.

LOCAL COVERAGE: A NEGATIVE AD CAMPAIGN SAYS IT ALL

A local news story appeared in the 1984 sample that indicated that negative advertising was used effectively to dominate the news agenda, media blitz fashion, to throw the opponent onto the defensive, quite publicly and visually. It appeared on Channel 5 in a major market area, Atlanta. Democratic incumbent State Public Service Commissioner Mac Barber, whose opponent, Republican Joyce Carter, was gaining on him, used a last-minute ad to charge her with "wanting to raise $125,000. . . . Now where do you think she's getting that money?" The question was innocuous enough, but it was raised in a fashion, which, according to Claiburn Darden, who was consultant to the candidate who developed and used the ad, created the "impression that there's something wrong there." The idea was that of a concept ad, focusing on a candidate statement and inquiring what the voter should do with the information. But sound effects and visuals drummed away, focusing on voter uncertainty about the honesty of politicians. Interviewed in Atlanta afterward, Darden said he believed the whole thing in politics is "emotion, emotion and emotion," and that "a candidate isn't expected to tell the truth about his opponent all the time. The whole thing is strategy—getting your opponent on the defensive." [22]

In this instance, "getting your opponent on the defensive" involved getting her onto the news defending herself on the issue. Channel 5's news story about the subject only drew attention to the question of Joyce Carter's integrity. She said she had raised only one-half of the alleged amount, and she had done so openly and ethically. She charged that her opponent was questioning her integrity and should apologize. Barber replied that his charge was based on a news story that said she "wanted to raise $125,000." He was just seeking the facts: Where was she going to raise the money? "I'm not casting aspersions," he said.

The use of sound and visual effects, however, contradicted Barber's conclusion. They lent an image dimension to the ad and did thereby cast character aspersions, but, as Darden said later, not through the use of specific *words,* but by "inference." The suggestion of wrongdoing remained in the air, with Carter defending herself on a phony issue, while the reporter concluded that Barber would not give Carter the apologies she demands. Barber won. [23]

In the absence of investigative reporting or editorials, or a clear definition of what is ethical in an ad campaign (which is a task not just of journalists, but of scholars and the political community as well), such an ad could set the broadcast news agenda in a major media market. This story in fact comprised one-eighth of the total 1984 Atlanta news sample of slightly over eight minutes devoted to candidate news in races below the federal level. Given the high cost of advertising in such a large market, without a large war chest to pay for response advertising, the candidate against whom such an ad is launched at the last minute may not only be thrown on the defensive, but may be unable to hit back. One ad containing a plausible, controversial, and therefore newsworthy distortion may carry the political impact not only of the ad itself, but of the subsequent news coverage. In this case, an ad was successfully to dominate the news agenda at a crucial point in a campaign.

THE SENATE CAMPAIGN PREDOMINANT—HELMS DEFINES THE NEWS AGENDA

Ads on the Senate level in North Carolina overpowered the news, 58 to 11 minutes in the 1984 sample. In the North Carolina Senate race, the ads thus *were* the campaign for many television viewers.

Yet the Jesse Helms campaign used the charge of a powerful and liberal news media to justify its heavy use of negative advertising. Gary Pearce, co-campaign manager for his opponent, Governor Jim Hunt, believed Helms's charge was a tactical one and that it was effective. "They performed judo on the mass media, destroying its credibility so that whatever it said about the race became suspicious. It was a brilliant campaign—liberal politicians connected with liberal news media, which cast everything into doubt, playing on people's natural suspicions."[24]

Research by Shanto Iyengar and Donald R. Kinder suggests that the consumer of news stories accepts the information contained in them as true more readily if he or she believes the source, that is, the news media itself, is credible. Repeated charges of bias, albeit unproven, would have an inevitable effect on the information process by raising public suspicion of the media or by promoting media defensiveness. Newspapers and television in recent years have exhibited concern about their public credibility, which is one of their major assets in a democratic society. Since much television news originates in Washington, the seat of the "big government" and thus the "other" against which conservatives often campaign, the charge is of concern to the news media. Yet students of television network news have found no pattern of liberal or conservative election coverage.[25]

In the stations included in the 1984 sample, Helms was not discriminated against. Rather, it was *his* issues that had established the local North Carolina stations issues agenda. In a generally issueless year for campaign news, his concerns stood out in the 1984 news sample: abortion, religion, and school prayer.

Nor did close analysis of the sample indicate that reporter commentary or editorials framed any of his issues in a fashion that kept Jesse Helms from being his uncompromising self. Two days before the election he closed the campaign with the school prayer issue, which ran in the evening news as confirmation of a concern on his part for religion that was greater than any political interest he might have. The story focused on the view he shared with "the president" that *"some* things" are more important than winning elections, and that the two of them (Helms and Reagan), like the average voter (and true believers throughout history), are persecuted for this belief.[26]

It was a lengthy story that, like all of the eight North Carolina Senate stories, was coded for no accompanying reporter or editorial critique. Helms spoke with no negative bracketing. He said that his advisors had told him to avoid the issue of school prayer, but "some things are more important" than winning elections. Ronald Reagan "gets kicked around a lot [for raising such ideas as prayer in the schools] just as you do, just as I do, but it doesn't bother him and I know it doesn't bother you." This story, which ran on November 2 on Channel 8, was almost a benediction on his major campaign theme—that he, unlike his opponent, was not "just another politician."

By contrast, in the 1984 ad sample Jim Hunt was embroiled in stories that raised questions about what he would do, including whether he would give clemency to a Death Row criminal and whether one of his issues, Social Security cutbacks, was demagoguery. Hunt brought in a "former Social Security commissioner" at the last minute to prove his charge that Helms had voted to cut Social Security, and he ended his final news conference by accusing Helms of violating the Federal Elections Law. No supporting statements were included in the news stories, nor were Hunt's assertions "bracketed" by favorable reporter commentary, in a fashion which would give them extra credibility. Neither were there investigative pieces or television editorials dealing either with Social Security or with the substance of the Federal Elections Law charge despite the fact that they were crucial to Hunt's case against Helms during the blitz. All stories were reported in straight source-countersource fashion, with Helms responding to the federal elections issue, for example, by asserting in his typically graphic fashion that the Hunt forces had "egg all over their faces."

Interestingly, the Helms and Hunt forces received almost exactly equal time, as if stopwatches were used not only by the postelection coders, but during the campaign in the local newsrooms as well. The horrors of negative campaigning itself grew into a major story, which gave no credit to Hunt, however, for moving to the attack only after his campaign had begun to believe that negative advertising had begun to work against him. There was no bias against the conservative candidate. Rather, the Helms media blitz threw Hunt onto the defensive, and he appeared this way on the evening news counterattacking on a set of issues that received no additional credibility from either reporter legwork or commentary or anticonservative editorials by local stations. Confirming the success of Helms's media blitz strategies described in the previous chapter, Helms was ultimately able to define his image on the local news as well as through his advertising campaign. He emerged finally as the charismatic leader less concerned about the horror show going on around him than with feeding his lambs.

CONCLUSION

Overall, this analysis of issues in the ads and broadcast news indicates that ads still play a significant role in the campaign information mix of the network television viewer. Comparing only candidate ads and news on all levels, the ratio is three to one favoring ads.

Further, close examination of the 30-second and 60-second spots used during the final days of the election indicated the prevalence of slogan ads over platform ads conveying issue commitments and rationales relating to various issues. Further, the choice of issues discussed in them was selective, lending support to single-issue theory rather than that which argues that the ads appearing on the air reflect broader societal concerns about issues.

Surprisingly, there were major variations by campaign level, with ads becoming more slogan oriented the higher one went up the federal campaign ladder. Thus, ads on the House of Representatives level were most platform oriented, and those on the presidential level were the least platform oriented. One issue, taxes, which involves both an easily comprehensible, specific platform statement and, as we shall see in subsequent chapters, the ready possibility of dovetailing an easily comprehensible candidate character message, played a particularly important role.

Still, as in 1972, the spots carried more issues information than the news, probably both because candidates on all levels did not always focus on issues and because news organizations focused on noncandidate stories and horse-race coverage during this period.

It is quite possible that there was more issues coverage earlier in the race. And there is great value in stories devoted to noncandidate electoral process such as the type that comprised a surprising 29 percent of the ad sample that was not examined in detail in this research. Before firm conclusions can be drawn, however, much more research needs to be conducted, both in relation to the coverage of such stories and of campaign news coverage of network-related, independent, and cable news stations in a broader number of market areas across the country.

From this sample, however, it is clear that there were differences in coverage of campaign issues on the various levels. This sample lends support to the view that mediality theory suggesting sole significance for news coverage applies, if at all, only on the presidential level. Such varied races on other levels as those involving Senator Jesse Helms of North Carolina and State Public Service Commissioner Mac Barber of Atlanta Georgia indicate that it is possible to use advertising to overwhelm the local television news agenda.

In relation to issues, there were differences in the quality of the local news coverage, with a greater emphasis on presidential issues coverage on the Los Angeles station and a strong emphasis on candidate backgrounds and issues in Indiana, particularly in West Lafayette, which was, however, not a typical station because of the small size of the market area and the elevated overall educational level of its community. Still, the Indiana station examined in this study demonstrated that a station that takes its *local* news seriously can compete with a large-town station and provide large doses of information about candidates and their positions on the issues.

Much more research into local campaign news should be conducted. But two things are clear: During the final days of an election, there is room for successful use by candidates of media blitz strategies that can overwhelm local news coverage. And although issues figure prominently in televised political advertising, they are but one part of a total message. We now turn to an analysis of that broader message.

NOTES

1. Thomas E. Patterson and Robert D. McClure, *The Unseeing Eye: The Myth of Television Power in National Politics* (New York: Putnam's, 1976), p. 108.

2. See Lynda Lee Kaid, "Political Advertising," in *Handbook of Political Communication,* ed. Dan D. Nimmo and K. R. Sanders (Beverly Hills, Calif., Sage, 1988), pp. 249–71. For more recent reviews of the literature on political advertising, see Susan A. Hellweg, "Political Candidate Campaign Advertising: A Selected Review of the Literature," and Roger C. Aden, "Televised Political Advertising: A Review of the Literature on 'Spots,' " papers presented at the International Communication Association Convention, New Orleans, May 1988.

3. See Chapter 1 for media blitz and mediality theories.

4. See also W. Lance Bennett, "The Ritualistic and Pragmatic Bases of Political Campaign Discourse," *Quarterly Journal of Speech* 63(1977): 219–38; and Robert Rudd, "Issues as Image in Political Campaign Commercials," *The Western Journal of Speech Communication* 50 (Winter 1986): 102–118.

5. Richard Joslyn found issues mentioned heavily in ads in his 1976 sample, but he also focused on the image dimension of such ads. Richard A. Joslyn, "The Content of Political Spot Ads," *Journalism Quarterly* 57: (1980) 92–98.

Writing in the fall of 1984, on the basis of his research on "several hundred 30- and 60-second spots from nearly 20 different campaign organizations from the 1980 and 1984 presidential primary races," Shyles concluded that by contrast with the production effects used in image spots, "the presentation used when issues are the primary focus is much simpler. . . . There is generally no music and no announcer. Instead, the candidate speaks for himself, looks directly at the camera and is formally dressed. In short, issue spots tend to use what has come to be called a straightforward talking head approach with few transitions." Leonard Shyles, "Political Spots: Images and Issues," *Video Systems,* September 1984, p. 20.

6. Kathleen Hall Jamieson, "The Evolution of Political Advertising in America," in *New Perspectives on Political Advertising,* ed. Lynda Lee Kaid, Dan Nimmo, and Keith R. Sanders ed. (Carbondale: Southern Illinois University Press, 1986), pp. 1–21.

See also Richard Joslyn, "Political Advertising and the Meaning of Elections," in *New Perspectives,* pp. 139–83. Joslyn argues that there are four purposes of political advertising that correspond to types of campaign appeals: "future oriented public policy promise," or prospective appeals; retrospective policy satisfaction appeals that "provide an opportunity for the public to evaluate past policy performance and to reward or punish incumbent parties and candidates", "benevolent leader" appeals, and highly ambiguous election-as-ritual appeals.

7. See Leonard Shyles, "Defining the Issues of a Presidential Election from Televised Political Spot Advertisements," *Journal of Broadcasting* 27, no. 4 (Fall 1983);

and for a careful methodology that focuses on the examination of production characteristics to make a distinction between image ads and issue ads, see Leonard Shyles, "The
Relationship of Images, Issues and Presentational Methods in Televised Spot Advertisements for 1980's American Presidential Primaries," *Journal of Broadcasting* 18 (Fall
1984): 405–421.

8. David Beiler, handbook accompanying the film *Political Advertising Classics,
Campaigns and Elections,* 1987.

9. See Chapter 1 for an explanation of the market areas.

10. See Appendix B, Tables B.1 and B.3.

11. Ibid.

12. C.R. Hofstetter and T.F. Buss, "Politics and Last-Minute Political Television,"
Western Political Quarterly 33(1980): 23–37.

In this sample the coding *slogan ad* was applied to ads in which the candidate does
not enunciate a specific way of dealing with a problem. In the case of attack ads the
charge is launched, but without evidence such as that which would be presented through
a how or why statement. The verb in such ads is vague: In relation to a presented
problem, the candidate might seek to "improve" or "stop" it or "attack something
head on" or he "has faced the problem of" it. Or the problem might be stated vaguely,
for example, "we don't want big government running our lives" or I'm "against the
big budget deficit" or "for jobs" or support "education" or a "right role for government."

In platform ads, however, the verb answers the question of what has been done or
will be done referring to a specific objective. This requires the statement of a policy
position and what the candidate will do about it, through the use of a specific verb, for
example "oppose" or "support". In attack ads the opponent's policy position is either
clearly stated or a backup statement gives a reason for why it is wrong.

Coding was done by means of transcribing the verbal content of all of the ads and
then examining this content.

13. Martin Franks is cited in an Associated Press article, "GOP Accused of Exceed-
ing Spending Limits with Ads," *Washington Post,* October 21, 1984, p. 4. The Republican National Committee and NRCC spent $10 million on ads in 1984.

Interview with William Greener, Director of Communications, Republican National
Committee, Washington, D.C. February 16, 1985.

14. Greener interview.

15. See Chapters 7 and 8.

16. For a review of the research on media coverage of congressional elections, see
Edie N. Goldenberg and Michael W. Traugott, *Campaigning for Congress* (Washington, D.C., Congressional Quarterly, 1984, "The Information Environment," Chapter
8, pp. 109–124. For an examination of newspaper coverage of congressional elections,
see Peter Clarke and Susan H. Evans, *Covering Campaigns: Journalism in Congressional Elections* (Stanford, Calif.: Stanford University Press, 1983).

17. Martin Schram, *The Great American Video Game: Presidential Politics in the
Television Age* (New York: William Morrow, 1987).

18. For an examination of the station characteristics, see Chapter 1.

19. Interviews with Mike Piggott, news director and Tom Combs, advertising director, WLFI-TV Channel 18, West Lafayette, third week of July 1985. Interviews were
also conducted with West Lafayette's Democratic and Republican state senate candi-

dates, who confirmed this role for the station, on which they bought numerous television ads which aired extensively during the 1984 blitz.

20. For the figures see *State Demographics* (Homewood, Ill.: Dow Jones-Irwin, 1984). Interview with David Summers, station manager, WXII, Winston-Salem, North Carolina, December 27, 1984.

21. See Chapters 8 and 9.

22. Interview with Claiburn Darden, chairman, Darden Associates, Atlanta, Georgia, March 19, 1985.

23. Ibid.

24. Wayne Boyles, office of Senator Jesse Helms, Washington, D.C., December 26, 1984; Interview with Gary Pearce, cocampaign manager, Hunt campaign, December 28, 1984.

25. Shanto Iyengar, Mark D. Peters, and Donald R. Kinder, "Experimental Demonstrations of the 'Not-So-Minimal Consequences of Television News Programs," *American Political Science Review* 76(December 1982): 848–858. For a review of the bias question in relation to television news, see Graber, *Mass Media and American Politics* (Washington, D.C: Congressional Quarterly Press, 1980), pp. 167–69.

26. For methodology used in examining the news stories for stories editorial bias see Montague Kern, "The Invasion of Afghanistan: Domestic vs. Foreign Stories," *Television Coverage of the Middle East* (Norwood, N.J.: Ablex 1981), pp. 106–128.

4

Hope, Pride, Reassurance, and Trust: Decoding the Cues in Emotional Appeals

Three considerations guided the effort described in this chapter to develop a content analysis of symbols and music in the 1984 ad sample theoretically intended as cues to tap the elusive "responsive chord," and to start the process of building a typology of ads that use sound and symbols intended to appeal to positive and negative feelings or affect.

But first, some definitions. In their simplest sense, symbols, as Charles D. Elder and Roger W. Cobb have argued, are "anything but the real thing" to get a message across. Establishing meaning by means of symbols involves both cognitive and affective aspects. "Affect," as Elder and Cobb define it, is distinct from cognition. It is

the direction or intensity of a person's feelings toward an object, i.e., whether the person views the object positively or negatively and to what degree. The cognitive component refers to the meaning a person associates with the object . . . all that a person "knows" about the object of what it stands for. . . . Such knowledge may be based on a sophisticated understanding of relevant facts and values, or it may be based on an uninformed opinion.[1]

A growing body of research in social science has focused on the importance of the building of emotional bonds, or affect, between candidates and voters. Richard Fenno described the major bond as a trust relationship. The candidate achieves this by establishing that he cares for the voter's interests, that he is "like him," and that he has qualifications for the office. There is also an increasingly sophisticated trend in social psychological and information-processing research that has focused on the use of symbols in political learning. As Elder and Cobb have cogently summarized this line of research, learning involves how a voter feels about an object or person, as well as what he or she learns through cognitive thought processes, and the basis for much learning lies in childhood.[2]

The second consideration was the body of critical theory, described in Chapter 1, that has focused on the use of symbols in film and advertising. One branch has focused on variables relating to such questions as camera angles. Semiotic theorists are attempting to develop a language of symbols and sounds used by filmmakers whose objective may be to draw viewers into an "experience."[3]

The third consideration was a series of 1984 postelection interviews with consultants and campaign managers responsible for airing ads included in the 1984 sample, which clarified the fact that emotional intent was included in consultant philosophical approaches. Research by Lynda Lee Kaid and Dorothy K. Davidson, who interviewed half a dozen consultants who had produced ads for 1982 Senate campaigns, found affect-laden purposes. Their findings were published in 1986 along with a videostyle typology. Further, an emotional category was included in Anne Johnston Wadsworth and Lynda Lee Kaid's videostyle typology in 1988.[4]

Such theoretical considerations led to the creation of a Delphic panel of viewers during the first three months after the 1984 election to examine the 1984 ad sample and develop a list of feelings to which the ads in the blitz sample were believed to appeal. The purpose was to correlate the viewers' responses with aural and visual cues in the ads (including group, family, and individual symbols as well as setting or location) in order to develop a typology of positive and negative ads based on affect-related cues.

THE DELPHIC PANEL

The first question asked coders was whether or not they believed each ad was directed to a feeling. If the response was positive, the further question was, "To which feeling do you believe the ad was directed?" The results are to be understood within the framework of these questions, and they remain to be tested further in a "live" setting with a statistically significant body of potential voters. The panel of four coders was multidisciplinary (representing communications, psychology, political science, and literature), bipartisan, with two Republicans and two Democrats, and multiaged, from 18 to 44. Two voted for Ronald Reagan and two for Walter Mondale.

The initial list of categories was influenced by interviews conducted with campaign managers and consultants immediately after the election. The tally sheet was pretested using a 10 percent sample of the ads before being presented to the panel of four coders. The panelists made their assessments separately, without consulting each other during the coding process.

COMPARABLE FINDINGS

During the 1984 election, there were small-scale and large-scale studies indicating affect-related responses to ads and visual images on TV. One of the former was conducted by the consulting firm of Edward Reilly Associates of Cambridge, Massachusetts, which tested the ads for the Mondale presidential campaign in ten-person focus groups prior to their use during the 1984 general election campaign. Some of their results are reported in Chapter 5. The Reilly group's reported reactions to the Democratic presidential candidate's ads were similar to those that the panel coding the 1984 ad sample found independently.[5]

Second is the emerging body of research in social psychology, which has determined not only that there are positive and negative responses to candidates but that specific facial gestures viewed on television can provoke such positive and negative emotional responses in a uniform manner across different societies irregardless of the partisan background or cultural environment of viewers who observe these gestures on television. Similar research has been conducted in the area of products advertising. The major criticism of this form of research is that it is next to impossible to divorce viewer reactions to a politican's facial gestures on television from other variables, such as assessments of his performance coming from other sources.[6]

There are valid questions concerning the universal affect-related response across cultures to a set of televised facial expressions viewed on television, and the reasons why facial displays can elicit affect-laden responses. But the research of a group of researchers drawn from the fields of social psychology and political science, and centered around Dartmouth College, has indicated quite clearly that affect-related responses to political candidates, including Ronald Reagan and Walter Mondale, occurred during the 1984 election cycle when their research was conducted. The time frame of their research was comparable to that of the panel whose findings are reported here, which examined the commercials in late 1984 and early 1985 when Ronald Reagan's popularity and favorable media coverage continued at a high level.

A third set of comparable findings is summarized in the Lowe-Marschalk wheel of emotions described in Chapter 2, which formulated emotions appealed to in commercial advertising in terms of overall positive and negative categories found both by researchers such as social psychologists Robert P. Abelson, Donald R. Kinder, and Mark D. Peters and the Dartmouth group and the researchers who worked on the categories developed here. Interestingly, most of the categories in the typology developed for this study also appeared on both the positive and negative side of the Lowe-Marschalk wheel of emotions, which was developed at approximately the same time.[7]

Finally, close examination of a large sample of 569 ads used in federal races in 1986 suggests that patterns found in the 1984 ads continued in the 1980s although it was not possible to examine all these ads for affect using a similar panel so as to make direct comparisons. The trend, however, was intensified use of ads that, on the positive side, were even more elegaic, lyrical, and connected with affect-laden symbols than in 1984. This chapter reports findings related to positive appeals, and the next chapter reports the results of the 1984 content analysis relating to negative advertising, along with a similar focus on their meaning in relation to the ads used in 1986.

SELECTING THE CATEGORIES

On the positive scale, nine targeted emotions were included in the final list given to the coders of the 1984 ad sample. (See Table 4.1.)

Table 4.1
Positive Affect-Laden Appeals

compassion—sympathetic consciousness of others' distress together with a desire to alleviate it

ambition—urgency to get something done

nostalgia—yearning for the past

reassurance—the feeling that everything is okay; includes the feelings of comfort and satisfaction

trust—confidence in the candidate

intimacy—close association, contact, or familiarity with those on screen

hope—desire accompanied by an expression of or belief in a good future

national pride—elation arising from some activity, possession, or relationship connected with the nation

local pride—elation arising from some activity, possession, or relationship connected with the local area

Of these feelings, the major ones in terms of number turned out to be those that Agres of Lowe-Marschalk had developed quite independently in his wheel of emotions: comfort-reassurance-satisfaction, trust, hope, and local and national pride. Together these five categories comprised the primary positive codings in the 1984 sample.[8] "Excitement" and "joy," which figured prominently in Agres's commercial advertising typology, were similar to a "wow, really" effect that the 1984 coders attempted to pin down under the category of "surprise." But the category proved impossible for the panel to code consistently and was therefore dropped. Perhaps it had more to do with an "arousal" value in political advertising; an "unexpected" or "what's next" or "arousal" can only be measured by researchers using nonverbal measurement devices.[9]

"Compassion," "intimacy," and "ambition" were all included in the 1984 sample, but not in the Agres list. Of these, "intimacy" received the most codings, but it was a category that contributed to the coders' overall failure to reach agreement. So also with "ambition," which was difficult to pin down. "Compassion" occurred primarily in Mondale ads, along with "guilt" (which in the Tony Schwartz philosophy reported in Chapter 2 might have been called "shame") on the negative side, which will be examined in the next section. It also appeared in a few other codings, for example, on the congressional level in Indiana and North Carolina, but it was not a real force in the 1984 ad sample.

Agreement between at least two of the four coders on whether an ad was directed to a given emotion, for example, "anger" or "uncertainty-suspicion," was reached in the case of one-half of all the ads. The coding device was a complicated one, a fact that could partially explain this finding. It left enough ads, for which two coders had reached an agreement concerning a specific affect, to justify further analysis of the content of the ads according to sounds, symbols, and in the case of negative ads examined in the next chapter, issues as well.

OVERALL RESULTS

As Table 4.2 indicates, the ads in the 1984 sample were coded heavily for emotional appeals. Ads coded entirely for specific positive feelings comprised the largest category single category, at 55.9 percent of all ads (See Table 4.2). However, 38.8 percent of the ads combined positive and negative codings, thus indicating that the wheel-of-emotions commercial ad form may well exist in the world of political advertising as well. By contrast with the ads that combined positive and negative appeals, purely negative ads comprised a significantly smaller amount, 4.2 percent, of the total time aired.

When the ads having at least some negative content are tallied, however, the total time is significant—43 percent. This was a sizable proportion of the ads during the period of the 1984 sample, particularly in view of pre-1984 theory which suggests that to be successful, the candidate should come on at the close of the campaign with positive advertising and give the viewer a reason to vote *for* him.[10]

The success of commercial techniques in political advertising, appealing to symbols relating to primary personal experiences, was manifest in the extensive use of childhood and family in the ads. In 1976 Richard Joslyn noted the decline in the symbolic appearance of a major political institution, the party, which had been a significant part of political appeals in decades past. But his analysis of the ads for that year noted that other group-related appeals, notably those related to labor and farmers, comprised a large proportion of his sample. It is a major finding of the symbolic content analysis, however, that in the 1984 sample the appeal was almost overwhelmingly either to the individual or to the primary social grouping, the family.[11]

This finding confirms the views of both independent analysis and political consultants whose views are reported in Chapter 2 concerning the personalization of political advertising. There are two experiences that all viewers have in common: childhood and death. The former involves shared experiences as children and the desire to "see our kids get ahead," as well as association with a period of great receptivity to political learning. Childhood is thus a popular

Table 4.2
"Emotions" Codings in the 1984 Ads (30 second and 5 minute spots)*

Number of Ads		No Emotions Coded	Time Aired			Total
30 Second	5 Minute		Positive	Positive/Negative	Negative	
102	5	2.5	127.0	88	9.5	227.0
			(55.9%)	(38.8%)	(4.2%)	(99.5%)

Note: Only ads containing a human figure are included in this analysis.

symbol in advertising. The latter, as noted in our next chapter, may well play its role in negative advertising.[12]

Approximately 25.3 percent of all adtime involving the use of symbols relates to life's stages with childhood (8.1 percent), youth (7.9 percent) and old age (9.3 percent). By contrast, 15.2 percent was devoted to human symbols representing economic interests, such as labor (8.4 percent) and business (6.8 percent). Socially defined groups, such as women and blacks, were also represented in the advertising, but in small numbers—5.5 percent for women and 4.8 percent for blacks—which were scarcely commensurate with their objective significance in society. The percentage of these labor, business, and black group symbols was higher in races in which a candidate was clearly backed by labor, such as the Democratic presidential campaign and the gubernatorial race of Democrat Wayne Townsend in Indiana. Overall, human symbols in the 1984 ad sample indicate greater significance for the homeplace as compared with the workplace.

Symbols of place used in the congressional ads were from the home state— particularly scenic vistas, outdoors, individual homes. From a referential advertising perspective, they were affect-laden symbols associated with home and reinforced through music that might connect the candidate with the viewer's prior positive feelings about his or her version of the state. That feelings associated with home and state are a part of U.S. political culture is scarcely news. Symbols, music, scenery, language, even the name of a state—Indiana—and its people—"Hoosiers"—might well evoke affect. One pithy aphorism expresses some of the feelings that place and, in some political cultures, statehood itself can evoke: "To be a Virginian, either by birth, marriage, adoption, or even on one's mother's side, is an introduction to any state of the Union, a passport to any foreign country, and a benediction from the Almighty God."

Symbols of place in candidate advertising might well be used in an effort to evoke such affect and transfer it to the candidate. The candidate "becomes Vermont," by which is meant that he or she partakes of the feelings the voter holds for his personal version of the state. The candidate is also assumed to feel just as the voter does about the state. In other words, the candidate is so much a part of it that he or she understands the way things—depicted lovingly on the screen—really are. The candidate may also be taken to hold views on policy matters evoked by symbols that are meaningful to people in the state. Recall the case of school prayer cited in Chapter 2.[13]

Symbols of group identity, other than those relating specifically to the political office that the candidate holds or to which he aspires, appeared rarely in the 1984 ad sample. In the 300 1984 Republican candidate ads viewed at the National Republican Congressional Committee (NRCC) candidate advertising, however, religious institutions made an appearance as Republican candidates from the South occasionally appeared walking out of church with their families.[14]

Other groups were not making an appearance in positive ads, perhaps because they had lost their political appeal to voters in the individualistic United States of the mid-1980s, and perhaps also because political advertising followed its commercial counterpart, which focused on individual appeals. As the results cited in the next chapter indicate, however, association with interest groups and other large, alien entities, including government, provided the negative symbols.

THE CANDIDATE IN THE ADS

Another overall set of results should be examined before turning to close analysis of the ads for symbolic characteristics of ads coded for specific feelings. This is the overall nature, whether positive or negative, of the ads in which the candidate makes an appearance. The issue is relevant because legislation was proposed in Congress in the mid-1980s that sought to achieve two objectives by requiring the appearance of the candidate in the ads. The appearance of the candidate, it was argued, would reduce the amount of negative advertising because candidates rarely want to be directly associated with negative ads, as they necessarily would if a picture of the candidate was required in the ad. Further, it was thought that such a requirement would result in the production of more talking head ads, which researchers in the past have indicated are more directed to discussion of the issues in campaigns than other types of ads.[15]

Generally, the opponents of candidate-in-the-ads legislation argue that, indeed, ads including the candidate may be less negative, but they are also less substantive, as the candidate rarely discusses the issues but might instead make a cameo appearance dandling a baby on his or her knee. According to Jeremy Gaunt of *Congressional Quarterly,* who followed this legislation closely, this argument was made quite effectively by National Conservative Political Action Committee (NCPAC) representatives in Washington during the 1985 legislative season when the issue was hotly debated.[16]

A further reason to be interested in the question of the type of advertising in which the candidate appears is the research of the Dartmouth group, which indicated that candidate appearances on television are not devoid of emotional content. People respond emotionally to visual symbols, for example, facial displays. Further, they respond most strongly when the facial displays are positive ones. Further, in May 1988, the Republican National Committee was making two major arguments. The first was that negative advertising works if no response is made to it. The second was that the best response is a direct candidate statement in front of the candidate. One thing is clear. It is that America's candidates appear in close facial shots in a fashion that is quite different from that in some British Commonwealth countries where close facial shots are avoided. There are a variety of reasons to examine ads in which the candidate makes an appearance.[17]

The candidate himself appeared in 32 percent of the 73 minutes of total adtime coded for affect in the 1984 sample. He appeared in two types of ads. The first was the brief onstage *cameo* appearance. Of all ads coded for feelings, 15 percent included cameo shots of the candidate. Of the 24.5 total minutes of 30-second adtime that included such cameo performances, only one-fifth was devoted to ads coded for *both* positive and negative feelings. There was greater negativity in cameo ads on the congressional than on other levels, for reasons that are not clear. There were fewer codings on the state and local than on other levels.

The second category of ads that included the candidate was the talking head ad. Overall 28.7 percent of all adtime included talking heads. Of this adtime, 19 percent was devoted to candidate talking heads, with other politicians and actors making up the difference. The panel of coders responded positively to the candidate talking head ads. Of those coded for emotions, 96.9 percent were coded positively. This was a figure higher than the 65.1 percent, positive codings of appeals that other politicians and actors made on behalf of candidates. In sum, talking head ads were coded more positively than the overall 1984 advertising coded for affect appeals, 55.9 percent of which were positive.

Finally, the pure candidate-to-camera talking head spot, discussed in Chapter 3 as the pure issues spot, has been altered because, as various analysts have suggested, camera angles and sound and pictures convey much more than words, or politicians are trained to "find" their proper voice and demeanor—in short to communicate "honest passion," that elusive quality said by wags to be most commonly missing among politicians and prize fighters. In the political world of the 1980s, however, dominated by an actor president, some media consultants were loath to trust the candidate. California consultant William Zimmerman explained his decision to use actors rather than candidates in political ads by observing that much more than words is conveyed when a person speaks to the voter on television. Candidates, he argued, frequently communicate in an inadvertent, unintended fashion. The content analysis indicated one thing quite clearly. The ads were coded heavily for affect. In short, much more than an issue statement is communicated in ads featuring the candidate.[18]

The relative absence of negative codings in the ads in which candidates make an appearance, however, indicates that candidates are indeed doing what both the Dartmouth researchers and the consultants who argue the danger of having the candidate appear in an ad, such as the "Crying Farmer" series, have described as being most effective. The candidate should avoid appearing visually in a negative ad for fear of being associated with the problem, not emerging as its resolution.[19]

Indeed, the trend in talking head ads growing out of the 1984 election, as the following close analysis of the ads coded for "hope" and "reassurance" indicates, may well be that of involving the viewer in a "total experience," not only through the appearance of actors and candidates with rhetorical and acting training telling folksy parables, but through sound effects, such as the music that was used even in Ronald Reagan's talking head ads picked up in the 1984 sample. The unadorned, candidate-to-camera talking head spot was little in evidence in the 1984 sample of political advertising.

CATEGORIES OF POSITIVE ADS

"Trust," the largest single category with 45 codings, overlapped heavily with most of the other positive codings, indicating that it is a complex category with appeals that tap positive feelings in a number of ways. For purpose of close analysis of the 1984 ads for production qualities and use, the decision was made first to concentrate on two major categories that emerged from the analysis and then to return to the phenomenon of appeals to the voters to trust the candidate. The two categories selected for close analysis were "hope" ads, which received 23 codings, and "comfort-reassurance-satisfaction," with 36 codings. The decision to concentrate on these two as opposed to "national pride" and "local pride," which are commonly believed to be the emotions to which advertising appeals, was made because the "pride" categories overlapped heavily with hope and reassurance and were easily recognizable because of their use of symbols such as the national flag, purely "American" music with no ethnic elements, or the local barbershop. The hope and reassurance ads will be examined closely, however.

HOPE AND REASSURANCE ADS

Arguably, "hope" ads seek to tap the feeling, through sound and very personal visual symbols, that it's not all gloomy, and that there is a personal future. This idea is expressed in terms the voter can relate to, most frequently through symbols of children and youth, but also through those relating to individual involvement in work and business activity. The clearest characteristic associated with this coding is the use of symbols of youth and children, which connect the candidate with the voter's future.

By contrast, the clearest coded symbolic characteristic of reassurance ads (coded for comfort-reassurance-satisfaction) relate to place—the homeplace. The ads link the candidate with symbols of everyday life that have positive meaning to the viewer. These symbols may relate to a national heritage (the attempt, for example was to make Ronald Reagan "America") or to ethnic or local heritage. Or, an ad that appeals to an older person may focus on a *small* space—a kitchen, with groceries, for example—with emphasis on each move on the part of the person whose space is becoming more circumscribed. The focus may be a kitchen, for example, where a bright green head of lettuce is taken out of a grocery bag and washed in the sink. Like the hope ads, reassurance ads make heavy use of music, and the question that should be raised is whether they link the candidate with the viewer's feelings about the way things are, in the place that he or she knows and loves.

These propositions emerged from detailed analysis of the symbolic qualities and use of ads in the 1984 sample coded for the feelings of hope and reassurance.

Talking Head Hope and Reassurance Ads

Talking head ads were disproportionately heavy in the 1984 ads coded for hope and reassurance. Of all the codings in these categories, 50 percent were talking head ads. The figure is notable, given that talking head ads comprised less than a fourth of the 1984 ad sample.

Reagan ads comprised one-sixth of all the reassurance ads and one-third of the hope ads, eight of which were cut on behalf of his own candidacy, and one for Jim Martin, the North Carolina Republican gubernatorial candidate. That Reagan speaking on video could have been coded so overwhelmingly positively on the basis of his facial expressions and the sound of his voice may or may not have been known to the "Tuesday Team," Ronald Reagan's Madison Avenue media consultants. But they took no chances, and in half of his talking head ads coded in these categories they included swelling "native" American symphonic music. It was the same music that was included in his non-talking head ads, illuminating the use in political advertising of techniques developed for commercial use, notably the use of music—even in a talking head ad, which had recently been declared the last bastion of the issues ad.

There were, however, other talking ads coded for hope and reassurance in the 1984 sample. Most of these were made by Republicans, notably Representative Jim Broyhill who spoke on behalf of his fellow Republican congressional candidates in North Carolina while anticipating a possible 1986 Senate race, and Guy Vander Jagt, the chairman of the NRCC, who had been a student of rhetoric and a graduate of a theological seminary. He opened his five-minute talking head commercial with parables. Like Ronald Reagan, Congressman Vander Jagt emerged as a warm figure who could relate well to the home video viewer.[20]

Who Used the Hope and Reassurance Ads?

A defining characteristic of the reassurance ads was their use by incumbents, who received slightly over three-fourths of the total codings; if the three Republican generic ads are removed from the reassurance ad sample the percentage is higher, 84.8%. Hope ads, although more heavily used by incumbents (55 percent, or 12 out of 22 codings) were also used by challengers such as Walter Mondale and North Carolina senatorial candidate Jim Hunt in ads with mixed positive and negative codings.

Hope ads ran most heavily on the presidential level. On that level 14 out of a total of 22, or 63 percent, were coded. Of these, 45 percent were Reagan ads. The reassurance ads were more generally used, with only 25 percent (9 of a total of 36) coded on the presidential level. The Reagan campaign produced all but one of the reassurance ads on the presidential level. In the case of the one Mondale reassurance ad coding, a member of the panel noted that prior trust of the candidate was required for seeing that intended effect in the ad!

Few of the hope and reassurance ads appeared on the senatorial level. Perhaps this was because the Senate race that used the most advertising was the Hunt-Helms race. It was heavily competitive. The Georgia Senate race, by comparison, was not. The incumbent, Sam Nunn, used only one ad, a five-minute spot coded for reassurance and a number of other positive appeals. On the gubernatorial level, reassurance appeals ran heavily, particularly by Indiana Republican incumbent Governor Bob Orr, whose talking head and production-style ads, which ran in equal amounts, coded heavily on the side of reassurance and other positive affect-related appeals. On the level of the Indiana State Senate, reassurance ads were heavily used, and included among them were many talking head ads.

Sculpting with Sound

Media consultant Robert Goodman of the emotional school, known for the panoramic vistas and swelling music that frame his candidates, commented on the two basic types of sound mix that characterize political advertising. The safe incumbent "can play violins and chamber music [while] the other person's going to try to throw off that sound mix." The 1984 sample of ads bore out this pithy aphorism.[21]

Reassurance and hope ads were, heavily, incumbent ads and fell into categories that, after pretesting, were labeled "swelling," "soft," and "country." The Reagan advertising used swelling music, which tells a story through sound, a sound that evokes the memory of myths and stories in childhood, which as noted, is a period of important political learning. Music, it could be argued, is a shortcut to recall of that earlier experience. The mythic experience evoked by the swelling music of the Reagan ads is one of a full and happy life, which is reinforced by visual depictions of bright lawns and rolling landscapes. As the cameras pan to a storybook world, the music starts gently, then builds, and finally rounds out the experience with a soft conclusion. The conclusion comes fully, but gently, with a soft twist or coda, as the story ends with the soft determination—or resolution—that the storybook life depicted in the ad is attainable. The music, in short, is almost a story in itself, reinforcing the visuals, beginning tentatively, rising, and then moving to a climax, leaving the viewer with the feeling that something has been settled. There is, in short, resolution as raised questions are settled in a happy ending.

Reagan's swelling music was symphonic music, and the final determination toward which it draws the viewer is reinforced with visual images of the United States as a proud nation, and with its residents as successful people. The music, like all of the Republican advertising, which was similarly coded for national pride, is nonethnic American music and is linked with an American past that in no way includes the jarring 1960s, a music which, oddly, the Mondale campaign used, in Goodman's felicitous phrase, "to throw off that sound mix." However, other Mondale ads, coded for hope and reassurance, used soft music, but there was in most of them little of the mythic storytelling that could be paralleled musically in the Reagan ads.

Location (or Setting) Defines the Reassurance Ads

If there is one symbolic attribute that defines the reassurance ad as a genre it is setting, or the location shot selected to develop bonds of identification and empathy between voter and candidate. Two types of setting, frequently in combination, occurred heavily in reassurance ads in the 1984 sample. One was professional, and since many of the reassurance ads were cut for incumbents, it was not surprising to find heavy use (38.3 percent of all codings) of such professional-qualification settings as the flag-draped office and congressional hearing room.

Identification locations, based on non-professional criteria, were frequently used, however, as has been noted in previous discussion of the congressional fisherman from Connecticut and the California House candidate strolling atop Big Sur with his wife. The congressman or senator might be depicted on the steps of the U.S. Capitol, for example. But more often the symbols are of the candidate returning to the district, which, unlike Washington, is depicted as the *real* world of front porches, picnics, dramatic local vistas, hometown Main Streets—and *real* people.

The most popular identification locations are *outdoor scenes* of field, farm, stream, and street, which together comprised 19.1 percent of all the location shots in the ads. Outdoor locations may also be used to introduce an element of humor into the race, thereby catching attention and establishing important self-deprecatory, human qualities about the candidate.

Home shots constitute the second-largest category of location shots in reassurance ads, 12.8 percent all told. The question that should be raised is whether these offer candidate identification with feelings of comfort and reassurance based on familial and small-group interaction. As in all of the symbolic categories examined for this study, it was a Reagan ad that carried this potential to its fullest—the home shot of a wedding scene just outside a church. Only 9 percent of the reassurance ads do not use location shots to establish bonds of qualification and identity.

Sentimental Interaction Defines the "Hope" Ads

If the defining production dimension of the reassurance ads is the setting, the defining element of hope ads is bonding between generations. Of the hope ads, 11 were non-talking head production ads, and of these 10 include a mix of generations, including one featuring the candidate's family. The intergenera-

tional relationship is pure and without reference to economic or political identification. The single exception among the hope ads is one for the North Carolina Democratic candidate for lieutenant governor, Robert Jordan. In it the youth
clearly represents labor, as the candidate works a crowd of workingmen wear-
ing hard hats.

Young people of voting age between 18 and 30 years are a prime target for
both parties, but the Republicans won their vote in 1984 on the presidential
level. The heavy advertising directed at this age group occurred on all levels
of the Republican effort, from congressional to presidential, in ads that mixed
generations and were designed not just to reelect Reagan but to draw this age
group into the Republican party fold. The cognitive message of the ads was
"strive and succeed on your own." The young, said Randy Moorhead of NRCC,
have a strong entrepreneurial instinct, and Ronald Reagan exemplified this.[22]

Ronald Reagan and the Republicans certainly stood for unfettered free enterprise, a concept that can be and has been debated rationally and extensively.
And this was certainly the issues content of the Republican message. But ironically, the symbolic message that dovetailed with the issues message of individual striving was one of intergenerational bonding. Further, what was offered
was a vision of the future conveyed visually, not rationally. Children are their
elders' link with immortality, and in the phrase of a 1984 Republican media
consultant, "what can we know of the future save through our children?" If
religious belief offers the promise of a bright future for some, *all* voters of
whatever age share childhood and youth on some deep emotional level, either
in memory or as parents.

In an age in which the reality was of family breakup on the personal level,
and failed presidencies on the national level, was it possible that symbols of
intergenerational bonding represented hope? Wanda Urbanska, a journalist who
conducted in-depth interviews with the 18–30 age group during the period examined in this study, noted the high percentage of divorce in the personal or
family history of this age group and concluded that it was a "singular generation" that was "more acquainted with endings than with beginnings."[23]

Continuity between generations in the campaign advertising offered hope to
those of the younger generation who sought it. For the older generation the link
with kids who in the visual fantasy world of the Reagan ads wear no Mohawks,
help their elders and then settle down to raise families, also offers hope for the
future. This intergenerational motif in advertising is bipartisan. It reached cul-
mination as an art form in the 1984 Republican generic and Reagan ads but
then found full expression the following presidential primary cycle in the candidacy of Democratic presidential candidate Michael Dukakis, whose ads focused on competence, caring, and the legacy he had received from his father.
When urged to take more specific positive issue positions on a number of issues, he would return to a critique of the opponent and offer a few positive
themes, one of which was the preservation of the all important institution of
the family.

TOWARD AN UNDERSTANDING OF HOW ADS SEEK TO BUILD TRUST

By drawing a connection between symbols and affective codings, two positive ad categories have been posited: *reassurance* and *hope* ads. These may well be linked, however, with the largest single coding in the 1984 sample, "trust." This is not surprising, given that attempting to make one's own candidate more trusted than the opponent is, as political scientist Richard Fenno and Republican Ed Blakely and political theorists would argue, the major task of a campaign.[24]

At the beginning of this chapter Fenno's three components of trust were examined. Ads include visual and aural cues directed to all three. They are designed to establish bonds of empathy and identity between candidate and voter and to establish his or her qualification for the office. Yet much more is involved than proving one's qualification for the job by demonstrating work experience. Along the route to establishing trust in the candidate come attempts at bonding by means of very personal symbols of home and family. These offer resolution: reassurance that the homeplace stands and that there will be a future in an uncertain world. In short, the candidate seeks to become valued and trusted by using aural and visual effects that associate him or her with the voter's own sense of place and aspirations.

Particularly sought after is the incorporation of the candidate into the trust circle of the family. In what may be identified as family trust ads, memories of the past are evoked, memories of times when, as children, we all dreamed, had ideals and as social scientists argue, learned about politics. Memories are evoked either in a complex fashion as in the Reagan ads or, more simply, as in a 1986 talking head ad cut by Roger Ailes for Republican Senator James Abdnor of South Dakota. The senator is sitting on the front porch with an orange pumpkin in the background. There is a minimal amount of music. He looks the viewer in the eye and says, "Ever since I gave up on being a major league baseball player, I've always wanted to run for office."[25]

In such ads, in addition to childhood, a second component of the trust-building process is employed, the symbol of *place*—in this case the big white house with a front porch swing and a pumpkin that your mother put out. It may all be entertainment—it may be a storybook house, and your mother may never have put out the pumpkin—but in that case it may attract attention, or in social-psychological terms "arouse" a reaction, because of a recognizable or exciting quality relating either to story or reality. In this genre, which might be termed a downhome trust ad, such symbols are employed to "make the candidate South Dakota," or Georgia, or the entire country if necessary. The location and scale may change; the technique remains the same.

A third motif is an attempt to establish trust which is built in what might be termed strength-building trust ads. Such ads require symbols associated in the viewer's mind with real or mythic events in which courage has been displayed.

Strength symbols which grow out of real-life situations in which courage has been displayed, derive from the world of sports and may in the intergenerational 1980 be directed at the multiage event, as was the case of the trigenerational football game in downtown Denver that was featured in an ad for successful senatorial candidate Tim Wirth in 1986, as he was seeking to ward off an attack from the right. Often strength symbols are related to the military: battleships, helicopters, helmets, camouflage pants, training exercises, and weapons. In 1986, for example, Senator Fritz Hollings of South Carolina campaigned for reelection with the help of an ad claiming that he had saved a vital weapons system from extinction. Strength symbols can backfire, however, as Walter Mondale discovered when he wore a football jersey and boarded the Naval carrier *Nimitz* as noted in Chapter 6. Michael Dukakis' comparable attempt to develop an image of strength by driving a tank also backfired in the fall of 1988.[26]

A major problem for women candidates stems from the fact that consultants have not discovered female strength symbols similarly derived from the culture. Analysis of the 30 ads produced by the major consultants for women in the 1986 election cycle produced one victorious candidate, Liz Patterson of South Carolina, talking with a veteran and another, Madeline Kunin, the governor of Vermont, riding in a helicopter. Otherwise, no strength symbols emerged. Jill Buckley, a female media consultant who until 1986 had represented a number of male candidates who defeated women candidates, said that generally it is assumed that women are compassionate. Therefore the idea is to demonstrate competence on the part of women candidates, which is frequently done by means of symbols of office and the presentation of legislative successes.[27]

What, then, of Fenno's final component of the trust-building process: establishing qualification for office? Two forms of trust-building ads are used for this purpose. One is the *accomplishment* spot that focuses on their records, on what they have done for voters. Here incumbents usually have a clear advantage. Such spots frequently include a character as well as an issues dimension, and Richard Joslyn quite perceptively called them ''benevolent leader'' spots. The trend in these ads in 1986 was, as noted in Chapter 2, to elegy, lyricism, and very personal, micropolicy-oriented storytelling in ads that focused on ''the power a life.'' In these, the candidate emerged as the final resolution to uncertainties raised in the ad.[28]

Thus, in ''River'' by Robert Goodman for 1986 Louisiana Senate candidate W. Henson Moore, the story is of one family learning the importance of community from a flooded-river ordeal. The candidate enters only at the very end, in his role of making sure that insurance is paid to the victims—the resolution, in short. In ''Letter'' by William Zimmerman for Representative Tim Wirth, running for the Senate in Colorado in 1986, the story is of a bunk-bed disaster. It is a story told by a bereaved father writing it up on his cabin typewriter for the local newspaper as a letter of appreciation for Wirth—who emerges late in the ad inspecting bunk beds in a department store with an eye to introducing consumer legislation. Or in "We" by Raymond Strother for incumbent Connecticut governor Bill O'Neill seeking reelection in 1986, tempo music flashes the viewer through his achievements at a mythic pace to the coda: "He took us through the dark economic times with a steady hand."[29]

The other form of trust-building *accomplishment* spot is the testimonial, which partakes of the affect-laden trend described in relation to talking head spots. In 1986 the number of testimonials by family members on behalf of candidates was quite remarkable. Howard Coble and Jesse Helms took advantage of this in House and Senate races in North Carolina in 1984, not just to present the image of the candidate as a family man, but to introduce the candidate's record on an issue. Marrying symbols of family with accomplishments in "Kelly," the teenage son of Oregon Democratic congressman Les AuCoin, testifies to the parsimony of "old Dad," as he personally washes the family car. In this example of dovetailing, he offers the requisite visual character side of the message "I will not raise taxes" from the perspective of a son whose dad is careful with the allowance. Who can offer better testimony on parsimony than a son? In another 1986 ad, a teenage daughter carries the message, before any attack has been launched, that her Republican congressman dad would *never* cut Social Security. A daughter can certainly testify to the caring character side of the Social Security message. Thus the circle is complete. Accomplishment spots designed to build trust return to a focus on the family.

Consultant Don Ringe conducted a successful media campaign for Republican gubernatorial candidate Bob Martinez in Florida in 1986. It was an important victory in a lean Republican year in statewide races, and he moved on to become media consultant to the presidential primary race of Republican presidential contender Bob Dole in 1988. In describing the Martinez race, he said that he learns through polls and by "hitting barrooms and Baptist churches" and determined early that people think a governor should be a manager, or provider of real services, and a "parental figure." The two concepts are related, for parents and governors both "provide." Thus, in introducing the candidate, he used a multifaceted family motif, along with a recital of his success as an elected city manager. A central focus is placed on the fact that it is through having children that Martinez first got involved in the community and then in politics. And at the conclusion of a campaign that was characterized by much negative advertising, Martinez returned to its original theme, one which Ringe believed was crucial on the final days of the election:

A governor is a father figure, or a female governor would be a mother figure. At any rate . . . that kind of bonding is what people really tend to look for in governors, by and large. This was the closing spot.[30]

In 1986, therefore, one trend was to build trust and establish the candidate's qualification for the job by means of family—a quality that dovetailed with

managerial competence, which is perceived to be a crucial aspect of job qualification.

Following a close look at the 1984 ads, which enabled us to develop some
cues to look for in advertising coded for positive affect, we might well hypoth-
esize that there are two categories of emotions appealed to in positive ads in
the 1980s: reassurance and hope. They are associated with pride, which we
examined less closely but they fit quite fully with a broader category, trust.

Further, from a review of representative work by the major 1986 consultants
in both statewide and congressional races, it can be suggested that the trend
was to highly personal appeals focused to building voter trust in the candidate.
These appeals incorporate symbols associated with the hope, reassurance, and
pride advertising, and they boil down to the following categories: family trust,
downhome trust, strength-building trust, and accomplishment spots.

From a review of all of them, one may ask, Have not highly personal, affect-
laden cues come into their own in the positive political advertising of the 1980s?

We turn now to an examination of negative advertising.

NOTES

1. See Charles D. Elder and Roger W. Cobb, *The Political Uses of Symbols* (New
York and London: Longman, 1983), p. 37.

2. Richard F. Fenno has defined the trust a politician seeks to establish as based on
perceptions of the qualifications of the candidate and empathy and identity with him or
her. Richard Fenno, *Home Style: House Members in Their Districts* (Boston: Little,
Brown, 1978).

Fenno's trust-building task involves both affect and cognition, so defined. On the
cognitive side at a minimum is qualification, demonstrating competence, experience that
a candidate can do the job the voters want done. Cognition does not require a stated
rationale, however. In fact, numerous studies indicate that much learning may take place
in childhood and that it may be based on cultural or political myths, which provide the
prism through which later issues are filtered. See Doris Graber, "Political Languages,"
in Dan D. Nimmo, ed., *The Handbook of Political Communication* (Beverly Hills and
London: Sage, 1981), pp. 195–225.

3. An example of a semiotic perspective focusing on political advertising is Judith
Williamson, *Decoding Advertisements: Ideology and Meaning in Advertising* (New York
and London: Marion Boyars, 1978).

Research that has focused on camera angles and perceptions of source credibility and
attraction include L.M. Mandell and D.L. Shaw, "Judging People in the News—Un-
consciously: Effect of Camera Angle and Bodily Activity," *Journal of Broadcasting* 17
(1973): 353–62; T.A. McCain, J. Chilbert, and J. Wakshlag, "The Effect of Camera
Angle on Source Credibility and Attraction," *Journal of Broadcasting* 21 (1977): 35–
46; and R.K. Tiemons, "Some Relationships of Camera Angle to Communicator Credibility," *Journal of Broadcasting* 14 (1970): 483–90. See also such debate analyses as
R.K. Tiemons, "Television's Portrayal of the 1976 Presidential Debates: An Analysis
of Visual Content," *Communication Monographs,* 45 (1978): 362–70; and S.A. Hellweg and S.L. Phillips, "A Visual Analysis of the 1980 Houston Republican Presidential

Primary Debate,'' paper presented at the International Communication Association Convention, Minneapolis, May 1981.

4. Lynda Lee Kaid and Dorothy K. Davidson, ''Elements of Videostyle: Candidate Presentation through Television Advertising,'' in Lynda Lee Kaid, Dan Nimmo, and Keith R. Sanders, eds., *New Perspectives on Political Advertising* (Carbondale: Southern Illinois University Press, 1986), pp. 184–210. See also Anne Johnston Wadsworth and Lynda Lee Kaid, ''Incumbent and Challenger Styles in Presidential Advertising,'' paper presented at the International Communication Association Convention, Montreal, May 1987.

5. Mondale-Ferraro Campaign Focus Group Reports, Vols. I–III. Unpublished document, MRK Research, 351 Newbury Street, Boston, Massachusetts, MA 02115.

6. A group of social scientists based at Dartmouth (hereafter the Dartmouth group) has been conducting research on transnational responses to facial displays on television. This research indicated that there were panels of coders in France and the United States who responded to the facial expressions in the same way. The politicians so coded included Walter Mondale and Ronald Reagan. See John T. Lanzetta, Dennis G. Sullivan, Roger D. Masters, and Gregory J. McHugo, ''Emotional Reactions to a Political Leader's Displays,'' in Sidney Kraus and Richard M. Perloff, *Mass Media and Political Thought* (Beverly Hills, Calif.: Sage, 1985). See also a brief popular summary of recent commercial research in this area, ''Modern Advertising: The Subtle Finding Out What Makes Us Tick,'' *Christian Science Monitor,* January 27, 1987, p. 16.

7. The wheel of emotions is included as a figure in Chapter 2.

8. The categories ''none'' and ''other'' were also included.

9. For a summary of and critique of literature based on this type of research see Annie Lang, ''Involuntary Attention and Physiological Arousal Evoked by Formal Features and Mild Emotion in TV Commercials,'' paper presented at the International Communications Association, New Orleans, May 1988.

10. See Larry Sabato, ''The Media Masters,'' *The Rise of the Political Consultants* (New York: Basic Books, 1981), pp. 111–220.

11. Richard A. Joslyn, ''The Content of Political Spot Ads,'' *Journalism Quarterly* 57 (1980): 92–98. See also his *Mass Media and Elections* (Reading, Mass.: Addison-Wesley, 1984).

12. According to Gary Nordlinger, Democratic media consultant, there are two things that everyone has in common: childhood and death. This makes the former, at least, a popular symbol in advertising. Gary Nordlinger, lecture at American University School of Communications, November 1984.

13. See Chapter 2.

14. Data gathered from a review of close to 300 Republican congressional campaign commercials, Republican National Campaign Committee, Washington, D.C., February 8, 1985. See also Chapter 11.

15. Leonard Shyles has written about the plain unadorned talking head spot as the last bastion of major discussion of the issues in advertising. This topic was discussed in Chapter 3. A reform effort that would require ads to include the candidate was proposed by the Center for the Reform of the American Electorate and included in the major campaign finance reform bill proposed by Senators Boren and Byrd and widely discussed in Congress in 1987 and 1988.

16. Jeremy Gaunt, ''PACs and Parties,'' Edison Electric Institute, Washington, D.C., lecture, October 26, 1986.

17. Dartmouth group. Republican National Committee, Candidate School, April 29, 1988. There is a significant difference between the video presentation of U.S. candidates and those from Canada and Australia, as was evident from political ads aired from Australia developed by TBA, Australia, and analyzed by Donat J. Taddeo, Concordia University, Montreal, Quebec, and presented at a panel, "Images of the Political Process," International Communication Association Convention, New Orleans, June 1, 1988. The U.S. candidates are much more likely to be presented in close head shots.

18. Interview with William Zimmerman, Los Angeles, California, June 24, 1985.

The "wag" is George Will, July 26, ABC Sunday morning program. He said this "honest passion," which is so lacking in politicians, was the reason the public responded favorably to Oliver North in the Irangate congressional hearings during the summer of 1987.

19. The Dartmouth group of researchers concluded that positive candidate facial displays were more favorably received than negative ones. For a discussion of the "Crying Farmer" ad series, see Chapter 2.

20. For the story of Jim Broyhill's effort in talking heads on behalf of North Carolina Republicans including Jesse Helms, see Chapter 7.

21. Robert Goodman, lecture at *Campaigns and Elections* Conference, Washington, D.C., May 9, 1987. A whole literature of music and affective theory is developing. See, for example, James Lull, ed., *Popular Music and Communication* (Beverly Hills, Calif.: Sage, 1987). See also Alan Wells, "Popular Music: Emotional Use and Management," International Communication Association Conference, Los Angeles, May 29–June 2, 1988.

22. Interview with Randy Moorhead, NRCC, June 2, 1986.

23. Wanda Urbanska, *The Singular Generation* (New York: Doubleday, 1987).

24. Blakely interview.

25. This ad, created by Republican consultant Roger Ailes, like most of the 1986 ads examined in this chapter, can be viewed in the film "1986 Political Advertising Classics," which can be obtained from *Campaigns and Elections* magazine, Washington, D.C.

26. Ads can also focus on inner strength, such as persistence, determination, and perseverance. Examples of verbal statements of this from earlier campaigns are included in Richard Joslyn, "Political Advertising and the Meaning of Elections," pp. 168–69, in *New Perspectives on Political Advertising,* ed. Lynda Lee Kaid, Dan Nimmo, and Keith R. Sanders (Carbondale: Southern Illinois University Press, 1986).

For a discussion of Walter Mondale's efforts to use a football jersey and the *Nimitz* as strength symbols, see Chapter 6.

27. Jill Buckley, interview for the film "1986 Political Advertising Classics," July 7, 1987.

The literature on political advertising by women candidates is scant. See Susan A. Hellweg, "Political Candidate Campaign Advertising: A Selected Review of the Literature," paper presented at the International Communication Association conference, New Orleans, May 1988; and Roger Aden, "Televised Political Advertising: A Review of the Literature on 'Spots,' " idem.

28. Richard Joslyn, on the use of records in political advertising and benevolent leader spots, in "Political Advertising."

29. "River" by Robert Goodman, "Letter" by William Zimmerman, and "We" by

Raymond Strother can be seen on the film "1986 Political Advertising Classics," *Campaigns and Elections,* Washington, D.C. The same is true of "Kelly," which follows.

30. Don Ringe lecture "Devising a Media Strategy," *Campaigns and Elections* conference, Washington, D.C., May 7, 1987.

5

Negative Advertising and Affect: The Soft and the Hard Sell

Little research has been conducted to systematically analyze negative advertising, which is generally defined as that which is directed to the failings of the opponent in relation either to character or issues. Patterson and McClure examined three negative ads in 1972 and found that they could change voters' conceptions of candidate issue stands and images. One line of academic research found varied reactions to such advertising depending on socioeconomic status of the viewer (lower socioeconomic status respondents found them to be both more informative and more unethical than did viewers with a higher socioeconomic status). Recently, experimental research has focused on factors relating to the possibility of backlash against the candidate who uses negative ads. Yet a recent analysis of presidential-level ads from 1952 through 1984 collected by the Political Commercial Archive found that fully one-fourth of them were negative.[1]

Little academic research has examined the context within which such advertising is used. Nor have there been attempts to develop typologies of negative ads, which include aural and visual symbols. Further, much of the experimental research into its effectiveness has focused on only one style of advertising, that developed by the NCPAC, which links the opponent with other politicians or groups who are negatively perceived by voters. Some consultants in the mid-1980s argued, however, that other forms of negative advertising were more effective because they decreased the possibility of backlash against the user. Some consultants have termed this ''cute'' or ''funny'' negative advertising.[2]

The original effort in this research was to draw a distinction between two styles of negative advertising: one that had been described as issues advertising intended to focus in a neutral fashion on a comparison between the candidate and the opponent in terms of records or issues, and another that draws more heavily on sound and symbols, which Shyles and others have associated with a more image-oriented or emotional rhetorical style. Review of the 1984 ad sample resulted in the important finding, however, that although there were comparative ads that drew distinctions between the candidate and the opponent in terms of issues, few were neutral, in the sense of being without sound effects and visual techniques that add a value or a theoretically affect-laden dimension to the total message. An original dichotomy was drawn on the coding sheet between comparative ads that contrasted candidates on issue and character dimensions. But this distinction came to be impossible to maintain because of the heavy use of sounds and visual production effects even in such talking head (or introspective) ads as those cut by Ronald Reagan, ads that relied heavily on symphonic music. A few clear issue-oriented talking head ads were cut by such Republican congressional leaders as Congressmen Jim Broyhill and Guy Vander Jagt. They were the exception rather than the rule, however.

This lack of appeals focusing solely on issues may be because the sample was taken from the air during the final days of the 1984 campaign after neutral issues ads had already been aired. Or it may confirm the hypothesis that the political advertising aired during the final stage of a race, which appears in more competitive than noncompetitive races, has come to be heavily influenced by an emotional rhetoric.

The fact remains that *neutral attack ads,* those that convey a concept or idea without a production tone that implies either a threat or a value associated with the candidate's issues or character, were rare in the 1984 sample.

A TYPOLOGY OF NEGATIVE APPEALS

Because of the rarity of neutral attack ads, the decision was made to focus on advancing theory by developing a typology of negative ads using theoretically affect-laden appeals. Comparisons could then be made about the use of such advertising in different contexts.

Overall, the proposition to be tested is whether or not negative advertising carries value and affect-laden messages that serve a purpose that is the opposite of positive ads. Is this purpose, indeed, not in part that of attempting to sever real or potential bonds of trust between candidate and voter? Further, is not such a connection, as Fenno suggests, one that is built not only on a demonstration of qualifications based on the issues and one's record but on affective bonds of identification and empathy between candidate and voter as well? The hypothesis is that this is indeed a purpose of negative advertising and that two major styles are used to this end: *soft-sell* and *hard-sell negative advertising.*[3]

Hard-sell negative advertising is comparable to that developed by the NCPAC. It utilizes dark colors and threatening voices to create what has been called harsh reality advertising. In this advertising, the case that the candidate is *different from the voters, and therefore not to be trusted,* is made in the strongest possible visual and aural fashion. Few light entertainment related appeals are used, and the focus is on a serious threat to the viewer.[4]

A second major form of negative advertising involves the soft-sell appeal. It makes heavy use of lighter entertainment values, humor, self-deprecation, storytelling, or the unexpected turn of events—for example, the young male professional in the ad who must work hard to jump onto the bandwagon, which the young female professional rides as a matter of course. Such advertising may combine issues with negative affective appeals, such as uncertainty about one's own personal decision-making process, an issue which contains a threatening dimension, or suspicion directed at an individual or class of politicians.

It might also be argued that there is a category of "get 'em-mad" ads, which are designed to stir anger at the intentions of the opponent. The use of such ads might not be all that uncommon when a strong reason is needed to overcome the voters' proven reluctance to vote against an incumbent. Pocketbook issues—sure-fire routes to viewer attention and potential recall—might well be raised in such ads.

One further proposition might be tested: Ads utilizing negative appeals are of two types, those that combine positive and negative appeals, and the far fewer number, as noted in the previous chapter, that fall entirely into the negative ad categories. The 1984 content coders found five categories of negative appeals: guilt, strong fear, unpleasant fear, anger, and uncertainty. The anger and uncertainty ads varied in intensity between a hard-sell and a soft-sell approach.

This analysis will focus first on the results of the 1984 codings, which, it will be argued, result in a typology that is as relevant for understanding ads in 1986 and 1988, and on into the 1990s, as it was in 1984. The analysis will then turn to an examination of most of the ad campaigns in competitive statewide races in 1986, which offer proof of the widespread use of such advertising.

CODING THE CUES OF NEGATIVE ADS

The negative side of the feelings spectrum was presented to coders as shown in Table 5.1.

Table 5.1
Negative Affect-Laden Appeals

guilt	culpability for offenses, past and present
fear-s	a strong emotion caused by extreme anticipation or awareness of danger bordering on doom
fear-u	an unpleasant emotion caused by awareness of a threat
anger	strong feeling of displeasure or antagonism, "get 'em mad"
uncertainty	feeling of anxiety, uncertainty, or suspicion

The five coding categories were developed for presentation to coders following examination of a sample of the 1984 ads.[5] Three of Agres's categories developed for the wheel of emotions, discussed in Chapter 2, were identical with those developed here: "fearful," "anxious," and "ashamed" (which is close to "guilt"). On the negative side, Agres included "emotions." These might be associated with entertainment values such as "bored" and "serious," for example. These were impossible to code. The Dartmouth researchers included only two negative emotions in their psychological analysis of viewer responses to candidate facial displays on television. These are what some social psychologists have described as the two primary negative emotions, anger and fear-evasion. The independently developed categories of appeals derived from critical analysis of the 1984 ad sample were thus comparable to the Dartmouth researchers' physiologically developed categories as well as those developed by Agres.[6]

Appeals to anger focused on a feeling of displeasure or antagonism directed at the candidate or those responsible for developing a ballot initiative or proposition because of stated or implied harm the candidate had or would cause the viewer. Fear, however, seemed to the initial coders to operate on two levels and was consequently included on the coding sheet in this fashion: as *fear-s,* a strong emotion caused by extreme anticipation or awareness of danger bordering on doom; and *fear-u,* an unpleasant emotion caused by awareness of a threat.

The milder form of fear (fear-u) advertising appeal was, however, often difficult to distinguish from the uncertainty-anxiety-suspicion category that emerged during pretesting of the 1984 ad sample. The latter, labeled uncertainty advertising, was a combination grouping that emerged because it was impossible to distinguish clearly between three concepts: personal anxiety, uncertainty about one's own decision making, and uncertainty about or suspicion of a politician's character and his or her positions, which frequently grew out of character. The result is a combined uncertainty grouping. Guilt, or shame, defined as a sense of culpability for past offenses, also emerged as a category during pretesting and was quite easy to distinguish.[7]

The complexity of the categories—there were five, in comparison to the two negative categories of the Dartmouth researchers—contributed to the fact that although, as indicated in the last chapter, there was a high level of agreement on whether ads appealed in general to the positive or the negative side of the spectrum, agreement on the discrete categories was possible in only half of the cases. Nevertheless, the categories are examined here in order to isolate variables useful for analysis in future research.[8]

Overall results of this half of the total sample for which there was agreement by two coders were as follows: The uncertainty and anger codings emerged as the major categories, with 42 and 40 codings respectively out of a total of 102 ads coded from among 122 collected from the air in the 1984 ad sample. This included all the candidate and generic party ads for federal candidate and statewide candidate and proposition campaigns. Both unpleasant fear (fear-u) and the stronger category, fear-impending doom (fear-s) overlapped heavily with one or both of these two, and received a lesser number of codings, 15 and 6 respectively.

Anger and Uncertainty Codings

The concentration is first on the production and use characteristics of the anger and uncertainty codings because they emerged as the major ones, with the greatest number of codings. Ads coded in both of these categories were most heavily used by challengers, with similar percentages in the case of both anger and uncertainty. Of the 32 anger codings for candidate races 22, or 68.8 percent, were in challenger campaigns (5 for Mondale on the presidential level, 4 for North Carolina Democratic senatorial candidate Jim Hunt, 4 for congressional challengers, and 9 for challengers in competitive state races). In the uncertainty advertising a slightly smaller percentage, 62.8 percent (or 22 of 35 candidate codings), were in challenging campaigns. Ads coded for both feeling-level appeals were used by incumbent candidates in highly competitive races, that is, races that were close and for which money was widely available. This fit into an overall pattern of greater use of negative appeals by both challengers and incumbents in advertising used in competitive races. There was little use of such appeals on the local as opposed to the state or federal level.[9]

Republicans used such advertising appeals more than did the Democrats. But the correlation between challengers and anger appeals at 68 percent and challengers and uncertainty appeals at 62.8 percent was greater than that between either party (Democrats 14 out of 34, or 41.1 percent, and Republicans 20 out of 34, or 58.8 percent). This indicates that the challenger rather than the party variable is more significant in relation to the use of such appeals.

The use of such advertising appeals was greatest in the California market, which was comprised largely of proposition appeals. These were more heavily coded than candidate appeals for such negative affect. Proposition advertising, in fact, was heavily negative on both the yes and the no side. The ratio of negative to positive affect-oriented appeals was 17 to 10. Given the high proportion of proposition advertising in California, this meant, in terms of total number of ads, that the California advertising coded for affective appeals totaled 18 negative to 5 positive.

Negative advertising began to be noticed by researchers and consultants in California in relation to proposition campaigns several years ago. By 1986 such advertising was a major feature of competitive senatorial campaign advertising as well. That year in the Cranston-Zschau Senate race, as well as on other levels, negative advertising appeals began early and lasted to the end of the race.

Production Styles

Non-talking head production style was favored in ads coded for anger and uncertainty appeals. Of the 34 candidate anger ads, 27 fell into this category.

If the proposition ads are included, the figure rises to 31 production ads out of a total of 40. In the case of uncertainty appeals, there is an even higher proportion of production ads, 37 out of 42.

Non-talking head production-style advertising was thus favored in this negative attack advertising. Interestingly enough, the talking head ads that were coded for anger appeals were taped by actors or former actors. Two were Ronald Reagan ads taped on behalf of specific Republican challengers, and two were by actor Jack Klugman, who taped proposition ads on behalf of the Democratic side of a reapportionment issue in California.

Unlike positive advertising, negative advertising coded for anger and uncertainty appeals never included the candidate and his or her family in more than a freeze frame at the end. The largest single coding in negative advertising was *no-characterization* or *nonuse of the human figure.* Such ads have variously been labeled comparative or issue ads. *Hybrid,* however, is the best term for them because the use of sounds and visuals can add a character dimension and affective style of argumentation to an ad that does not use human symbols and is therefore concerned with issues, but only as one part of a broader message.[10]

How an ad that uses frames, words, and no moving character symbols can nevertheless be value- and character-, and, at least theoretically, affect-related, is illustrated by an examination of one of the ads in the sample, a 1984 Reagan-Bush ad entitled "Mondaleconomics." In this ad economic policies take on a character dimension. Indeed, by means of voices, sound effects, and visuals, they become inextricably linked with personalities, in this case ones that are certainly larger than any single human being. Policies are not just ideas; they are personified forces associated with the candidate and his or her opponent.

Thus, no human symbols are visible in "Mondaleconomics," save for a picture of President Reagan at the end under his slogan, "Leadership That's Working." *His* force is that "Reaganomics" is larger than life, and indeed it is U.S. economic prosperity, as the president has come to represent the nation. This personified force is in fact the resolution to the dilemmas presented by "Mondaleconomics," a negative personified force that is splashed across the screen in fluorescent blue colors to harsh sound effects. "Mondaleconomics" is a living threat, indeed, one which could result in the viewer losing something, his or her hard-earned income. It is a comparative ad, but much more than issue differences are connoted. A choice is laid out in an ad whose video rhetoric focuses on uncertainty, and anger moving at the end to trust with the picture and voice of the popular president. Thus, consider the choice presented in the frame:

Reaganomics	*Mondaleconomics*
Cut taxes	Raise taxes
Cut spending	Raise taxes
Create job growth	Raise taxes

REFERENTIAL ADVERTISING USING HUMAN SYMBOLS

In the majority of the ads coded for negative appeals that use human symbols, greatest use is made of what was coded as *other personalities,* that is, individuals who are not the candidate. The largest component of this grouping is other politicians who polling may well have indicated were already viewed negatively in the area where the advertising was aired. Thus, the question which should be raised concerns whether the appeal involves an attempt to transfer or "refer" negative affect associated with them to the opponent. Republican negative ads featured such negatively perceived "other personalities" as Walter Mondale and Geraldine Ferraro; Jerry Falwell similarly embellished some Democratic advertising. In the more entertainment oriented environment of the California proposition ad wars, "crooks" and "gamblers" who came straight from central casting served the same referential purpose.

Frequently, the opponent as well as many of the negatively viewed individuals with whom he or she is linked appears in what photographers call a dead shot. This is a still frame of past or "dead" action. The dead picture frame is often etched in black and white, contrasting sharply with the colorful action film surrounding it. The latter is the television world that defines Americans' video environment and whose purpose is to touch a responsive chord, drawing the viewer into an "experience." Visually, however, the question should be asked, is the purpose of the dead shot to add negative affect to the symbol of the "other" with whom the opponent is linked? Such devices might well be expected to surface affect that would either prevent the development of or break the bonds of qualification, identity, or empathy that are a necessary part of the trust relationship between candidate and voter.

When the various "other personalities" are tallied, they comprise the largest single grouping of human symbols in the 1984 advertising coded for anger, with 12 out of a total of 40 codings (30 percent) and a lesser, but still high total figure in the uncertainty advertising (11 out of 42, or 26 percent). The figures are even higher for the ads coded for even stronger affective advertising appeals, such as fear.

Another defining characteristic of the ads coded for anger and uncertainty appeals is that unlike either positive advertising or the advertising as a whole, one-fifth of the human symbols represent economic and social minority groups. As noted in Chapter 3, interest groups were making their appearance in negative, not positive, advertising during the final period of the 1984 campaign.

The Association of Anger Codings with Pocketbook Issues

The anger codings were heavily associated, not with any particular symbol, but with ads combining production effects and one type of issue—the pocketbook issue. Symbols, sounds, and mythology—indeed, there was a David-and-Goliath storytelling quality about these ads—together add up to the fact that a large and powerful entity, certainly one more significant than the viewer, is after his or her hard-earned cash. Further, such ads were much more than just issues ads.

Indeed, they were character ads as well, dovetailing an issue that could "make you mad" with readily visualized negative character qualities. In short, the opponent is associated with Goliath and, indeed, may well have a financially beneficial relationship with him. Visual symbols offer proof of links between the opponent and that large entity in a fashion that might well alienate the uninvolved voter. Limousines, actors playing the opponent stepping out into a fancy Washington party or taking expensive vacations—all link the opponent with moneyed interests.

Presentation of the Goliath with which the opponent is linked enables the candidate to emerge as David, a mythic hero, resolution in fact to the dilemmas raised in the ad. Checks are flourished and charge cards are crunched to the accompaniment of nerve-grating dissonant sounds that reach no conclusion, that do not move back into harmony. Resolution is possible in the form of David, who fights for the common man.

The pocketbook dimension of appeals in such ads, coded for anger, is clear. Of the 40 anger codings in the 1984 ad sample, 15 related to taxes; 12 others related to other ways the opponent and the large institutions with which the opponent was associated would "take your money" (See Table 5.2). These relate to political action committee (PAC) money the opponent was taking: "money earned by the opponent as a Washington lobbyist"; money the opponent will "take from you" because he is linked with utility interests; and in the case of a proposition campaign, money the state legislature should have "given back to you" as did the legislatures in other states. In the California proposition ads included in the 1984 sample were also "politicians stealing your money" and money the opposition would like to "steal from you in a game called reapportionment."

Movie Stars, not Politicians

Interestingly, in California, the center of America's entertainment industry, the only reference to "politicians" in the 1984 sample was in ads depicting them in such a negative fashion. Actors appeared more frequently than politicians in ads on the nonpresidential level. The only politician who appeared in such an ad was Republican congressman Bill Dannemeyer, who was apparently developing statewide name recognition for a future Republican primary race. In the California portion of the 1984 ad sample, therefore, it was actors, not politicians, who carried political messages.

An example of the type of advertising featuring movie stars is Proposition 39, opposing reapportionment, which was developed by Republicans who were poorly represented in the state legislature and believed this was because California legislative districts had been gerrymandered. The ad was cut by Jack Klugman, and its implication was that voters should respond to a Republican

Table 5.2
How the Opponent Is "Shafting" You in Anger Ads
(N = 40)

Issues	Money	Social	Other	Total
Taxes	15	5	7	27
Other	12			12
Jobs	1			1
	28 (70%)	5 (12.5%)	7 (17.5%)	40 (100%)

redistricting plan like individuals whose pockets are being picked. Klugman's "no" side carried the issue, thereby offering support for research that has proven that in California's proposition wars *any* "no" position is easier to carry than a positive position. The "yes" side must make a complex case for change, and it is difficult to make that on the visual media where the "nonpartisan" contest is largely fought.

SOFT-SELL UNCERTAINTY ADVERTISING

There are two theoretical types of ads utilizing appeals to voter uncertainty. The first are soft-sell ads, which were sometimes coded in the 1984 sample for both uncertainty and anger. In such ads entertainment devices are utilized to keep the attacker from appearing mean. Still, their purpose can be to tap feelings of uncertainty in the mind of the viewer. Such feelings may be related to previous political decisions, to the viewer's future, economic or personal, or to the positions or character of the opponent—or any combination thereof. The opponent or opposing party's candidates may also be linked with uncertainty about the future of the voter's children.

Also utilizing soft-sell uncertainty appeals are what are sometimes called cute negative ads. They attract the viewer by means of entertainment devices, such as a light-hearted comment, self-deprecation, or the unexpected and sometimes humorous revelation of a human foible. Then comes the message.

Examples of soft-sell uncertainty ads come from the Republican generic ads included in the 1984 sample. "Bandwagon" theory relating to the possibility of being outflanked by a competitor is used in one, designed for upwardly mobile young professionals (yuppies). Thus, in "Bus Stop" attractive male and female young professionals (yuppies) wait at a bus stop on a bright day whose clear colors bespeak the promise of success. Yet the conversation includes the following:

"Bus Stop" (excerpt)

She: Is your Democratic congressman for higher taxes?

He: I'd better find out. (The bus pulls up, she gets on it, and it pulls away. He is left behind, looking confused.) I'd better find out what time the next bus is, too.

In this bandwagon advertising, it is clear that the male yuppy will "miss the bus" or be left behind by a female counterpart if he continues his habitual pattern of decision making. Solution: finding out whether his congressman is not concealing something. Democrats are linked with the governmental Goliath in a fashion designed to suggest that the male professional (yuppy) might also be outdistanced by a female colleague if he does not vote Republican. Questions are raised about individual decision making, not through rational arguments, but through symbols and the sound of a missed bus.

In other soft-sell uncertainty ads, characters representing varied age groups appear in the visual symbolism of ads similarly suggesting a successful future. But in contrast to the hope ads, which also use a generational mix, as described in the previous chapter, symbols are used that raise questions concerning what the future will hold if the voter does not choose the action suggested by the ad.

In both "Father and Son" and "Grandpa and Susan," which ran heavily during the period of the 1984 sample, the pleasantness of the outdoor and home environments offers the promise of success, of life itself. Yet there is an undercurrent of uncertainty in the use of such characters in the ads as a father and a son, a granddaughter and grandfather. The action suggested is that of "doing the right thing" for a close relative. In "Father and Son" the son questions whether the father is "still" going to vote for a Democrat, an action that, it is implied, would hurt the son; in "Grandpa and Susan" Grandpa offers his firm view that it is up to *her* generation to right the wrongs of the past by voting against Democrats who raise taxes.

Uncertainty is raised about an economic issue and, in the crucial dimension that gives such advertising a dovetailing affective dimension, about personal decision-making as well. This is achieved in part by means of a very personal cast of characters. In both cases the protagonist tells the immediate relative of a "threat," which in the case of the son speaking to his father involves taking things "back to the way they used to be," a phrase that can have many meanings beyond economic ones. Resolution, however, is to be found in *right* action: voting Republican.

"Grandpa and Susan"

(Very old man sitting down in mythic, light-strewn living room. His grand-daughter comes up to his rocking chair. They exchange affectionate glances.)

Susan: It's my first time voting.

Grandpa: Did you know the Democrats have controlled the House for the last 29 years?

Susan: Really?

Grandpa: And now they're threatening to raise taxes again. Well, maybe *your* generation can do something about it.

Susan (with pensive look): I hope so.

Whether softly, in such "cute" soft-sell uncertainty ads featuring intergenerational relations, or more starkly in hard-sell negative ads, those that link the opponent with a more clearly defined threatening entity, the question that emerges is whether the purpose of the ad is to prevent the development of bonds of identification and empathy between the opposing candidate and the viewer by linking the opponent with a threat. That this should be an economic one on the ad's conceptual level of meaning is hardly surprising, given the fact that economic well-being is a crucial voting variable. That ads focusing on such threats should also feature an intergenerational cast of characters producing an affective side to the total complex mix that is the attitudinal appeal in political advertising is highly compelling.

HARD-SELL UNCERTAINTY ADVERTISING

Hard-sell negative ads are distinguished from soft-sell ads by their use of stronger, indeed harsher, language, sounds, and visuals.

One hard-sell format is what might be termed the secret villain ad. The candidate is battling not just an idea but its personification as well. In this genre, common in the 1984 ad sample coded for uncertainty, positive and negative codings are both prevalent. The threat is presented either by means of a human symbol and/or verbally and aurally through jarring special effects in ads that contain no human symbols but may give an organization, institution, or an idea human or storybook-villain form.

In the 1984 sample the secret villain genre was most frequently used by challengers and endangered incumbents. A Democratic version was used by North Carolina gubernatorial contender Rufus Edmisten, for example, as he was losing to Republican Jim Martin, as well as by a number of other endangered or underdog Democrats in the 1984 sample whose races are examined in the strategy chapters. In Edmisten's ad, "Enemies He's Proud Of," the opponent is linked with a negative entity drawn from the world of business.

"Enemies He's Proud Of"

Video	*Audio*
Camera focuses on checks written to Jim Martin.	"This is a *different* kind of candidate . . . He has enemies he's proud of: big chemicals, big utilities, and big oil. He's won battles for the elderly and the poor . . . so no wonder *they* . . . are so proud of Jim Martin. Ever thought? If *they* win *you* lose."

The difference between this advertising appeal and soft-sell advertising is that the threat is more starkly drawn. This is done by means of clear verbal messages ("enemies" and "if *they* win, *you* lose") as well as by jarring symbols (pens scratching on checks, which point to sleaze) and other dissonant sound effects.

In the Republican version of the secret villain genre, using similar language, the culprit whose interest the opponent is serving is *big government*. This culprit was the staple of the Reagan advertising in the 1980 presidential election, but it was seen more in its "government as big taxer and spender" version in 1984. In ads that Reagan cut on behalf of several nonincumbent Republican gubernatorial candidates, however, the big-government villain emerged in its purer verbal form. Reagan refers to the bad days before he came into office, when "government in Washington was the *enemy.*" For North Carolina Republican gubernatorial candidate Jim Martin, it is the "state legislature" that is the secret villain, bilking the public of its just economic rewards. Key is the fact that in the hard-sell uncertainty ads few light-hearted or engaging entertainment devices are used.

There are many other forms of the secret villain with whom the opposing candidate is linked in such hard-nosed ads included in the 1984 sample. In the California proposition ads coded for uncertainty, harsh black-and-white colors and jail cell and smoke-filled room scenarios underscore the verbal and visual message of criminals and eastern "gamblers," villains with which the opposing camp is linked. In Georgia, it is "northern liberals." In North Carolina, it is "sex abusers," the religious right, and national Democrats.

THE DOUBLE MESSAGE OF FLIP-FLOP ADS

Another formula used in both hard-sell and soft-sell negative advertising uses changes in an opponent's position over time, his *record,* in other words, as one side of a double message relating to character or integrity. The familiar *flip flop* ad is frequently about more than just a record. It also concerns the candidate serving only his or her own interests, thus fulfilling the voter's suspicion that he or she is "just another politician."

An award-winning 1984 ad cut for Indiana Democratic congressional candidate Art Smith by Steve Powell of Cerrell Associates illustrates how the flip-flop ad can contain a character dimension relating to integrity as the reverse side of a dovetailing character-concepts message:

"Bouncing Ball"

(A ball bounces back and forth across the screen.)

Narrator: Can you follow the bouncing ball? On October 1, 1982, John Myers voted for a balanced federal budget. June 3, 1983, he voted against a $7 million office expense reduction for himself and every other congressman. John would like to have us believe that he's a friend of the taxpayers, but on December 14, 1982, he voted himself a $9,000 raise at our expense. Maybe it's time we got in the game and gave him the bounce by making Art Smith our next congressman.[11]

The ball metaphor catches attention while it represents inconstant character.

THE ABSENTEE

Another approach used in both hard-sell and soft-sell negative advertising in 1986, as in 1984, questions the opponent's lack of effectiveness or qualifications by suggesting that he is an absentee congressman or congresswoman or state legislator.

All of these approaches, in some degree, link the opponent with ongoing public suspicion about the integrity of *all politicians*. By the 1986 midterm elections, pollster Peter Hart was observing that the lone overarching "issue" in the midterm congressional races was character. "The messenger is the message" was his oft-quoted aphorism.

HARSH REALITY ADS

The strongest form of the hard-sell uncertainty genre is the ad that was coded in the 1984 example for uncertainty, but there were other, stronger codings as well. These were fear, and sometimes anger as well. Such appeals are *harsh reality* ads because they represent reality in a stark fashion. All of the elements of other uncertainty ads are in place, including threats and referential linkage of the opponent with negatively viewed "other personalities." But the level of the attack is raised through the use of sound effects and visuals that link the opponent with a feeling of vulnerability on the part of the voter.

The special quality of such harsh reality advertising is the use of the color black combined with sound effects that can only be described by such labels as *doomsday music* and *insinuating voices,* which raise the possibility of imminent danger. If absorbed by the viewer, and viewers certainly vary on how they would react to this, as they do to any other advertising, such ads would leave them with the impression of vulnerability before a threat. The threat in such ads is all the more frightening because it appears to be hidden. This possibility is underscored by sound effects and insinuating voices implying that there is something fearful about which the voter is uninformed. Howling wind and what one might call portentous music and sound effects, defined as those that raise expectations that something negative could happen, are all used.

THREE TYPES OF AFFECTIVE APPEALS

What this experimental research reveals is three major types of negative affective appeals that are used in ads that combine affect, concept, and, frequently, storied images drawn from childhood memory. They might be summarized as follows. First are *uncertainty appeals,* which involve questions relating to the decision-making process, intergenerational issues, and the opponent's honesty, that is, whether the opponent is deceitful and would deliberately commit an act contrary to the voter's best interest. Second are *"get 'em mad"* (or *anger*) *appeals,* which focus on whether the individual will be "ripped off" economically by large forces favored by or associated with the opponent. The additional quality of the third, *harsh reality appeals,* relates to the question of individual vulnerability in the face of uncontrollable, powerful forces.

In relation to the latter, the codings for North Carolina and California in the 1984 sample, as well as the West Virginia Senate campaign ads broadcast from Washington, indicated that the harsh reality ad was alive and well in competitive races in 1984.

Nonpresidential use of the special effects that were a characteristic feature of these ads was greatest in the 1984 ad sample in North Carolina and California. In North Carolina they were found not only in the Hunt-Helms race but on lower levels as well, including the attorney general's race.

STATE DIFFERENCES IN SOFT-SELL AND HARD-SELL NEGATIVE ADS

Overall, in relation to both major categories of negative advertising appeals—soft-sell and hard-sell—there were differences between the level of affect-related appeals in the various states. In Los Angeles, California, the tone was heavily negative, a tone offset in our sample by the fact that in the second large media market, Atlanta, Georgia, all was sweet lullabies during the final days of the 1984 election (a fact which, as Chapter 9 on Southern congressional races indicates, belies the heavy use of negative advertising earlier in the race). The biggest contrast during the final days of the election occurred between North Carolina and Indiana, the two states that ran the greatest number of ads in the 1984 sample because the media markets were smaller and rates were more affordable for candidate advertising.

In both cases little negative advertising existed on the state and local levels. However, there was a great deal of it on all federal levels in North Carolina. In Indiana the greatest amount occurred on the congressional level, but as the chapter on Indiana congressional races indicates (Chapter 9), there was only one competitive race in the 1984 sample, a fact which kept the negative level lower than in North Carolina, where three competitive congressional races were included in the sample. Both states had competitive gubernatorial races, and the higher negative advertising figures in the state with more competitiveness increases the possibility of the use of negative advertising.

Selecting an Early Negative Issue

In the Indiana gubernatorial race, there was less negative advertising at the end largely because the open-seat North Carolina race between Democrat Rufus Edmisten and Republican Jim Martin was more competitive than that between Republican incumbent governor Robert Orr and Democratic challenger Wayne Townsend, but also because Townsend was running out of money at the end. He had selected a negative issue at the beginning of the race and developed an advertising campaign around it: It was "corruption" in the state system whereby the ruling party receives the car license renewal fees.

The issue of corruption in the state system was selected, according to Townsend's pollster, because, according to projective polls that had tested for intensity of response when both new and old issues were presented to the viewer, it was the one that people did *not* know about and therefore had no opinion about. But when people found out about it, the issue of corruption "moved the numbers." Thus, it was selected for use in the campaign's early political advertising over the issue of education, which, although rated high in other polls as a matter of public concern, was not "felt" with the same intensity as license branches in the projective polls. Contrary to expectations, Townsend made a close race of it in this fashion, focusing first on a negative issue, license branches, to make the race competitive, and then on education and jobs. Orr was narrowly reelected with 52 percent of the vote to Townsend's 48 percent. In 1986, a similar poll was conducted, license branches was again selected as an issue, and the candidate—in this case Evan Bayh, who pulled ahead from ten points behind during the final two weeks of the race focusing only on the license branch issue—won a state office. The pattern used in this race was repeated on other levels of this research and is examined in detail in subsequent chapters.[12]

ADS IN COMPETITIVE RACES IN 1986

Ads by major consultants used in a sample of 1986 statewide gubernatorial and senatorial races were also examined, although not as closely for each appeal in each individual ad as was the case with the 1984 sample taken from the air. The 1986 sample included 146 gubernatorial ads from 17 competitive and 3 noncompetitive races and 210 ads from 19 competitive and 8 noncompetitive Senate races. The fund-raising community frequently defines a competitive race as one in which the front-runner drops below 60 percent. In this study the categories are defined by whether the final vote tallys produced winners who won by 60 percent or less.[13]

The 1986 ad analysis indicates that 1986 deserved its reputation as a year of negative advertising in competitive races. It was also a year in which heavy use was made of soft-sell uncertainty ads, that is, ads that utilize entertainment devices but are nevertheless negative. This is because although such devices were used to attract attention and promote recall, the focus was on the character traits associated with pocketbook issues, whether relating to agricultural policy or regional economic disparities (as between prosperous New York and California, and the troubled U.S. Midwest). David-and-Goliath myths also predominated, focusing on the little guy in relation to large negative forces, which might be criminals or drug dealers as well as Wall Street.

SLICK ADS IN TINSELTOWN

1986 was also a year in which ads built on the idea that the opponent was somehow phony because he used political advertising. It was ironic that such a message might appear in a negative ad, but indeed it did. Thus, a character issue might be raised in terms of "slick advertising," as was the case in Democratic senator Alan Cranston's initial early negative ads against his opponent, Republican Ed Zschau. Two of Cranston's soft-sell uncertainty ads, "Film" and "Advertising," raised doubts or uncertainty about the character of his opponent by mimicking his ads, using dissonant clicking film and clacking projector sounds. That a candidate's character could be questioned in an ad because he had aired ads is just another irony of campaigning in the video age.[14]

Not only was there innovation in soft-sell negative advertising; there were also creative new developments in the area of hard-sell negative advertising that used not only dark colors and heavy sound motifs but bright colors as well. Life, depicted through bright, personal visuals, was juxtaposed with the "subtle shock" of tragic recognition. This might occur in an ad in Washington state that relates what could happen to your child if a toxic waste truck exploded; or in Florida, what could result if your family walked outside at night alone, or home to an empty house, lovingly depicted in bright colors as one in which your grandmother might have lived. Home and comfort are contrasted for extra impact with a violation of this intimate space. Hard-sell negative advertising still utilized dark colors and quick-response techniques, however, and Bella Abzug, Jane Fonda, and indeed Angela Davis, the alleged 1960s communist, all appeared in referential ads that associated the opponent with a negatively perceived "other personality." In what should have been, but apparently was not, a warning to the 1988 Democratic presidential nominee, gubernatorial candidates were charged not only with being soft on crime, but were linked in highly personal ways with tragedies caused by criminals.

The 1986 sample included ads from all but four of the competitive gubernatorial races, and from all but three of the competitive Senate races. It is clear from this analysis that soft-sell and hard-sell negative advertising are common campaign tools in such races. They were used in all but one of both the gubernatorial and senatorial races included in the sample; and not only by challengers, but incumbents as well used them. These figures offer compelling proof of the heavy use and great significance of negative advertising in competitive statewide races during 1986.

CONCLUSION

This content analysis has focused on theoretical categories of affective appeals. It located in the 1984 ad sample appeals comparable to those found by psychological and commercial researchers, including uncertainty, anger, and even stronger negative emotions such as fear. Future research should be conducted on the spot, when the ads are being aired, using a representative sample of voters. It might also well further analyze such production characteristics as camera angles. Still, patterns of use in human and nonhuman symbols, sounds, and one type of issue in the 1984 ads appearing on the air were isolated, and patterns were found that continued in 1986 in most of the nation's competitive statewide races.

Overall, it is argued there are two categories of negative ads. Both categories include an affective rhetorical dimension focused around questions of empathy, or identification between voter and candidate, as well as a concept issue. Soft-sell ads utilize entertainment devices such as humor, self-deprecation, and storytelling to blend within the message environment of a visual medium such as television. In the process that we have isolated and called dovetailing, ideas become human, or visual. An economic concept is not just a theory. It is flesh made manifest on a highly personalizing electronic medium.

Hard-sell negative advertising uses dark colors, strong sounds, and human symbols of alienation that are more bluntly expressed. It can, however, as the trend in 1986 indicated, also use bright and enticing visuals and combine these with attempts to appeal to uncertainty and even fear. The strongest codings of both soft-sell and hard-sell negative appeals were to uncertainty, a coding that combines issues with appeals to uncertainty about personal decision making, intergenerational bonding, and suspicion of *a,* perhaps *all,* politicians, and to anger, which may well be strongly associated with pocketbook issues, specifically whether the voter will be "ripped off" by large, frequently mythically personified forces favored by, or associated with, the opponent. Harsh reality hard-sell advertising adds to all this the further dimension of individual vulnerability.

This research has also focused on variation of use in two large market areas, Atlanta and Los Angeles, where candidate advertising is expensive, and in two parts of the country, Indiana and North Carolina, which varied on factors relating to the incumbency, the competitiveness of races, and levels of voter education. It found that in the Los Angeles market, which featured competitive proposition campaigns, a highly negative environment existed below the presidential level—one dominated by figures from the entertainment industry, not by politicians. It also found more negative advertising on the federal level in North Carolina, which was a more competitive but less educated environment than Indiana.

Issues are certainly an important part of negative ads. But this analysis has focused on how they are part of a total, broader message. This should not be unexpected given recent research that has focused on a broad definition of what an "attitude" is and the fact that communication occurs on a storytelling electronic medium that is best attuned to presenting the world in microcosm through compelling visuals.

NOTES

1. Thomas D. Patterson and Robert D. McClure, *Political Advertising: Voter Reaction to Televised Political Commercials* (Princeton, N.J.: Citizen's Research Foundation, 1973); Stuart H. Surlin and Thomas F. Gordon, "How Values Affect Attitudes

toward Direct Reference Political Advertising,'' *Journalism Quarterly* 54 (1977): 89–98. Recent experimental research focusing on viewer reactions to negative advertising was conducted by Gina M. Garramone, ''Voter Response to Negative Political Ads,'' *Journalism Quarterly* 61 (1984): 250–59; and Lynda Lee Kaid and J. Boydston, ''An Experimental Study of the Effectiveness of Negative Political Advertisements,'' *Communication Quarterly* 35 (1987): 193–201.

Research has determined that negative advertising is more extensive on the presidential level than previously assumed. See Anne Johnston Wadsworth and Lynda Lee Kaid, ''Incumbent and Challenger Styles in Presidential Advertising,'' paper presented at the International Communication Association Convention, Montreal, May 1987.

2. Surlin and Gordon defined what they called ''direct reference,'' or negative advertising, in the fashion that has governed most subsequent research: It is advertising that directly refers to and attacks the opponent, his or her issues, or the opposition party.

More recently, B.E. Gronbeck identified three types of political ads, still based on their focus. The ''implicative ad'' involves an implication or innuendo about the opponent but no direct attack, unless it is quickly slipped in through phrases such as ''unlike my opponent.'' The ''comparative'' ad incorporates an explicit comparison between the contenders. The ''assaultive ad,'' provides a direct, personal attack on the opponent's character, motives, associates, or actions, usually with little or no reference to the originator of the advertisement. B.E. Gronbeck, ''The Rhetoric of Negative Political Advertising: Thoughts on Senatorial Race Ads in 1984,'' Paper presented at the Speech Communication Association Convention, Denver, November 1985.

For analyses of the literature on negative advertising, see Susan A. Hellweg, ''Political Candidate Campaign Advertising: A Selected Review of the Literature,'' paper presented at the International Communication Association Convention, New Orleans, May 1988; and Roger C. Aden, ''Televised Political Advertising: A Review of the Literature on 'Spots,' '' paper presented at the International Communication Association Convention, New Orleans, May 1988.

3. Richard Fenno, *Home Style: House Members and Their Districts* (Boston: Little, Brown, 1978).

4. This style has been frequently tested in the literature cited in Hellweg. See also ''fear'' appeals cited in Wadsworth and Kaid, ''Incumbent and Challenger Styles.''

5. ''None'' and ''other'' were also included on the coding sheet.

6. See Chapter 4.

7. For Tony Schwartz's view on ''guilt'' appeals see Chapter 2. For the use of such appeals, see Chapter 6.

8. See Chapter 9.

9. See Chapter 8.

10. Shyles on hybrid ads. See discussion in Chapter 3.

11. This ad was made for the 1984 Congressional race of Art Smith of Indiana. For its context, see Chapter 8.

12. Interview with the polling and media consultants Dick Dresner and Dick Sykes, who were the strategists for Townsend's race, New York, September 23, 1985, and Doug Schoen, who was the pollster for Democrat Evan Bayh, the son of Birch Bayh, who was pitted in a campaign for the position of Indiana secretary of state against the son of popular former governor of Indiana Otis Bowen. Schoen believes it was heavy use of this issue and this issue alone during the final ten days of the race that brought Bayh up from 12 points behind to a 54–46 percent victory. Doug Schoen, ''Integrating

Polling and Media,'' paper presented at the *Campaigns and Elections* Conference, Washington, D.C., May 6, 1987.

See also the discussion in Chapter 2. The pattern of early negative advertising using an affect-oriented issue is discussed in Chapter 8 and 9 for the congressional level.

13. See Appendix C.

14. For the chance to view these ads and others from the Zschau-Cranston race, see the film *1986 Political Advertising Classics,* (Washington, D.C.: Campaigns and Elections, 1987).

6

Democrats Reach for the Presidency: 1984 and Yet More Enduring Lessons

Walter Mondale's 1984 presidential campaign illustrated how even the most philosophically informational media campaign could turn to an emotional style. The campaign set out, as Mondale expressed it, to "grind away," educating people to such complex issues as the deficit and the consequent need to raise taxes. A part of this effort was to prove that his opponent, incumbent president Ronald Reagan, was "blow-dried," a seeming success simply because he was a good video communicator. Ironically, when pressed both during the primary and general election campaigns, the Mondale campaign itself turned to a highly emotional style.[1]

A "mixed," or new informational, Democratic media campaign failed resoundingly, and Walter Mondale lost every state except his native Minnesota and found to his dismay that the public overwhelmingly accepted his opponent's version of both the character and issues of the two candidates.[2]

From this experience the 1988 Democratic presidential candidates learned important lessons. The first one was the value of the Reagan version of an emotional style of campaigning. While they might disagree with Reagan on the issues, the style he represented came to be predominant. One consultant observed that if 1984 was a year of transition, 1986 was the year of triumph for commercial principles in political advertising. What happened on the presidential level in 1984 was a major reason for this. The lessons were those of the winning Reagan campaign: acceptance of affect- and entertainment-laden messages, a focus on myth, the dovetailing of character and issues messages, and the careful integration of news and advertising efforts. Most important, perhaps, was an understanding of the importance of early candidate imagery.

Because the race was such a significant one in terms of the evolution of political advertising, it will be examined in some detail, but from the perspective of the 1984 ad sample. The lessons learned from this race, as will be seen, were implemented by the 1988 Democratic candidates.

The 1984 Democratic advertising challenge was indeed a difficult one. Mondale was 20 points behind President Reagan on Labor Day, having emerged wounded from a series of bitterly fought primaries and a divided convention and having further selected a running-mate without regard for the regional requirements of victory. Walter Mondale needed all the help he could get in the South and the West but hurt himself both by his selection of a vice-presidential candidate from New York and then by his reversal of a decision to appoint Georgia's Bert Lance to a high campaign position. The Bert Lance affair and Mondale's failure to screen the finances of the vice-presidential candidate, followed by his failure to insist that the national campaign manage press coverage of John Zaccaro's financial irregularities, were major blows not only of substance but also of communications strategy. They foretold a campaign in which Mondale appeared to be helping Reagan achieve his landslide, a landslide that had an important communications dimension.

THE 1984 SAMPLE

The Mondale ads in the 1984 sample point to acceptance of the premises of an emotional approach to political advertising. In his last-ditch effort during the final days of the campaign, Mondale drew on an emotional advertising strategy as old as the "Daisy" commercial that had linked Barry Goldwater with nuclear irresponsibility. This time, voters were asked not only to "teach your children well" but also to protect them from the consequences of Reagan's military policies.

As the strains of "Teach Your Children Well" die down, and the faces of an old woman and a blue-collar worker ("you can decide on how she lives and whether he works") pass by, we are left with two young children. They look up, concerned, their play interrupted. The narrator renews his appeal to the viewer's sense of responsibility, perhaps even to feelings of guilt. *"You* can speak for those who cannot speak for themselves," he says. A missile is launched, and we see the world from outer space.

In "Elderly" the camera focused on a series of defenseless, lonely elderly women whose faces are pinched. Their voices express deep uncertainty as they speak of their desperate plight and inquire what they will do now that Reagan has cut the food-stamp program. As the camera pans away, one concludes that these women just want to "get by."

In a third advertisement, a series of characters representing traditional Democratic constituencies bemoan hard times, and a laborer concludes that Reagan doesn't understand how poor people live. "He's just an upper-class man."

These and other Mondale spots in the 1984 sample were coded for a negative rhetorical style. Four out of nine Mondale 30-second spots which ran 25 times in the 1984 ad sample were coded for anger, centered around themes of economic injustice and uncertainty, a coding which includes the view that the ad appeals to feelings of uncertainty, insecurity, or suspicion. One was coded for guilt, or the view that the intended recipient of the message (who was ignoring the plight of the poor) was not acting responsibly. Although there were few codings on the positive side, there was one coding for compassion, or an appeal to the viewer's desire to help others. This was quite unusual among the 1984 positive presidential codings, which were dominated by the Reagan advertising focus on trust, hope, reassurance, and national and local pride.[3]

Mondale's negative emotional appeals differed from Reagan's positive ones in that they were those of a challenger trying to stop the music, to interrupt the sound of the incumbent's violins.

Mondale officials interviewed during the final days of the campaign said that the final 1984 ad sequence was intended to identify the candidate with doubts about Reagan's sense of fairness and commitment to arms control. But according to one, it was also an effort to give the viewers an emotional jolt. "We've put our argument in emotional terms, in gut-wrenching ways," said one advisor. "If there's going to be a major shift in voter's preferences, it's got to come from the gut level." According to another, it was an advertising campaign designed to tap liberals' sense of "guilt," bestirring the party's traditional supporters on Mondale's behalf in this period when the campaign knew it would lose but hoped to narrow the gap.[4]

The issues that Mondale had originally intended to stress, and that reporters from the campaign trail described Mondale as being happiest discussing, finally emerged in these closing ads, which were flown to him from the offices of Texas consultant Roy Spence for his review on the campaign trail. The Mondale of these ads in late October and early November was a traditional "compassionate" Democrat who favored strong government intervention on behalf of the poor and was profoundly concerned about arms control. This was the Mondale of the campaign's original plan. But it was a Mondale who had never fully emerged earlier because the decision had been made after the Democratic convention to focus in the fall campaign on articulating issues that would build a strong leadership image for a candidate who, as the polling and focus-group research indicated, was perceived to be "weak," or indeed "just a politician." The issues that would strengthen the candidate with the crucial 25–40-year-old voters were favored in the process of issue selection. It was ironic that Mondale's return during the final days of the campaign to the issues he cared most about was perceived as yet another retreat from a previous advertising plan, yet another sign that his advertising was not helping him control the total televised-message agenda.[5]

For both an anonymous "former Mondale media consultant" and Republican consultant Roger Ailes, quoted in the *Wall Street Journal,* the final ads were a sign of desperation. The fact that former Mondale media consultants were divulging their views on the pages of the *Journal* and agreeing with Roger Ailes was a sign of major difficulties in yet another area: lack of unity in the campaign in general.[6]

According to Richard Leone, who held responsibility for Mondale's paid and unpaid media message at the beginning of September, the problem was that by fall there was so little else that seemed to hold promise that the advertising effort became crucial, but decisions were made by a committee of whoever happened to be around. Leone, a protégé of Jim Johnson, who had devised Walter Mondale's original campaign strategy, was, during these final days, engaged in a spirited disagreement with the "people who run the campaign" who had moved the advertising in what he considered a futile negative direction. Indeed, there were many other signs of disunity in the campaign. One was the fact that such media consultants as Leone and Roy Spence had limited access to the upper echelons of campaign decision making. From this, Spence later concluded that he would never be in a campaign again "where I'm not in control." [7]

The Mondale effort was also heavily outgunned in terms of spot airtime during the final ten days of the election. Mondale's 30-second and 1-minute ads were overshadowed 3 to 1 with 27.5 to Reagan's 79 minutes of airtime. If Reagan's 30-minute ad, broadcast the night before the election, is included, his lead in the 1984 sample airtime rises from 3 to 1 to 4 to 1. The Mondale campaign's modest efforts to focus the debate on questions of food stamps, education, agriculture, and economic opportunity were also overwhelmed in terms of issue advertising airtime by the Reagan themes of government size, inflation, interest rates, and taxes. Part of the difference between the two campaigns during this period, of course, may be due to the fact that Mondale pulled ads from a number of states during the final blitz (including North Carolina and Georgia, the two states included in this sample) in his last-ditch attempt to prevent the loss of Minnesota. [8]

Human symbols and music both confirmed the throwback during this period to the traditional group-oriented Democratic focus of the ads in the 1984 sample. Unlike the Reagan advertising, and much of the other advertising in the sample, the characters represent traditional constituencies. The appeals offered more of an interest-group than an individual orientation, confirming an approach that was more political than commercial. The music was not the broad, swelling sound that would appeal to everyone; it was a Crosby, Stills, and Nash tune designed to rally the aging 1960s liberals who had to turn out if the whole effort was not to become a 50-state rout.

THE IMPORTANCE OF EARLY IMAGES

For months the Mondale presidential primary media campaign had been guided by the need to develop themes that the strategists, pollsters, and focus groups determined would move large numbers of people for immediate ends. Thus, with the whole Democratic primary field committed to arms control, the candidates did not develop an advertising focus on this issue, which the polls indicated was an area of vulnerability for Ronald Reagan. As a result, no groundwork was laid for a race against Reagan in the fall general election. Reagan, whose polls indicated that he was also vulnerable on the age issue (he was a septuagenarian) and on the possibility of "Democratic return to the fold" in the fall, was thus given plenty of time in the spring and summer to develop a carefully coordinated advertising and news media effort to "inoculate" himself on such issues.[9]

At one point in the hard-fought primary season running ahead of Gary Hart in Ohio, the Mondale campaign launched a first salvo against Reagan by running a "Star Wars" ad. But Mondale lost Ohio to Hart, who focused on "hard times" in the traditional industrial states and launched a hard-sell negative integrity attack on Mondale as a "changeling" politician who was not "like us" but at the beck and call of the "special interests."

Mondale returned with a similar attack—in what was clearly becoming the negative coin of the presidential primary race. The commercial was called "Red Phone," and it was of the hard-sell negative genre in its appeal to feelings of public uncertainty, relating fear of nuclear war to the opponent's qualities, in this case not having held public office. Would one want to elect an "inexperienced" president who might not know what to do when that "Red Phone" rang?

This particular ad achieved its objective. According to Texas media consultant Roy Spence, it was inspired by the urgently blinking lights and ringing phones encountered on a hospital visit to his wife, who was imminently expecting the birth of their child while he was under his own deadline to come up with an ad to use in the bitterly contested Hart-Mondale race.[10]

Joe Trippi, who ran the Mondale primary effort in Pennsylvania, said that

"Red Phone" was used to respond to everything they threw at us. In this case, fear of nuclear war worked for us. The other guy would be arguing, "No guts, no belly, owned by labor." We didn't address that. We spent millions of dollars on that ad.[11]

Not surprisingly, the negative campaigning—in which the "no-guts" and the "dangerously inexperienced" candidates faced off—left a bitter legacy not only in the public opinion polls, in which Mondale started the general election campaign with "high negatives," but also with disaffected supporters who had favored his opponent in a number of states. One of these was California, the largest general election battleground, where many Democrats who gave Hart the nod during the primary remained unrequited into the fall general election.

Campaign manager Robert Beckel later commented that Mondale was damaged by the primary season, in what he described as a "lack of set-up" going into the fall campaign. "We were in the fourteenth round to start the fight. When you can't see light until Labor Day, what are you going to do?" Further, according to Beckel, "we ran an issueless primary campaign as the 'pick of the lot.' " The problem was, thus, that the negative referential primary advertising laid the foundation for Republican attacks on Mondale's character, making them credible. Hart's "no-guts, no-belly" attacks hit home, dovetailing with publicized speeches the candidate had given in seeking interest-group support over three years of campaigning for the nomination. The public suspected he was the "interest-group candidate," and this was confirmed for many by the fact that Mondale had not actually established what he stood for. Reagan could beat him using Mondale's own thesis, as developed in "Red Phone," that the candidate with less experience might endanger the nation. If Mondale had spent four years a heartbeat away from the "Red Phone," Reagan had spent four years even closer to it, and the United States was still at peace.[12]

The hope, according to Mondale media coordinator Richard Leone, was that in the general election campaign, it would be possible to achieve an objective similar to that envisioned by the Reagan campaign: *to make the Mondale-Ferraro candidacy "America."* As Leone expressed it, the idea was to make the campaign the vehicle *for Americans to achieve their own "hopes, dreams and symbols."* (italics mine). The advertising effort should

build a new vision of America, of this new party featuring Mondale and Ferraro. A good many of the visual symbols and the whole initial media campaign planned by Roy Spence was around that set of themes—family, and patriotism and progress, equality and women.[13]

Although the first three of these were similar to those articulated in the Reagan media, the latter—equality and women—was different, as was the consistent set of issues ("part of Jim Johnson's initial plan") that would also be presented. These were

fairness, which people felt Reagan might be vulnerable on, war and peace, and the looming problem of dealing with the deficit. At least that was Mondale's conception of what he should make his campaign about, and that's what he wanted his media to be about.[14]

The first task of the campaign, however, was to rehabilitate Mondale, moving him forward from the "Carter-Mondale" image. His "negatives were bad before the convention, and the Lance thing was really bad. Then he came back remarkably quickly." This whole approach "had to be scrapped, however, when the initial scandal broke around Ferraro, the candidate who by the end of the campaign was the least popular in the race."[15]

FOCUS-GROUP FEEDBACK

Thus, in late August and early September, with the story of John Zaccaro's finances dominating the news, the wounded Democratic campaign tested image and issues ads to use in the race against Reagan. The findings of focus groups conducted by Edward J. Reilly of Boston say a great deal about the problems Mondale faced and offer feedback concerning how a presidential campaign can evaluate its advertising effort. The lessons might equally apply to any candidate attempting to develop a coherent message after his or her credibility has been severely damaged.

In a series of "Mondale to Camera" ads tested on September 4, the Reilly group concluded that respondents were "distracted by the visuals and by his presence" and "had difficulty understanding the message" concerning education, taxes, and the deficit. Several remarked that Mondale may be right on the issues, but they didn't "see how he's going to do it." One undecided farmer reached the conclusion most feared by the Mondale campaign: "He reminds me of Carter in those ads." Of one, in which the candidate appeared in a football jersey in an effort to strengthen his image, an undecided heavy-equipment operator remarked, "Mondale is not a football player, and I think it looks stupid to have him walking around in a sweatshirt." [16]

The view that emerged from such focus groups was that the public believed Mondale was weak. This perception contributed to the development of the campaign's foreign policy message. The Reilly group tested a number of foreign policy ads. In one, Mondale outlined a position favoring arms control negotiations. The report concluded that there was a problem with them. People did not believe Mondale would be a tough negotiator. The focus group leader concluded, "This type of thing would work much better with a third party of stature describing his strengths in foreign affairs." Another 60-second spot, "Arms Unlimited," argued that every president except Ronald Reagan had achieved an arms control treaty. Reagan, instead, "has embarked on a massive arms race and . . . refuses to discuss banning weapons from outer space." The text referred to arms control agreements concluded from Eisenhower through Carter, over visuals depicting treaty-signing ceremonies. It ended with a quote from Kennedy's 1961 inaugural speech: "Let us never negotiate out of fear, but let us never fear to negotiate." [17]

The focus group revealed a public confused by efforts to use spots to articulate an arms control position based on its historic context. Participants related better to specific presidents and the "process" in its most general sense, rather than to any results. For example, Reilly noted that they were "confused by all of the different information [presented in "Arms Unlimited"] but responded positively to the Kennedy quote." Further, participants favored "talking" over "treaties" as a solution to problems caused by nuclear weapons. Treaties were perceived as legal documents "that got us into the trouble we're in." [18]

Ads were tested that scored Reagan for a joke in which over an open mike he inadvertently suggested imminent bombing of the Soviet Union. It turned out that viewers did not perceive this as a serious mistake. The only ads that worked were "Reagan-Chernenko," which noted the advancing years of *both* leaders and scored them for holding "the same stalemated ideas for so long, that they cannot find anything new to think," and "Conference Table," which connected this idea with an empty table. Use of the latter was recommended because voters "want dialogue, and the conference table is a neat, clear, and dramatic example of Reagan's record." [19]

Polling data confirmed the focus groups' conclusions that Mondale was perceived to be weak. The campaign accordingly avoided the arms control issue, which was in any event, as the testing indicated, difficult to express visually. This decision represented the triumph of visual as the fact of talking itself—which is what people perceive in television coverage of summit meetings between the heads of states, rather than the results of those talks—*became the Mondale issue*. Thus, failure to talk as symbolized by an empty table was the campaign's main arms control issue. According to Beckel, the feelings of the 25–40 age group were decisive in campaign decision making in this vital area in which the campaign had long realized it must differentiate Mondale from Reagan. The group, quite simply, did not care for the complexities of the arms control process. Concern for the views of this elusive age group also contributed to the decision not to open with "fairness," which implied "big government." [20]

This was a generation raised on television, with its individualism and heroes, and visual memories of a series of ambitious but failed presidents culminating with Jimmy Carter, with whom Walter Mondale was repeatedly linked by fellow Democrats during the primary and by Republicans during the general election campaign. "Our way of dealing with the *wimp* factor," according to Trippi, a youthful addition to the Mondale campaign,

was the "Nimitz" ad—Mondale on deck, on an inspection tour with jets flying overhead. But after two years of not doing anything to make the average guy think he's a hero, this may have brought attention to whatever may have been causing the problem." [21]

The Reilly group concluded in late August that

nothing about Mondale stuck, relating either to his family, or his career, or whatever, because there was no sense of an ideological core, something he stood for. . . . Because voters believe that Reagan's ideology is strong, they view his pragmatism in positive terms . . . while Mondale holds up his finger to see which way the wind is blowing. . . . This is particularly disturbing because it leads respondents to a position where they are willing to believe that Reagan is more of a family man, more religious, and more of a decent person. Without a sense of Mondale's soul, respondents were quite willing to take the symbols of Mondale's life and synthesize them into a Mondale that is developed more by the image of Jimmy Carter than Walter Mondale. . . .

The sense of "not knowing" Mondale really is a desire to know if there is anything Mondale is willing to fight for regardless of political risk. The tax-truthfulness issue [developed at the Democratic convention] was beginning to do exactly that but has been obscured by recent events [surrounding the Ferraro disclosures]. [22]

DOVETAILING: STRESS ON AN ISSUE TO
BUILD CHARACTER

Further development of an issue—the deficit—was therefore recommended in September to give Mondale definition as a person of firm beliefs. The deficit issue would work for Mondale because it

is becoming a term that is representative of personal fears about the individual's economic viability . . . [and] there is frustration with the enormity of the problem, a feeling of helplessness. Respondents, however, demonstrated a clear desire to begin to "clean up the mess" provided they were shown a plan that would work, and that was fair to them personally."[23]

The conclusion was that the campaign should attack on the issue in a way that would "shake up the framework" of economic satisfaction but, equally important, present a plan for what should be done.

Testing of components of a proposed plan, however, produced mixed results. Respondents questioned Mondale's commitment to spending cuts and his ability to be more effective in this area than Reagan, and they were confused by efforts to explain his "15 percent minimum corporate tax." As the respondents' reactions in the arms control area also indicated, it is difficult to explain a complex issue in a spot. The campaign was aware of this but decided to go heavily with the deficit. Beckel said it was necessary to "create issues because people aren't going to go for slogans. 'This guy's better.' Would people believe that? No. So we tried to make the deficit an issue, contrary to people's thinking, first at the convention, and then in September when we had to explain Mondale's position. . . . And Reagan did a very good job of keeping out of that issue."[24]

If the idea was to make Walter Mondale the issues candidate, in part as a way to build his character, to make "being a politician work for him," it was also an attempt to provide some "symbolic negatives" to carry a negative message about the character of Ronald Reagan. The idea was to enhance, by means of a very real issue, the idea that Reagan was a demagogue or "salesman." Despite its general conclusion that attacks on Reagan didn't work, the report recommended that the campaign go with a type of negative ad, "Taxes," which quoted Reagan and Bush inconsistencies on taxes, based on news coverage, and concluded with a Mondale statement: "Mr. Reagan will raise taxes, and so will I. He won't tell you. I just did." The recommendation was based on the view that after seeing the ad, respondents' description of Reagan changed from "leader" to "politician."[25]

Reilly said the campaign should "use actual footage of Reagan 'dancing' on various issues, i.e., new taxes, to politicize him, and move him from the image of an ideological purist to that of a demagogue." At the same time, it should use two negative ads by New York media consultant David Sawyer, "Deficit

(Father)'' and "Roller Coaster" to bring the deficit issue home in a way people can understand.

Hard-Sell Negative Ads

Both "Deficit (Father)" and "Roller Coaster" were hard-sell negative ads featuring mixed generations, as described in Chapter 5. They were the mirror opposite of the positive Reagan ads that mixed generations. "Roller Coaster" opens with visuals of the hands of a man and boy holding the bar of an ascending car to the sound of the roller coaster's mechanism, "click, click, click." The announcer describes how the deficit could drive interest rates through the roof, cause unemployment, and send "us into a recession again. But . . . most people don't seem to be worried . . . not yet." The car reaches the summit and then begins a precipitous fall down the tracks. The voices become anxious, "Uh-oh! Here we go!" and the last sound is that of the boy taking a deep breath. There is a freeze frame and a super: "If you're thinking of voting Republican in 1984, think about what will happen in 1985." [26]

The report indicated that the spot "worked well. . . . Viewers laughed and nodded as the car went up, and they all knew the fear of the impending decline. The spot induced fear and apprehensiveness . . . [but] when probed for further response, they rejected the impending decline as the fault of Reagan or the Republicans." [27]

"Deficit (Father)" also opens with a close-up of hands, this time the father's, which were wringing in dismay at the burden of his debt. Finally, he asks, "Could I ask you to pay it back?" A child's hand reaches into the frame, takes the man's hand, and comforts him as a small voice says, "Sure . . . Daddy. I'll try." The announcer chides the Republicans for their lack of a plan to deal with the huge national debt and for their willingness to "pass it on to our children and grandchildren."

According to the focus-group report, viewers did not respond very well to this. They were "defensive" about the deficit being "their fault." Like "Roller Coaster," the format was the opposite of the Reagan hope ads, using an intergenerational family mix to raise the level of voter uncertainty about the future. Both conclude, "If you're thinking of voting Republican in 1984 . . . just think of what could happen in 1985." They were ads that, according to the commercial language of the 1980s, tried to create an "experience" or take the viewers across a wheel of emotions. But there was no alternative, no resolution, at the end: There was no "fast, fast relief" in the form of a credible candidate. [28]

Reilly's recommendations on the deficit advertising were followed, despite the argument of some in the campaign that negative advertising against Reagan would not work. The Reilly report also warned, however, that such ads would not work unless they were accompanied by positive ads that would outline Mondale's approach to the subject. And so an effort was put into developing a plan that would be used for this purpose to influence both the paid and unpaid media. The plan came out on the very day that Geraldine Ferraro stole the headlines with details of her husband's finances.

This represented a failure in what is emerging as a key measure of media campaign effectiveness: timing in relation to network news. Both messages were under the control of the Mondale campaign. That it could not control the messages of the two prongs of its campaign, so that one would not interfere with the other, was a sign of problems.

Ultimately, the campaign ran one ad after another on the deficit and other issues, but none ran long enough to dominate the television agenda. For Beckel, this was in part because the campaign had no message that "people wanted to hear." But there was also a problem of simply running *any* one ad long enough for it to take hold. Not just a theme, an *ad*. Mondale's media buyer, Judy Press Brenner, was credited by Leone with spending in a fashion that maximized impact and saved money for the campaign. But her superior, campaign cochair Bob Beckel, believed there was a problem of penetration:

We had this smorgasboard of stuff that we were trying out. And the problem is that in a lot of major markets we were only running 150–200 points on some of those spots, which I found out after the fact. . . . You had to infiltrate Reagan. You had to get in and undermine him from underneath. . . . That takes time and an awful lot of exposure. . . .

We were running at a pretty high level [on the deficit issue]. But on particular ads, we were running at low levels. That's one of the things that I complained about. The message may be that we've got a deficit . . . [but] you've got to *see* the same thing over and over again.[29]

Republican consultant Roger Ailes agreed, but he believed the problem was that Mondale was indecisive, unable to launch one theme and stick with it. Ailes, whose anti-Huddleston "Bloodhound" ad scarcely failed for lack of repetition and was believed to be the most effective ad of 1984, also believed the Mondale campaign would have done better to adopt what became known as the "David Sawyer approach" and stick with it. Sawyer's approach was instead a source of internal campaign disagreement.[30]

Beyond the Deficit: Negative Ads on a Social Issue?

Sawyer believed that by September the Republicans had recovered from their initial waffling on the deficit issue. The Democratic presidential campaign might use deficit ads briefly, but it should move on to tough attack spots on social and religious-freedom topics. Speaking after the campaign, Beckel concurred. "In retrospect, the most important decision and the one that could be questioned—I question it myself now—was to go with the Sawyer theory, which was to shock the hell out of people, in a very negative way, [with] a very negative campaign." Sawyer developed one tough social issues ad, "Abortion."[31]

"Abortion"

Video	Audio
A black card with white type: "1985."	
"1985" fades into darkness. Bedside lamp turned on. Viewer sees bedside table with lamp, clock radio, and phone. Man's hand reaches for phone.	Phone begins ringing.
	Man: "Hello?" *Young woman:* "Daddy? It's Mary Ellen. Daddy . . . something terrible . . . Daddy." *Another man's voice on the line:* "Mr Sawyer? This is Lieutenant Kennan at police headquarters. Your daughter has been raped. . . . Now, she's not been harmed, but if you and Mrs Sawyer . . ." (voice fades)
Camera moves in on phone, perhaps toward picture of kids on the table.	*Announcer:* "The Republican Party platform says that it will be a law . . . if a woman is raped . . . she must carry the child of the rapist. That abortion will be illegal, even in cases of rape or incest. Think about that. If you vote Republican in 1984 . . . think about what they will do . . . in 1985."
Superimposed on the image: *If you vote Republican in 1984, think about what they will do in 1985.*	
	Young woman: "Daddy? Tell me everything's going to be okay."

The Reilly group tested the ad and recommended further testing before using it.

This spot created a powerful reaction. Respondents put their heads down, they avoided eye contact with the moderators, they tried not to speak to the issue. . . . Without any questions, this spot generated more emotion than anything else tested. What remains unclear is to what end and does this acute discomfort serve Mondale-Ferraro. With respect to drawing a sharp issue distinction with Reagan-Bush, it worked. As far as agreement with our position, it was unanimous. I would like to see further testing of this before airing.[32]

Leone, to whom the Reilly group reported, said he opposed all negative advertising. Beckel said he opposed the Sawyer approach because the ads concluded with the slogan, "If you think you've got problems in '84, wait till '85."

My problem with those ads, although I thought they were done very well, was that people didn't think there was a problem in '84. Thus there was no reason for them to think there was going to be a problem in '85. I'm not sure if in the choice of who would be their leader, Mondale or Reagan, Mondale would have won that debate.[33]

Thus, "the fear of the future under Reagan was a theme that was debated, and we didn't take." Mondale was not inclined to do it, but Pat Caddell's polling showed that any attack on Reagan along the lines of the Sawyer ads would "backfire [on the sponsors]," unless the attack was preceded either by "prior education of voters" on the issue, or "some positive reinforcement of Mondale."[34]

There was, as Leone noted, little consensus within the campaign during "the weeks that followed the Ferraro thing." Decisions were made by a

committee, whose membership seemed to change depending on who was in town and who wasn't. It was a product of a frustration, of everybody recognizing that the numbers weren't very promising. And thus opening the campaign to anybody who might seem to have an idea.[35]

According to Leone, Sawyer would have probably had more influence had he been in town—he was spending most of his time working on the Hunt campaign in North Carolina, where he recommended use of the same abortion spot. Pat Caddell, who had worked for Gary Hart in the primaries, gained influence, with his mid-September polling showing the campaign 20 points behind, the first challenging presidential campaign to fail to pick up votes in September.[36]

For Beckel, a "winning strategy required a yuppie emphasis." Ultimately, while they couldn't be reached on economic issues, the right-wing agenda on social issues was the one thing that moved them. It was thus decided to introduce attack advertising linking the administration with Rev. Jerry Falwell and a checklist for judges. Further, there was a switch to a heavy emphasis on anti–Star Wars advertising in late September, early October. "As we continued to probe and probe," Beckel reported of this period after Caddell joined the campaign:

The other weakness we found in Reagan was that there was still a little bit of the warmonger problem. That's when we went heavily into weapons in space, trying to attract women who were weak Reagan supporters, and also in our unending quest for the baby-boomers.[37]

The California Mondale campaign did not believe the resulting "Star Wars" ad was effective. California's young males, surveyed in a focus group that the local campaign found credible, "loved the lasers." According to Joe Trippi, who moved to work with the California campaign during the general election, the ad confirmed their belief that Mondale was weak and "did not want to be strong." California consultant Jules Radcliffe, who worked with the Mondale campaign in the general election, said Californians believed the "shield was dandy." They didn't care one whit about complexity. People "like a good, simple, clean fight. The Republicans tapped into that." [38]

Radcliffe, who said he favors "redneck advertising," argued that the "blip" in Mondale's favor in late September, early October, had nothing to do with arms control. It was a decline in Reagan's "comfort level" as people, who were not sure about Mondale, recognized that Reagan "has connections with unsavory people, and a [rich] lifestyle, with riding boots, that's hard to relate to." The difference with Mondale, the son of Presbyterian minister, who was in actuality much more a man of the people, "should have been pointed out." [39]

Instead, the campaign was unwilling to take advantage of the "rich boy" attack theme, which would have given a character side to the Mondale deficit message. Instead, the campaign decided to explain the issue in the abstract. Radcliffe viewed this as an impossible task in a media campaign. "Mondale is gifted, bright, and has his heart in the right place. From an intellectual standpoint, he's right. Life is more complex." But "people won't buy any message from a cerebral liberal. We're suspicious of it." Part of the national campaign was not impressed with the California critique. According to Leone, "Why should the views of a group of Democrats which had *never* been able to win a race against Ronald Reagan be given any credence?" [40]

"Star Wars" ran in California in a 3–2 rotation with ads tailored to the local market. These included "Toxic Wastes," a Gary Hart endorsement spot, and a Geraldine Ferraro ad. This latter was a novelty. Ferraro did not appear alone in any national ad because of her growing unpopularity. But the California campaign fought for, and ran, this one. Tensions within the campaign erupted at one point as the California consultants believed that headquarters had leaked a memo in order to undermine the efforts of one of them, Mickey Kantor. California was, however, a must-win state for Mondale. Locally, likely voters' response would be examined through tracking polls after an ad had run for a few days; if it was determined that the ad wasn't "working," it would be "yanked." In California, the Reagan advertising effort outgunned that of Mondale during the final days of the election. [41]

Like the majority of previous challenging presidential campaigns, it moved heavily into attack advertising. According to Leone:

Mondale became increasingly convinced that he had to attack Reagan . . . It was not a very effective strategy. But from a great many strategies that didn't seem to offer much promise, that was the one he selected. [42]

There was controversy not only over the selection of advertising themes but in the crucial area of news strategies as well. Leone attempted to prevent attacks on President Reagan from dominating the news. But in September . . . the television coverage he was making, and she, Gerry, was making was largely attacking Ronald Reagan. . . . The campaign had very little success, particularly with Gerry, in getting the candidate to move from that approach. Gerry was on the news every night, attacking, getting cheers, and thinking that she was being effective."[43]

THE IMPACT OF AN INDIVIDUALISTIC VIDEOSTYLE

Walter Mondale later believed that his lack of television savvy contributed to his loss. There were significant structural problems:

We were running at a very inopportune time against a very popular incumbent when the nation was starved for continuity with the economy performing well and international problems more or less off the stage at the moment.[44]

But his own inability to communicate through television was important. "I'm not trying to excuse what happened in 1984 on the basis of television technique even though I think [Reagan's] a genius at it and I'm not very good at it." And as for wrapping its message in the flag, Mondale later commented, "I just wasn't in that ballgame."[45]

Mondale's discomfort with television is hardly surprising in view of a further finding: the focus group's conclusion that the campaign's message was "negatively impacted by his presence." The heavy news coverage of John Zaccaro's finances was also reported to have upset him, so that he decided to avoid the press by traveling in an airplane compartment off limits to reporters. He did not take advantage of opportunities to appear on talk shows and avoided camera sessions with his media consultants. They said he was willing to sit down with them only twice, leaving them with the task of sorting through tons of camera footage to find visuals from campaign speeches—hopefully from an early period of the campaign when he didn't have bags under his eyes. Further, there were complaints that at a rally he would launch a theme that was not a part of their media strategy, thus accentuating discontinuity between the paid and unpaid media.[46]

Yet the advisors who traveled with him, according to Leone, "talked about [what was going to be on the news] but in fact the day wasn't structured around it, and that was all that Reagan's day was structured around." The campaign was "old fashioned." And whether because, as Leone thought, Mondale and Ferraro succumbed to "the most frequent mistake candidates make in a campaign, which is to confuse the experience they're having with the experience the voters are having," or for other reasons, there was no unified effort to pitch the campaign to the home video audience rather than to the crowds. As a result, in Leone's view, the voters "were having the experience of seeing Walter Mondale and Geraldine Ferraro yelling at Ronald Reagan."[47]

Declamations that work well with crowds, the candidate's audience in an earlier, people-centered era, do not go over well on national television in an era of "intimate" communication on television. "I" statements, which work with an audience, appear egoistic in the living room. Nor was the recurring "I" persona who appeared on the screen in the new coverage dovetailing with Mondale's attempted issue positioning during the final days of the campaign: that of a "caring" government that should serve the needy. The candidate made a rare appearance in the blitz ads, which were taken from rally tapes. In one, "Cincinnati," which L. Patrick Devlin described as Mondale at his "communicative best," animated and sincere, with tears welling up into his eyes, Mondale appeared as a man of service to others. This ad was part of the final 1984 ad series examined here. Its creator Roy Spence described it as "emotional." [48]

Still, in contrast with the Reagan ads, in which the candidate always used the pronoun *we* and focused on the fact that his life was only a reflection of the American spirit, of *American* greatness, in "Cincinnati" Mondale testified to his own life as an example for others, and he used the first person ten times. "If it hadn't been for the GI bill, *I* couldn't have afforded law school, *I* don't think," he said. *"I* paid the government back several times, *I* don't mind it" (and neither should the young girl, young man in uniform, black man, and older woman whose images appear on the screen presumably representing this targeted audience). "And *I* want your generation, of all generations in American history, to get the best. *I* want you to learn, *I* want you to challenge yourself. . . . *I* want you to stretch [hands to temples] that mind, think of new things and dream new dreams. *I* want your life to be thrilling and *I* wanna help ya."

"Who won the debate and projected an image of the future?" he also declaimed at a rally in New York the day after his successful first debate, the first real break in his campaign. *"I* did," he concluded. This was the 20-second snippet concerning the debate that appeared on the news that evening, amid speculation about the as yet perhaps incompletely formed public reaction to the debate. It was an especially significant news segment because, as Patrick Devlin pointed out, the campaign cut no ads to prolong the video life of two of its major communicative successes: the convention and the first debate, relying instead on the news coverage to carry the message. Thus to have what appeared to be bragging appear on this crucial segment was a blow. Whether for this or for other reasons, the campaign was disappointed in the amount of life Mondale's actual debate performance afforded the campaign. Mondale used *rally style,* not videostyle, which did not project well on an intimate medium. [49]

Some claimed that it was the pitch of his voice, which was high. When Mondale was forced to shout over the din of boos and chants by hecklers, it was reported that his voice became "whiny." Thus, at a University of Southern California rally, an effort at self-deprecating humor backfired: "I got these bags the hard way. I earned them" came out "strident and challenging." A critique he similarly launched on Reagan's arms control policies was reported to be "shrill, harsh, sometimes menacing." By contrast, Reagan's whole career, like those of such Hollywood figures as Jack Benny and George Burns, has been built on self-deprecating humor, which has long been key to successful communication on the entertainment-dominated commercial electronic media.[50]

Family Imagery

Some aspects of videostyle can be dealt with by changing the format—by putting the candidate more often into a living room, for example, or before a smaller crowd. Although the reasons for the decision making are unclear, it is clear that Mondale tried to make a virtue out of this problem. Instead of taking voice or facial expression control lessons, or campaigning primarily from his living room, he set out to prove he was the only non-"blow-dried" candidate in the race. This took the practical form of avoiding camera sessions with his media consultants, who complained bitterly.[51]

But the family image, which would prove to be highly significant in the 1980s in developing empathy with voters, was left to Reagan, who could use it very effectively. Not only did all of his ads from the 1984 sample feature intergenerational bonding, his lengthy ad segment "My Nancy" at the Republican National Convention ("She has been my first lady since long before the White House. . . . I can't imagine life without her") caused University of Texas speech professor Kathleen Hall Jamieson to say, "When he talks about his closeness to his wife, he's sharing his feelings about someone important to him, and people trust him because he's confided something to them." Early in the campaign, Mondale's aides instead shielded his family life from public view, reinforcing the public's perception of the candidate's natural reserve.[52]

Whether because of this reserve—or, in Reilly's view, because of the fact that in the absence of a strong sense of Mondale's "soul" nothing else about his personal life stuck—family life, which most candidates and voters have in common, did not help the Democratic candidate develop a connection with the voters. As various polls indicated, the U.S. public did not believe it truly *knew* the candidate. Joan Mondale toured extensively on behalf of the campaign, but as her press secretary commented, nationally Mrs. Mondale was a "sleeper . . . somehow the [media] has missed her." Mondale had never been divorced and his whole family was close. But image, not reality, was the issue.[53]

LESSONS

The Mondale advertising in the 1984 sample was highly emotional, part of a last-minute effort to hold the fort against a Reagan landslide. It illustrated how even a philosophically informationally-oriented campaign used emotional appeals. The emotions appealed to, while confirming the campaign's acceptance of the premises of an affect-laden rhetorical philosophy, were almost the reverse of those in the Reagan advertising. In terms of our categories, whereas the latter's ads appealed to hope, reassurance, and pride, Mondale's appealed to insecurity, uncertainty, and even more complex negative emotions. Compassion was also a part of the mix. During the general election, as during the primary, the Mondale campaign turned to referential and wheel-of-emotions negative advertising.

One original purpose in the general election campaign advertising was to associate the candidate—wounded in a divisive primary that had featured hard-sell negative spots—with an idea, a courageous stand on the deficit, and the associated need to raise taxes. This was a way of building character, of making "being a politician work for him." The challenge examined in this chapter was that of Walter Mondale's attempt to build a positive image after lengthy receipt of body blows ("no guts, no belly") during the primary, and a campaign in which he had consequently run as the "pick of the lot."

From this effort, with all of its pitfalls, other presidential candidates and their consultants would learn a few important lessons. Michael Dukakis began his presidential campaign believing that early images focusing on family are important. Dukakis's commercially trained media consultants thus developed such entertaining and mythic ads in 1986 for his barely contested gubernatorial re-election effort. The ads stressed family myths: that he owed all he had become to lessons learned from his parents and to the joy and humor of individual entrepreneurial efforts, as was made visible in an ad set in a Greek restaurant. Throughout the primary and the 1988 general election campaign Dukakis used the institution of the family as a prism through which issues such as income and jobs could be best understood—rather than using disembodied statistics or general social or political theory. Thus, if Mondale might be forced into using negative intergenerational bonding motifs to explain the deficit late in the campaign, Dukakis had early in the campaign laid out his approach to a few simple issues such as jobs, directing his comments squarely to the incumbent Republican party. And so Dukakis would say in Ohio on July 1, 1988:

Yes, I know that today there are more Americans working than at any time in our history. But average family income in America is right where it was 20 years ago, even though there's been a tremendous increase in the number of families where both parents work.[54]

It was of course not just the Democratic candidates who learned the lessons of 1984. The Democratic party also learned its lessons and advised candidates to avoid excessive negative campaigning. Thus, the Democratic presidential primary contenders, including Dukakis, were more careful than had been the case in 1984 in the *type* of negative advertising that was used. Negative ads would still be used. But the intent was to prevent the escalation of *all* their negatives leaving the victor, like Walter Mondale in 1984, badly damaged heading into the general election.

Seemingly by common consent, during the 1988 Democratic primaries attack ads were kept on the soft-sell rather than hard-sell side of the negative spectrum. There were no threats that the world would come to an end if the opponent won, as had happened in the case of Mondale's ad against Gary Hart, the "Red Phone." Nor did character attacks quite reach the level of the Hart "no-guts, no belly" attack. Instead, when virtually the entire field used negative advertising against Richard Gephardt, for example, who emerged from Iowa with major momentum in the days prior to the southern regional primary, Super Tuesday, the disposition was to use soft-sell negative advertising rather than hard-sell negative appeals. One anti-Gephardt ad, for example, used a flip-flop approach that featured a gymnast. The *CBS New York Times* poll reported that this combined negative attack, which did include an integrity dimension, was quite effective. This was because it was directed at a southern population that was undecided and knew very little about Gephardt. According to this poll, negative ads "worked," but the attack was not a harsh one.[55]

It is a fact that advertising including a modified wheel-of-emotions style is attention getting and was therefore used. Dukakis used this motif in his own advertising to establish an early, positive image. Of his 1986 test ads, one featured a nurse thumping on the chest of a heart attack victim; another, people walking through mind-numbing traffic, stopping trucks. A caring and competent governor, Michael Dukakis, and his dovetailing issues—welfare and highway programs—emerge as resolution to the dilemmas raised by the ads.

Another problem of Mondale's 1984 campaign was the difficulty of communicating Mondale's issues, which were considered to be electorally quite important by the campaign. They were the deficit and arms control—process issues which could require complex explanations. In the case of arms control, the general election campaign thus focused early on the visually communicable concept of "talks." The problem was that in the spring the Reagan campaign had already recognized this as an area of vulnerability and developed "inoculation" advertising based on staged, heavily televised news media events, including large-scale, mythic overseas trips focusing on visually compelling aspects of life, death, and sacrifice. The trips were to Korea and Normandy Beach long before Mondale won the nomination. Ads based on these trips, featuring myths of small-town life, intergenerational bonding and sacrifice, in which Americans of all religions, genders, and races could participate, continued to run throughout the campaign and on into the 1984 ad ample. During the general election campaign, the Reagan campaign further preempted the visual imagery of "talks," the Mondale campaign's ultimate, if uninspired, version of the issue, by developing a heavily televised presidential meeting with Mikhail Gorbachev.[56]

The lesson? Focus on character, early. Avoid tackling complex issues that are difficult to explain on the visual media before character has been well established. Michael Dukakis followed this strategy during the 1988 primary election campaign. His rival, Paul Simon, by contrast, was forced into attempting to explain a complex social welfare plan that might require a tax hike, and then he foundered on the issue.

Walter Mondale, a product of the backrooms of a political culture that preceded the video age, hired what were clearly described as "political" or issues-oriented consultants. The campaign was not able to focus its efforts on the affective and entertainment side of issue expression, and it never found ways to deal effectively with the deficit or the arms control issues in these terms. Nor did the candidate find a way of presenting himself as a positive alternative to Ronald Reagan as a resolution to the complex issues raised in his ads.

Ultimately, the campaign failed to offer resolution to the dilemmas of war, deficits, poverty, which it raised. Thus, in the "Roller Coaster" ad the children rode the deficit roller coaster with their parents, but it roared back down the track without an alternative to the dilemma raised by the ad. And the child in the 1984 national deficit ad, reminiscent of "Daisy" from an earlier era, was offered no resolution in the form of a reassuring presidential voice. If Reagan's ads offered hope, reassurance, and pride, Mondale's ads painted an uncertain picture of the future.

In short the very themes that Mondale attempted to develop were just the ones that the Reagan campaign used in its early advertising and news media strategies, which were coordinated throughout the campaign to effectively "inoculate" the candidate. There were in fact areas of potential vulnerability for the president. These were unearthed in an early poll conducted for the president, according to Lou Kitchen, southern director of the Reagan-Bush campaign. They were the candidate's age, anxiety about the possibility of war, and the possibility of Democrats returning to the traditional fold at the end of the campaign. All these questions were dealt with in early Reagan advertising according to the best principles of "inoculation" theory.[57]

But the Mondale campaign also experienced serious problems in developing and executing a consistent political advertising policy. There was uncertainty in the campaign, bred of frustration, and an ongoing debate over the nature and value of not only family issues but also negative advertising and the on-line "where's the beef" commercial advertising approach to campaigning. There were major failures to develop any consistent approach to campaign advertising.

Later presidential candidates of both parties would instead take care to try to develop a single common thread that dovetailed a character and issues message, one, for example, that could be used in both paid media and relations with the press. And, on the Democratic side, they would direct their attention to key figures in the opposing party, early. Thus, for example, Michael Dukakis's preconvention critique of Ronald Reagan, reported on the network news program on June 29, 1988, was that he was "confused." This was an acceptable attack message in relation to a popular president, and it was one that could dovetail with his primary issue: that government is out of control and in need of a competent manager.

Later candidates also sought to overcome their personal limitations in relation to the video environment. Dukakis, who learned how to perform on television by being the emcee of PBS's "The Advocates" between terms as governor of Massachusetts, further learned how to deliver effectively a crucial speech at the Democratic National Convention, one which though short on explanations of his issue positions included a teary-eyed reference to how proud his father would have been of him. The speech was highly praised.

Still, the 1988 Democratic campaign did not learn some of the major lessons of 1984: that negative advertising works, that it is symbolic and sloganistic, and that single issue attacks are becoming the norm.

Nor did his campaign seem to be aware of regional differences in advertising. In the more competitive and negative Southern portion of the 1984 ad sample, for example, Ronald Reagan used negative advertising not used elsewhere. In 1988, George Bush built not only on the experience of family values and national myths, but on other lessons of 1984 as well, most notably Ronald Reagan's careful "media blitz," controlled-news, advertising-oriented press strategy. After the 1988 election Democrats would again need to rethink how they would conduct a mass media election in a highly professionalized, now-Republican-dominated era of thirty-second presidential politics.

NOTES

1. Mondale quoted in the *Washington Post,* May 8, 1985, p. 2.
2. ABC post-1984 exit polls.
3. See also Chapter 4. Doug Watts was media coordinator for Reagan-Bush relations with their New York commercial advertising team. Watts confirmed the fact that the Reagan ads were appealing to these coded feelings. Interview with Doug Watts, Washington, D.C., December 13, 1987.
4. Mondale campaign officials quoted in an article by Robert W. Merry and David Shribman, *Wall Street Journal,* November 5, 1984.
5. Interview with Robert Beckel, Mondale campaign manager, Washington, D.C., October 23, 1985.
6. Merry and Shribman.
7. Interview with Richard Leone, director of communications, Mondale campaign, New York, February 1986; Spence is quoted in L. Patrick Devlin, "Contrasts in Presidential Campaign Commercials in 1984," *Political Communication Review* 12 (1987): 37.
8. Data from logs of Atlanta, Georgia, television stations obtained on the author's visit to the stations, March 1985. The logs indicated that Mondale pulled ads from the air during the last few weeks. The reason for this was confirmed by Leone.
9. Interview with Lou Kitchen, Southern regional director, Reagan-Bush campaign, Atlanta, Georgia, March 20, 1985.
10. Interview with Joe Trippi, Washington, D.C., June 20, 1985.
11. Ibid.
12. Beckel interview.
13. Leone interview.

14. Ibid.

15. Ibid.

16. Edward J. Reilly, MRK Research Confidential Focus-Group Report, *Mondale/ Ferraro Campaign, Boston* I, (unpublished document), p. 17.

17. Ibid., p. 58.

18. Ibid., p. 52.

19. Ibid., p. 58.

20. Beckel interview.

21. Trippi interview.

22. Reilly, Focus-Group Report, pp. 6–7.

23. Ibid., p. 7.

24. Ibid., p. 12; Beckel interview.

25. Reilly, Focus-Group Report, p. 43.

26. Ibid., p. 41.

27. Ibid.

28. Ibid., p. 40.

29. Beckel interview.

30. Interview with Roger Ailes, New York, January 16, 1986.

31. Beckel interview.

32. Reilly, Focus-Group Report, p. 47.

33. Beckel interview.

34. Ibid.

35. Leone interview.

36. Ibid.; for Caddell see Jack W. Germond and Jules Witcover, *Wake Us When It's Over: Presidential Politics of 1984* (New York: Macmillan, 1985).

37. Beckel interview.

38. Trippi interview; interview with Jules Radcliffe, Los Angeles, California, July 25, 1985.

39. Radcliffe interview.

40. Radcliffe and Leone interviews.

41. Trippi and Radcliffe interviews.

42. Leone interview.

43. Ibid.

44. *Washington Post,* May 8, 1985, p. 2.

45. Ibid.

46. Leone interview.

47. Ibid.

48. Devlin, *Contrasts,* p. 40.

49. Ibid., p. 42, on the campaign's failure to follow up on its most significant moments by means of ads.

50. William Dickenson, ''Mondale's Image Is the Victim of the Public Eye,'' *Washington Post,* October 5, 1984, p. 4. See also Paul F. Boller, *Presidential Anecdotes* (New York: Oxford University Press, 1981).

51. Leone and Radcliffe interviews.

52. Jamieson quoted in William Dickenson, *Washington Post,* October 5, 1984, p. 4.

53. Donnie Radcliffe, ''Trouper Mondale: The Candidate's Wife Focused on the Finish Line,'' *Washington Post,* November 2, 1984, p. C1.

For a discussion of family trust, one of the components of the trust-building process in political advertising, see Chapter 4.

54. Robin Toner, "New Image for Dukakis in a Midwestern Swing," *New York Times,* July 1, 1988, p. 86.

55. E. J. Dionne, Jr., "Candidates TV Ads Produce Shifts in South, Survey Finds," *New York Times,* March 4, 1988, p. 1. The gymnast ad was created by Dan Payne, who said its impact was doubled by the national media coverage. Payne interview.

56. Reagan ads collected from the air for this study and given to the author on tape from earlier in the campaign by William Greener of the Republican National Committee. A complete study of the 1984 Reagan communication effort is in preparation for future publication.

57. Kitchen interview.

7

The Hunt-Helms Senate Race: Finding What Works in a Negative Campaign

During the final ten days of the 1984 North Carolina Senate election, the television audience watched their senior senator, Jesse Helms, conduct a flyaround of their state's major media markets, calling his opponent, their governor Jim Hunt, a "liar." They also read front-page news stories reporting his suggestion that Hunt should install a toll-free telephone line to give out his "falsehood of the day." It was a coordinated news and advertising media blitz that raised the additional moral question of whether Hunt felt a sense of *shame* for his crass behavior. Four upright North Carolinians, their faces tight with disapproval, appeared in an ad to state that Jim Hunt had no decency, he was *just a politician* "who wants to get elected too bad." In his equally negative flyaround the unrepentant Hunt launched a different attack. Jesse Helms was the leader of a right-wing network, which was a sinister force engaged in a worldwide quest for power.[1]

The race received extensive national and even international attention because it was viewed as a battle for the soul of the South and Jesse Helms was a potential chairman of the Senate Foreign Relations Committee. It also demanded attention because it was clear that the race would set a record not only for spending but for early and extensive use of negative advertising.

LESSONS: ACTUAL AND INDIRECT EFFECTS

Above all, the Hunt-Helms race provided major lessons for U.S. campaign specialists, lessons that were applied in 1986. One was that it is possible for a campaign, in Helms's case one that was able to raise millions of dollars through direct mail, to dominate the message agenda on television, overwhelming news coverage of the race.[2]

The second was that it was a successful test for the quick-response philosophy of advertising that relied more heavily on news than commercial advertising style. 1984 was a year of innovation in quick-response polling and advertising technologies. With 7,000 ads broadcast during the last five weeks in the Hunt-Helms contest and daily polling for their effectiveness, the ads *became* the race. Ads responded to ads and were answered in turn, in a pattern that was repeated in 1986. Helms, with the help of such polling firms as Black, Manafort, Stone, and Atwater, led the field in innovation. Four hundred people, including Michael Murphy and Alex Castellanos, were professionally involved in the effort.[3]

They were less concerned with beautiful pictures of North Carolina and sentimental interaction than with hard-sell negative harsh reality black-and-white ads that focused more on facts and newsprint thrown onto the screen—all of which may have been put together overnight. The idea, as Murphy indicated, was to make the ads look like news. In this they were successful. Timothy John Walker examined the 1984 Helms ads and found that 65 percent replied directly to a Hunt commercial or drew on a current news story.[4]

Qualitatively, however, the Helms campaign was also better at finding visuals to use in the advertising that were simply unassailable in proving important points, points which left the Hunt campaign without a viable response. The Hunt campaign attempted to follow suit under the guidance of New York media consultant David Sawyer, who had been media consultant to Hunt's gubernatorial campaigns in 1976 and 1980. But their campaign, as we shall see, was thrown onto the defensive early, and their daily polling for reactions to individual ads began in the fall, long after the Helms campaign had perfected its daily polling effort.[5]

The Helms legions were the true innovators in the quick-response Ad Wars that resulted in achieving the primary goal of political advertising: establishing the campaign's issues as the major ones in the race. This goal was achieved, as the 1984 sample indicates, in no small part by overpowering the news coverage in total airtime.[6]

Another lesson concerns advertising effects, a long-debated issue. Did its advertising campaign, which was better able to control the television agenda, make any difference in the outcome of the race?

The view of major consultants, from both the Hunt and Helms campaigns, as well as those who applied the lessons of 1984 in 1986, was that advertising did in fact make a difference in this race, one which was particularly significant in its earlier stages when Helms's advertising and direct mail lowered Hunt's favorable margin by as much as six percentage points before the latter began his advertising effort. Further, there were indirect effects. Interviews with the Hunt consultants indicate that evidence of Helms's agenda control threw them onto the defensive from the beginning, and they never fully regained the offensive ability to establish their own issues and character messages as the dominant ones. Advertising was also believed to be helpful in mobilizing key constituencies—fundamentalists in Helms's case, blacks and moderates and liberals for Hunt.

Overall, direct mail rallied the committed, and grassroots efforts and the excitement generated by a presidential campaign helped get out the vote. But the conclusion that must be reached is that the Helms campaign's final margin of victory was slim, and its ability to overpower the news and make its case effectively with the undecided and persuadable voters who watch television made a difference.

The advertising was less significant during the latter part of the race, as thousands of dollars were spent to influence the same group of 200,000 undecided voters, swayed back and forth between the two candidates. According to a Hunt consultant, a specific ad might move as much as 5 percent of that group, which was then capable of being moved by a responsive ad back in a different direction.[7]

Finally, the Hunt-Helms race and other high-tech races in Kentucky, West Virginia, Texas, and Illinois in 1984 offered similar lessons that had the indirect effect of influencing subsequent decision making. The political community came to believe the integrity attack was effective. It can weaken the opponent, whose later messages are therefore not credible. And contrary to the experimental literature that has focused on the possibility that negative advertising has the primary effect of backfiring against the candidate who uses it, the candidate who launches such an attack can win. The primary conditions for this are making sure that the attack is *perceived to be fair* and that the *attacker represents a positive contrast to his or her opponent*. Or, in terms of wheel-of-emotions theory, the attack must provide a positive resolution to the issues raised in the ads.[8]

Many would question the effectiveness of the harsh reality aspect of Helms's hard-sell negative advertising. But the principle of the successful attack on an opposing candidate's integrity would continue to resonate. Indeed, it would become a serious concern for candidates on all levels in the late 1980s. This is in no small part because the successful early Helms ad campaign, based on this idea, was perceived to be effective by both campaigns; in fact, it most probably was effective. Because of its significance, the race's strategies are carefully examined.

HUNT'S EARLY STRATEGY

By the time the Hunt campaign developed its advertising strategy in the late spring of 1984 (which normally would have been plenty early, but never again could a campaign afford the luxury of such a late start), it had watched its ten-point lead dwindle to four points after 12 months of Helms's campaigning, which included negative television advertising and direct mail.

Until the late spring of 1984 the Hunt campaign had followed a strategy of allowing the popular governor to lose ground in the polls. Campaign cochair Joe Grimsley said, "We made a conscious decision to allow them to shed some blood—so we wouldn't run out of money." For his cochair, Gary Pearce, money was not the only issue. "We had enough money." It was a question of overconfidence. Grimsley agreed about this, saying that a contributing factor was an article in the *Washington Post* in early 1984 that called the race a sure Hunt win, fueling complacency in the Washington PAC community. Grimsley said, "I went to Washington. People had been reading that article 'by a friend of mine,' which argued that the Hunt election was a lead-pipe-cinch. They saw no reason to launch a major effort on behalf of the campaign."[9]

Analysts planning for future races said the decision not to use heavy early advertising was a fatal mistake. Indeed, this lesson became the new political wisdom of 1986, as it has also become the wisdom of academic researchers. Donald Cundy has established that early ads can protect a candidate from later attack, while Michael Pfau and Michael Burgoon have established that candidate liabilities discussed early can provide later protection when such issues are raised. They "inoculate" a candidate against later attack. Thus, early ads should have been used to establish Hunt as a man of character and strength by focusing on the courageous decisions he had made—just as was done, *after* these lessons were learned, in the successful 1986 Senate campaign of Democrat Terry Sanford.[10]

Simultaneously, an early attack should have focused the agenda in both advertising and news on the weaknesses of Helms's unpopular positions, which, in such areas as Social Security, were more conservative than those of his constituents. This issue would have dovetailed with a negative character message about Helms: He cared more about ideology than about the state's elderly people.

Another argument was that, further, the campaign's strategists should have known that Jesse Helms's Congressional Club typically launches early advertising attacks in newspapers and then moves onto the broadcast media before people are focusing on the elections and while they still have their defenses down. Democratic Senator Robert Morgan had been destroyed by such advertising in 1980. Like that in the anti-Morgan campaign, the attack on Hunt began early in newspapers with pictures of labor and black leaders, such as Lane Kirkland and Jesse Jackson, extolling Hunt's virtues.[11]

If the effectiveness of negative advertising was a lesson of 1980, the planning for 1984 indicates both how short-lived such lessons can be in the political world and how important the "wisdom" of the previous year can be in influencing subsequent campaign decision making. Leading Democratic consultants in 1984 were comforted by more recent precedent: the failures of the negative advertising of the Congressional Club during the 1982 congressional elections. The "Reagan recession" was believed to have had an impact on these races, but the impression among such leading Democratic consultants as Raleigh's Mike McLister was that negative advertising backfires. A 1982 North Carolina Democratic congressional candidate such as incumbent Representative Ike Andrews had in this view won due to a reaction against "those very heavy negative ads of the Congressional Club . . . which fail to show deference to the voters."[12]

Speaking to Raleigh's Triangle Club in February 1984, McLister noted that Helms (who had already begun his negative advertising) had come up ten points, while "Hunt's gone down ten points from the polls of last summer." This was the erasure of what the *Congressional Quarterly* later described as Hunt's "formidable lead," which it, like the consulting community, attributed to a series of "Where Do You Stand?" ads filmed by Murphy and Castellanos. At the time McLister indicated that he was not sure what caused the change, but one factor might be a "settling down of the electorate."[13]

McLister was also expressing classic theory, which was the 1984 conventional wisdom for a Democratic frontrunner. It was to stay positive, letting the challenger run the risk of backfire caused by using negative advertising. The Hunt campaign was also issues oriented. It firmly believed Helms was building a Senate record that would make him an easy target. This included his 1982 Senate vote favoring a tobacco tax and a "right-wing" agenda that the Senate roundly rejected.

Still, there was a problem of consistency in the Hunt campaign's thinking. It was directed by no single issue, or "fanatic common thread," in the language of political media in the 1980s. Further, the Hunt campaign combined what might be described as gentlemanly thinking about avoiding negative emotional appeals with their use by other elements within the campaign. This was clear when the North Carolina Campaign Fund distributed a fund-raising letter that called Jesse Helms a "dangerous right-wing demagogue" engaged in "racial bigotry." Speaking on behalf of the Hunt campaign, Richardson Preyer subsequently backtracked, suggesting the charge was a political one developed for fund-raising purposes. "We want to be very careful that we don't end up savaging people and talking in terms of anger."[14]

If the campaign's direct mail was at fault in this area, current research is indicating that the charge applies to the entire field of fund raising and lobbying through direct mail that frequently utilizes "bogeymen" to bring out the dollars. Few who engage in this activity admit this as openly as did Richardson Preyer, a respected former liberal-moderate congressman from Winston-Salem. The Hunt campaign's admission signified its difficulties in controlling the press-message agenda. It also fed into the opponent's major charge against Hunt, that of his "political" motivation, that is, spinelessness. It appealed to voter skepticism about leaders and political institutions.[15]

HELMS AS "CONTRAST": THE MYTHIC MORAL CRUSADER

Preyer's awkward public defense of the use of the term *bigot* pointed to another Helms advantage: While elements in the Hunt campaign were uncomfortable with negative campaigning, this division was not apparent in the Helms campaign, perhaps because Helms himself had engaged in attacks on the character of his opponents since the 1950s while maintaining an image as a moral crusader of mythic proportions. Indeed, his leadership style was what Helms aide Jim Lucier described in 1982 as "prepolitical." Through both his fund-raising letters and television ads, Lucier explained that he projects

principles that have been around for thousands of years: The family as the basis of social organization. Faith in the transcendent world—that God is the creator of this world that we live in and there is a higher meaning than materialism. Property as a fundamental human right—the idea that your home is your castle.[16]

An essential element in such a style is to "crusade" against a variety of evils. It was thus never out of character for Helms to point a finger not only at Hunt but at outsiders and those who did not share North Carolina values. Further, the fact that he took what Pearce called "extreme stands on issues which people often don't speak out on" made him "credible on other issues" such as Social Security, an issue on which the Hunt forces believed him to be vulnerable.[17]

Helms ran as a moral crusader, concerned with home, property, and family and also as a Christian televangelist long versed in the art of crusading for the right and godly and pointing a finger at all those "outsiders" who would undermine such virtues. Further, like the notable religious leaders with whom he identified, Helms was "persecuted" for his efforts, by "northern liberals" and the press. He combined these images of himself with the art of the communicator, or entertainer, who must first of all catch and hold an audience. The stories he told in his earlier career as a radio broadcaster and continued to tell in the mid-1980s were stories with heroes and villains, most of the former loyal Americans and most of the latter a more mixed bag of communists and "others."

Ironically, the Helms campaign was also not averse, as former Democratic Committee chairman Russell Walker pointed out, to "inserting a documentary [attacking Hunt for supporting a 1983 tax raise] during the Miss America contest right in there with the bathing suits." Helms utilized entertainment, a simple message, and attempts to provoke a reaction (the advertising Triad) in a process that did not detract from his role as a moral leader.[18]

Helms's early "mythic" use of media along with his "proreligious" stances in the Senate were a mobilizing force for grassroots fundamentalists who ultimately played a key role in turning out a crucial 100,000 votes in the swing I-85 corridor of the Piedmont.

HELMS'S FOUR COMMANDMENTS OF REFERENTIAL ATTACK

In maintaining the positive image and the perception that attacks are fair, which are crucial to a successful negative campaign, Helms had learned how to use great care in the phrasing of referential attacks, linking his opponent with a clearly scorned or feared "other" who might inspire anger or suspicion, but *visually* in a *verbally* deniable fashion. By contrast, the term *bigot,* as used in the early controversial piece of Hunt direct mail, was quite verbally explicit in laying the burden of proof on the user of the term. Nor is the term *bigot* easily made visual in the television era. What image most readily represents this concept and can be beamed to a general audience?

Further, as all reporters who had ever covered Jesse Helms knew, the candidate and his friends could cite numerous instances of his friendships with blacks, for the benefit of the press and other sophisticated audiences. His press secretary, Claude Allen, was black. It was an appointment that could be pointed to as a fact, thus disproving opponent charges of appeals to racism on the part of the Helms campaign. This occurred particularly in relation to the national press. Although negative affect might surface in relation to the advertising, this was deniable.

Helms thus used referential advertising that might link his opponent with negative voter attitudes without backfire in part because he was able to deny that he was doing so. Helms's success in the area of maintaining deniability—and therefore his status as a moral leader—suggest Four Commandments for the referential attack:

1. Use symbols appropriate to the visual media, rather than words, which have specific, identifiable meanings.
2. Remember that each message on television has several audiences.
3. Stay on the offensive.
4. Never acknowledge a "political" motivation.

What this all meant for news media strategy was that the Helms campaign avoided discussing strategy outside trusted campaign circles. Commandment 4 includes fear of being dehorsed and thrown into the murky world of political calculation where the white knight might be labeled just another politician. Reporters covering the Helms campaign found the campaign manager largely unavailable. The frequent explanation was that the press was pro-Hunt, which was also the *raison d'être* for Helms's ad campaign.[19]

It is also clear, however, that Helms's reluctance to discuss strategy contributed to his ability to launch an attack while maintaining white knight status. It was a modern media blitz strategy that involved coordination of all messages in news and advertising around a central line of the day—rather than open interchange with reporters—and it was successful. It worked by overwhelming the news coverage *and* by allowing the candidate to never appear "political" because such motivation was never acknowledged in strategy discussions with reporters (which could result in the Senator appearing to be "political" rather than "prepolitical").

The author experienced this combination of emotional and symbolic attack accompanied by silence while sitting for two hours in the Raleigh offices of

Jefferson Marketing awaiting the arrival of Helms's campaign manager, Carter Wrenn, for a scheduled interview. Wrenn was also associated with Jefferson Marketing, which raised the money for the Helms and other campaigns sponsored by the Congressional Club. Wrenn failed to keep the appointment, offering the explanation that the two-hour wait, with secretaries aware of the author's presence, was in the wrong office. Wrenn was in his "law office" in the same building. It proved impossible, however, to schedule a second appointment.

During the lengthy wait the author was treated to a full frontal view of the barrel of a gun pointing out from a television set as bold-face type proclaimed a "second assassination attempt on President Reagan." The gun was the "teaser" on a fund-raising envelope that linked the target of the Congressional Club's incipient fund-raising campaign, CBS television, with a most dreaded "other," whose evocation could produce nothing but fear—the criminal assassin who with one bullet could throw the nation into chaos.[20]

One of the "others" with whom Helms linked Hunt during this early period in his direct mail, and later in his referential TV advertising, was Jesse Jackson, whose 1982 photograph discussing a North Carolina voter registration drive was published in an advertising appeal. It was referential advertising in the sense that white voter attitudes or feelings relating to blacks might surface and be associated with the targeted opposing candidate. But the verbal question raised in the ad related to money, not race. The caption under the picture of Jesse Jackson engaging in voter registration activities was "Is this a proper use of your tax dollars?" The caption disassociated the questioning candidate, a man of proven concern for lean government, from the charge of racial bigotry. Further verbal focus could be shifted to "acceptable" discussions of "outsiders" seeking to "run things" in the state, not racial issues.

The same "How much does it cost?" theme and deniability were invoked when Helms used the publicity advantage of incumbency to proclaim his opposition to congressional legislation to make Martin Luther King's Birthday a federal holiday. By making an issue of the amount taxpayers would have to pay for the institution of the holiday, Helms could alert anti-black voters to his empathy with their concern, without alienating those who think of themselves as nonracists.

The combination of invoking both the symbolism and the deniability of racism was also used in spots that touted Helms's stance on the birthday issue and inquired of Hunt, who had already taken a position, "Where do you stand, Jim?" With Hunt registering black voters, who, it was believed, would vote for him, Helms sought to make headway with white Democrats in a state that was registered 3 to 1 Democratic. This issue and its associated advertising ran heavily as Helms gained on Hunt in the campaign polls.[21]

Although attitudes associated with such primal issues were most probably there to tie to your opponent through newspaper ads and the electronic media, the constant overt Helms theme was character, Hunt's alleged spinelessness.

"Where do you stand, Jim?" was the theme of the quick-response commercials created by Murphy-Castellanos that were credited with erasing Hunt's lead. According to Hunt campaign manager Joe Grimsley:

They saw the same polls we did. They had to destroy his popularity, they had to destroy him personally. It was an "integrity attack" not based on any issue. Its theme was *"Where* do you stand, Jim?" on issues on which we'd already taken a position, such as the MLK holiday. But it was not just one ad, it was that every ad had a negative sense, and was repeated for months and months and months. It was a masterful job of eliminating the history of Jim Hunt.[22]

The issues were there, such as racial justice and taxes, which arose during the 1983 summer General Assembly sessions. But, as Grimsley said, the character aspect of the message of the attack ads was important. Source credibility is essential to viewer acceptance of a message, and a character attack might be expected to reduce Hunt to the point where nothing that he might later say either about himself or his opponent would be credible. If the "Where do you stand?" ads were developed by Murphy-Castellanos, credibility as a viable theme was later credited to Bob Harris. He was a 26-year-old bedridden conservative with advanced muscular dystrophy who advised Tom Ellis, founder of the Congressional Club. Unlike Governor Jim Hunt, Harris was a political conservative who had never had to convince state legislators to act, that is, to focus on political process, which might involve a personal shift of position.[23]

According to Ellis, Harris developed this theme, and it convinced Helms, who was discouraged by poll results developed for the Congressional Club by conservative consultant Arthur Finkelstein, which showed Hunt ahead. Indeed, according to Ellis, Helms was considering not running for reelection, but Harris convinced him to make the effort, arguing, "You know, Hunt is vulnerable; he flip-flops on the issues; you don't know where he stands." Ellis said, "I bet he sent us 400 flip-flops of Hunt over the past eight years [many of which appeared in the Helms ads]."[24]

NEGATIVE ADS WORK AND HUNT RESPONDS

In March 1983 the Helms print-media advertising campaign began; it moved to radio in April. The Hunt campaign waited to respond until September 1983, by which point, according to Joe Grimsley, Helms's advertising had "closed the [pro-Hunt] gap to eight points," from 48 to 40 or 46 to 38. When the underdog, in this case Helms, moves to where he is within a ten-point spread, the fund-raising community defines the race as competitive, and money is more readily available. Thus, at a minimum the early advertising, like that on the House of Representatives level, which is examined in the southern portion of the 1984 ad sample, made Helms "competitive."[25]

The Hunt campaign's first response was not a bull's-eye counterattack designed either to respond to Helms's charges or to shift the agenda. It was, rather, designed to test the waters and boost the morale of the Democratic campaign workers. "What we wanted to say," according to Democratic state chairman David Price, "was 'here are some economic issues that need to be raised.' " [One ad said] "if you make more than $50,000 a year, then you've got a senator in Washington working for your needs. . . . If you worry about Social Security . . . then you ought to be worried about your senator in Washington." In February 1984 with the poll results still "strongly in our favor," the campaign ran its first heavy and, in Grimsley's view, largely positive ad campaign. The ads ran for three weeks and "drove the numbers back to a ten-eleven point spread." The Hunt campaign then went off the air for two months, and by the end of this time, the Helms advertising had picked up extra issues while continuing to question Hunt's credibility. The one ad Grimsley recalled as being especially effective was an ad that dovetailed a message about character with an issue: excessive, unnecessary government spending. In the ad a helicopter was the visual symbol that focused on the character side of this issue: Was Hunt being honest about how much was being spent, or wasted, on such gubernatorial "perks" as helicopters?[26]

The helicopter may well also have served as a symbol of class, working to distance a governor who rides in choppers and is thus clearly "not one of us" from ordinary Tar Heels. Its effective use, according to the Hunt campaign's polls, indicates how such symbols of office as a helicopter—which is an otherwise popular "strength" symbol because, in the language of television, it "wiggles" and therefore catches attention on a visual medium—can also be used on the attack side of an issue.

The conclusion must be reached that the Helms campaign, rather than the Hunt campaign, excelled at the selection of symbols that dovetailed with simple, readily comprehensible issues appropriate to visually driven campaigning. Further, prior to running its first ads, the Helms campaign leaked the helicopter expenditures story to the news media in a fashion that would redouble the impact of the ads. Not only did they dovetail character and issues, but the ads piggy-backed on the credibility-associated news stories. This strategy—coordinating news strategies with advertising—is clearly a hallmark of media strategy in the 1980s.

A divisive Democratic primary did not help matters for Hunt. In May 1984 a Gallup poll indicated that Helms had pulled ahead 50–46. With alarm bells ringing in Raleigh and Washington, there was a shake-up in the Hunt camp, with the result that Joe Grimsley and communications director Gary Pearce became cochairmen. Heavy advertising began, Grimsley says, and the campaign ran one ad "seven days a week at full rating points [400 grp]" and then "ran the next one, continuing for six or seven weeks."

The ad battle, which drove the campaign until November, was for 6 to 10 percent of the population, which did not change throughout the campaign. "We were dealing with approximately 200,000 people" moving in and out of the undecided category. "One expects that in the worst circumstances."

The campaign was based on the four E's: economics, education, the elderly, and the environment. The numbers showed that these were our strongest areas . . . areas where we had clear dominance in North Carolina. . . . We still have an edge on these issues. The only issues that Jesse could outdo us on were foreign policy, national defense, and moral values. Even on these, however, Jesse had only a slight advantage, around 4 percent.

But when the election got down to personalities, that was all she wrote.[27]

From May to July and again in September, in an attempt to gain control of the issues agenda, the Hunt campaign launched two "hot button" messages. The first focused on Helms' position on issues of concern to the elderly, particularly an attitude of "callousness" underlying Helms's positions on Social Security and Medicare. There was also his "ineffectiveness" on farm issues.[28]

The second, which was again present in Hunt's advertising during the final ten days of the campaign as indicated by the 1984 ad sample, was an attack on Helms as a leader of "radical right wingers." According to Grimsley, the polls indicated that they were not the "model people of America." In May 1984 hard-sell negative ads linked Helms with right-wing dictators, such as former Argentinian president Leopoldo F. Galtieri and Roberto d'Aubuisson, the leader of the El Salvador ARENA party, who was running against Reagan administration–backed Salvador Duarte in El Salvador's election. The point was that Helms was a loose cannon to the right of the administration and Congress, alienating congressmen whose friendship was needed to pass measures important to North Carolina, such as the beleagured tobacco price support bill. Again, indicating concern in paid media strategy for *total* impact on the visual medium, this attack was timed to take advantage of the fact that Helms was in the news with his solitary support of d'Aubuisson, which set him apart from Ronald Reagan.[29]

SELLING THE "EVIL EMPIRE"

Even given this advantage, however, in the last week of July the Hunt campaign proved the difficulty of this effort to successfully push an opponent into the arms of the "radical right" on the visual media. An ad was launched that according to Pearce, was intended to point out that Helms was at the "beck and call of an *evil* empire, the radical right." It opened with a scene of dead children who were killed by the death squads, who were linked with Helms's friend, Roberto d'Aubuisson.

The ad presented a basic dilemma in negative advertising: Why did it "backfire"? No one could approve of the killing of children, which apparently had been done by death squads associated with d'Aubuisson. The Hunt forces had polls indicating that d'Aubuisson was not popular. Yet to the degree that this was true, how intensely this attitude was held was another question. It was a hard-sell negative ad, which used referential human symbols linking the opponent with voter attitudes relating to cruel treatment of children. A key question relates to the depth of U.S. concern for what was essentially a mediated rather than a personally developed experience. How real was either d'Aubuisson or the death squads to voters? It is a question that must ultimately be raised in relation to significance of foreign policy issues in elections, and the depth of the global understanding of U.S. voters.

One must not assume that simply because a news story is on television it will be deeply felt. The Hunt forces may have made just this mistake. The mid-1980s was an era of the personalization of politics, and the question may be raised concerning whether death squads may have been an issue similar to contra aid in 1986—a year before the whole issue had been magnified by the Iran-contra scandal of the Reagan presidency. While most voters opposed contra funding in 1986, what they felt more deeply, according to one Democratic strategist, was resentment at having to think about the troubling issue at all. Was it possible that in the absence of prior information about Helms or his right-wing associates linking them with existing concerns or uncertainties, viewers considered the ad farfetched and therefore exploitative? Unlike Jesse Jackson, with whom Helms linked Hunt, Roberto d'Aubuisson was not in North Carolina working on voter registration. Further, by this time Hunt's credibility as a source of information had, according to Hunt's polls, been effectively challenged.[30]

THE ENDURING LEGACY OF THE HELMS IRATE CITIZEN

Helms responded quickly with "Scare Tactics," a man-in-the-street talking head ad that focused on close-up faces of North Carolina citizens who spoke a few words, carefully and deliberately. They were words that said, Tony Schwartzian fashion, *shame* on you, Jim Hunt, for using "slick" advertising, taking "cruel" advantage of the voters. It was a full-frontal, close-up talking head ad whose style would be used extensively in the future, and with a clear backward glance at the effectiveness of Helms's full-frontal irate citizens. It was used by Republican consultants Bailey-Deardourf in Missouri in 1986 after Harriett Woods was charged with using a "slick" advertising campaign, that of the "Crying Farmer." The format of an irate citizen crying "shame," of course, has many antecedents, but as admitted by both campaigns, the effectiveness of the Helms ad, used again and again to respond to Hunt's attacks, was recent and compelling.[31]

The faces of the citizens are extraordinarily expressive and their appeal in Schwartzian terms is "shame on you." But the ad uses words spoken very slowly, which as Woods's consultant Joe Slade White observed, can lower the "emotional" temperature of a campaign.[32]

Further, in the relentless fashion of all Helms's quick-response commercials, the ad turned the issue back onto taxes. To the "batter-up" challenge "What are Helms's views on Central America?" the response was, as Murphy argued in a different connection, "The sky is blue. But what about *my issue,* Hunt's evasive character, and the threat which it raises to your tax dollar?" Following this pattern of staying on the offensive, the ad concluded with the irate citizen declaring that Hunt was *again* trying to evade the fact that he "voted for a $217 billion tax increase at the February National Governor's Association."[33]

TO LINK A "GOOD" WITH A "BAD" DEMOCRAT: USE MUSIC

Hunt had tried to avoid the label of liberal or any linkage with national Democratic politics. Michael Murphy described how the process of linking Hunt with the national trend began with the use of a referential ad. We have seen how the focus of the first stage of Helms's advertising was on Hunt's *credibility*. The second stage would link him with a national trend, in this case Democrats, who were negatively perceived. The same pattern—raising questions of credibility and then linking the opponent with a national trend—would emerge from analysis of 1984 House races. The problem, according to Murphy, was that "you had a southern Hunt who was a good Democrat. He needed to be linked with Walter Mondale, who was perceived to be a bad Democrat. You can't call them both Democrats, so you need a symbol to link them together."[34]

The solution, described by Murphy, was an advertising strategy that focused on the link between the two candidates: the fact that both were supported by unions. A key Murphy-Castellanos ad used sound effects, Schwartz's short-cut to "evoked recall." "Look for the Union Label" is sung at the beginning in a woman's voice. A list of labor unions flashes across the screen and the narrator intones, *"All* of these unions support Jim Hunt for governor. You may not know *where* Jim Hunt stands, but you know who he stands with." The ad concludes with the song. Symbols and sounds transpose Hunt from the North Carolina to the national context.

The coup de grâce in this effort was delivered visually by means of unanswerable home videos of Hunt raising his hand at the February National Governor's Association Conference. Words underscored the visual "lie" of his denial that he would raise taxes. The ad that grew out of the conference, "Raised Hand," had double impact because it drew on the credibility of the news format. As if this were not enough, Walter Mondale, who Hunt had once supported and with whom he was now linked, declared that he was going to raise taxes at the 1984 Democratic National Convention in San Francisco.

For Pearce, "Raised Hand" was the nail in the coffin for Hunt on the tax issue. "The picture of Hunt raising his hand made it visual. Mondale gave it credibility.'' With Mondale's plan the Helms charge was confirmed: ''You can see we're going to do it.''[35]

For Grimsley, Mondale's announcement at the 1984 Democratic National Convention that he was going to raise taxes was the moment when Hunt lost the election because he was firmly identified with the wrong side of a national trend:

North Carolina is a low-tax state—our top tax rate is 7 percent by Constitution. People may agree on programs, and generally *want* programs, but they cut off the head of people who provide them. There's a *something for nothing attitude*. . . . Republicans run against Democrats, who've been the dominant party, saying ''you've got too many taxes on you'' and if this issue gets caught up in a national movement, it can be important.[36]

In this case, the no-tax position was being espoused by Ronald Reagan, who was running 18 to 25 points ahead of Walter Mondale in North Carolina.

Hunt's effort to distance himself from Mondale on taxes only underscored his credibility problem, for he had said he supported Mondale. This support, and the conclusion that should be drawn from it—''He's a Mondale liberal who will raise your taxes''—ran heavily in the Helms postconvention ads, but only minimally in the final ten days of the election. The exception was ''$157 per Month,'' the cost of a down payment. The argument is made by means of a visual of a buyer in a car showroom and this figure plastered on the top of a car. Like all the Republican advertising that used this figure, it was an estimate of how the Mondale tax plan would affect the average viewer. Hunt opposed raising taxes, however, so it was pure fantasy in relation to his stated position. But like ''Scare Tactics,'' which ran in an earlier version in relation to Social Security, and ''Raised Hand,'' it must have been considered a classic by the Helms campaign, since it ran on into the final ten days of the election period under the highly competitive condition of daily polling by the Charles Black market research group.

For Pearce, the tax issue had broad implications. Around it swirled all the factors that led to Hunt's defeat. Among these was the Reagan phenomenon, which included the presidential image to which Helms successfully tied himself, despite his ''grandstanding in the Senate,'' which Hunt had been trying to play up in ads such as ''Death Squad.'' Reagan campaigned in the state, confirming Helms's characterization of himself as a resolution, or contrast, to the dilemmas raised by the campaign. Reagan called Helms ''a lonely crusader'' and came on with Helms testimonial ads. But for Pearce the tax issue was ultimately a disaster because around it swirled, in addition to Hunt's credibility, a number of attitudinal factors: the governor's credibility, religion, outsiders versus natives (''a phenomenon in North Carolina politics''), and ''race as well, because people didn't want to give money to blacks.''[37]

It was clear by the time of the airing of ''Raised Hand'' that the Hunt campaign had lost the battle to control the issues and character agenda on television. A divided campaign tried both defensive and offensive response strategies in its aftermath. The initial response was defensive. According to Pearce, Hunt said, "I will not raise taxes." And Richardson Preyer, the former congressman and Hunt campaign official "who had considerable credibility in North Carolina," cut an ad in direct response to the "Raised Hand" commercial: "You've seen this ad that Jim voted to raise taxes. He didn't. It's a lie." "But," in Pearce's view, "this wasn't credible in the context of his positions: his plan to substantially increase defense spending, and his criticism of Helms for cutting Social Security. The voters probably said: How is he going to do this and not raise taxes?" In Pearce's view, further *defensive* statements on the tax issue should be avoided because the truth was that Hunt might in fact decide that it would be necessary to raise taxes.[38]

THE VOTERS KNEW HUNT

"Listening to the focus groups," Pearce said, "people didn't know Helms. But they knew Hunt just about as well as I did." Hunt was a consensus politician, and under certain circumstances, "he might have raised taxes." Pearce accordingly believed the governor's offensive strategy should be strengthened. He believed the right-wing linkage offense inaugurated in May should be pressed. This strategy involved an uphill battle, however, he argued later, because, unlike the Helms supporters who were used to their candidate's heavy attacks, Hunt's supporters began to murmur, "He's no better than Helms," following the airing and rapid dropping of "Death Squad."[39]

With Hunt four points ahead in August, according to the polls, the campaign turned to positive advertising and would have remained on a track, which Grimsley described as *"stay with the party of fairness, but scare with Social Security"* (italics mine) had it not lost the lead after Labor Day. Campaign cochair Grimsley made this comment:

Positive stuff may wiggle the numbers. The first day the [positive] ads do some good. Then the numbers go down. We saw the only shot we had was to take Jesse to the mat. . . . It wasn't the undecided voter we were dealing with [at this point]. It was the people going with the trend, ignoring issues in the two campaigns—they believed in Reagan."[40]

Hunt's media consultant, David Sawyer, said eight ads were cut and they were effective.

If Jesse Helms didn't respond to one of our ads, he lost a point. People say they don't like the negative ads, but our polls showed they changed people's minds. On Social Security you could watch a ten to fifteen percent shift depending on who was on the air.[41]

Helms responded with ''Scare Tactics,'' which was essentially the same ad used to reply to Hunt's d'Aubuisson linkage spot, with its irate North Carolinians crying ''shame,'' ''he's just a politician who wants to get elected too bad.'' In this case, the ad was used to respond to Hunt's Social Security ads. Illustrating the degree to which Helms finally controlled the message agenda, it was, as has been noted, ''Scare Tactics'' rather than Hunt's Social Security ads that continued to play on the air during the period of our 1984 ad sample.

THE ARGUMENT FOR AN OFFENSIVE STRATEGY

Trailing slightly, it was in the hourly ad battle after Labor Day that the Hunt campaign returned to the ''right-wing'' offense in order to refocus the race. For Pearce, this was too late. ''Any kind of communication works only when people believe it, and start out believing it.'' People vote for leaders, and they were tending toward Reagan and Helms because they were viewed as standing up for what they believed in, whether or not people agreed. Helms would say, ''You may not agree with me, but at least you know where I stand.'' Much earlier, Hunt should have come back with, ''You might know where he stands, but do you always agree? We didn't say well enough, or *graphically* enough: do you know where he stands? Do you know *who he stands with?''* [italics mine]. The challenge was to make the right-wing groups with which Helms was connected ''real.'' Pearce, like Murphy on the opposing side and the consultants for House campaigns examined in a subsequent chapter, believed that a winning campaign cannot be played out on the defensive side. The Hunt campaign

could have done as good or a better job of weakening Helms. But they diverted their money and resources into dealing with new issues, such as taxes. Without the tax issue, we could've continued to go for Helms' weaknesses.[42]

He believed the d'Aubuisson ad should not have been dropped. There was no poll evidence to support the view that it had backfired. ''If we had pressed that ad and stayed with such attacks, we might have won.'' The Hunt campaign should have ''educated the public early about what would happen if these [right-wing] people got their way.'' They would, for example, select school textbooks and teachers. ''But the campaign didn't have the boldness.'' In short, there was no ''fanatic common thread,'' which offered, in his opponent's apt phrase, ''the sky is blue,'' as a rejoinder to an attack, ''But what about the right wing?''[43]

Pearce's idea was to take advantage of the visual media to personalize the right-wing issue. He believed the Human Life Bill, which Helms had introduced in the Senate, was proof that new controls would be exerted in the area of human sexuality if Helms's supporters go their way. Pearce supported focusing advertising on this issue in a way that made the right-wing real, and he believed the campaign did not focus on this issue early or strongly enough.[44]

Finally, it was raised in the last weeks of the campaign with an ad that focused on Helms's position on birth control pills and ran on top youthful Top 40 radio. "I knew it had hurt them bad," Pearce said, "because Charlie Black called David Sawyer [Hunt's media consultant] and told him they thought they were losing, and with the yuppies, to whom this ad was directed." But also because the Helms campaign changed its flight of television ads and brought on Mrs. Jesse Helms, which was "an extraordinary thing to do." [45]

AFFECT-LADEN SYMBOLS: A MOTHER CRIES SHAME

In the final demonstration of its quick-response television advertising technique, the Helms campaign brought on white-haired Mrs. Jesse Helms from her living room to declare that her Jesse would *never* outlaw The Pill. "Jim Hunt, you know that," she declared, her soft southern voice full of moral rectitude, "and you ought to be ashamed of yourself. Some people will do *anything* for a vote."

The ad echoed the Schwartzian "shame" theme used earlier in the campaign. Further, Mrs. Helms was known in North Carolina as a mother who had gone out of her way to care in very concrete ways for those less fortunate than herself, including an adopted child. She could have been admonishing an errant member of her Sunday school class. Her husband won this round, for the Hunt "Pill" charge played only on radio, and the home video audience could scarcely ignore this unusual spin on the 1984 "family" motif. Nor would there be much sympathy in some parts of North Carolina for a governor who would force a wife and mother to go before the cameras and talk about birth control.

The ad played uncontested despite the fact that any reading of Helms's bill would support Hunt's charge. Why this lack of a reply, since Hunt raised the issue? Pearce believed the Helms campaign was more adept at response ads, a conclusion it would be difficult to dispute. In regard to Mrs. Helms, she followed a tendency that would become even more prominent in 1986. But the 1980s trend had been launched by Representative Barney Frank's mother, who came on the air in 1982 to carry the case for her son, the congressman, on Social Security.

The appearance of Mrs. Helms, and the opposing campaign's failure to find a response to her, offers a prime example of why highly personal family ads have come to be used. It is difficult to answer them. Is it credible that a nurturing family member, with whom each member of the audience can identify, would distort the facts? Particularly a parent who is responsible for the moral upbringing of children? Would *your* mother do that? A mother is the ultimate referential human symbol—one that holds affect-laden value for all individuals and is therefore difficult to ignore in an advertising message. Mrs. Helms set the seal on the Helms campaign's innovative use of symbols—and Mrs. Mac Mattingly, wife of the Georgia senator, would appear in 1986 in a reelection ad attesting to her husband's concern for drugs. Not surprisingly, Mattingly's campaign was also advised by Murphy-Castellanos. Few mothers could strike quite the tone, or the ultimate irony, of Mrs. Helms crying shame on her husband's opponent for using slick advertising, however.

How to respond to her? The Hunt campaign was divided about what should be done. Two ideas emerged: One was that Hunt himself should respond to Mrs. Helms. The other was that the initial Top 40 radio ad should be made into a television spot. "There was a whole lot of nervousness and insecurity" on the issue, however, said Pearce. And even Pearce, the self-described "Young Turk," couldn't see his way clear to going further on an issue they were responsible for catapulting onto television. "Even I couldn't quite visualize my [small-town] grandmother accepting the governor going on television on the issue." [46]

So much for the effort to use the "Ad Wars" to hoist Helms on the petard of his ideological positions. The other effort to link him with right wingers, which dominated Hunt's 30-second ads in the 1984 sample, fared no better. The capstone was a 30-minute Hunt documentary that ran on the Sunday before the election. The Helms campaign argued that it was "McCarthyism" because it failed to prove Helms led an alleged "close-knit" right-wing network that linked domestic leaders, such as Phyllis Schlafly and Rev. Jerry Falwell, with Rev. Sun Myung Moon and "right-wing political and military dictators around the world." Asked, however, to justify the Helms-Moon link, Hunt was able to cite only an article on the Hunt-Helms race in the *Washington Times,* which was owned by Moon's church, and a former *Times* editor's donation to the Helms campaign. Further, the 30-minute ad was narrated, not by a North Carolina "good old boy," but by Zero Mostel, of "Fiddler on the Roof" fame.[47]

The 30-minute ad could not have helped and may have hurt. Campaign polls indicate a shift in Hunt's favor from four behind to even on the Saturday before the election. The ad played on Sunday, and Hunt lost, narrowly, on Tuesday.

THE LAST-MINUTE PROBLEM OF CLUTTERED AIRWAVES

Although a 30-minute commercial is difficult to miss, it is of course possible that few noticed the ad. Both campaigns were running 2,000 gross rating points, far above the normal political ad level, at the end. Statewide, the North Carolina market was more heavily saturated than others in the 1984 ad sample. Grimsley questioned whether the late advertising had any effect at all. There was "a new ad each day in the end and people can't remember that volume." He reached this conclusion based on focus-group reports to which the campaign turned for reactions. Even when the ads were running at a "high volume of six or seven a month," respondents could not remember two-fifths of the ads. During the final few days the candidate Jim Hunt also echoed this view, noting that because the airwaves were so cluttered, "We can't get our message across. We can't use TV like we've done in the past. It won't get through in the current climate." Grimsley believed, "In the end, we washed each other's messages out." For other, later, statewide campaigns, the lesson was advertise early. Ironically, the Hunt campaign wound up with an unspent $1 million in the bank.[48]

The final Helms advertising also provided a positive contrast to Hunt. The content analysis indicated that there were more positive Helms than Hunt ads during the final days of the 1984 election. According to wheel-of-emotions theory, this could have been important in a negative race.

But this positive imagery did more than provide resolution, or an answer to the dilemmas raised by the ads. It broadened Helms's image with moderate Republican voters. An independent campaign committee spearheaded by moderate elements in the North Carolina Republican party and headed by Jim Broyhill helped make this possible. Helms had activated the fundamentalists and other religiously oriented and socially conservative voters—including those who were quite frankly racist, earlier in the race. According to the Fund for a Conservative Majority, which paid for the campaign, an ad sequence was developed because polls taken by a leading Republican pollster, Lance Tarrance, indicated that Helms needed to develop support among traditional Republicans in the western part of the state who knew and supported Broyhill but were only "soft supporters of Helms." [49]

The task at the end was similar to that of Ronald Reagan after the 1984 Republican National Convention broadening his image and electoral appeal. In Helms's case this meant forging bonds with moderate Republicans and clutching the increasingly moderate Ronald Reagan's coattails. A Fund for a Conservative Majority analyst later argued that these ads achieved their purpose, contributing to united traditional "moderate" Republican support that, when combined with the "eastern Jessecrat" vote, was crucial to the Helms reelection effort. Whether or not this was the case, Helms enjoyed united east-west support that the losing Broyhill did not enjoy in his 1986 Senate campaign.[50]

For those less extreme on social and religious matters, and generally from the western part of the state, the positive advertising featuring moderate congressman Jim Broyhill of Charlotte also sought to assuage doubts. His talking head testimonial ads in the 1984 sample featured "words" and a calm demeanor that may have helped not only to unite the troops under the "true" leadership of a Helms but also to tone the race down at the end for Helms. In a campaign marked by advertising that was both referential and involved heavy use of wheel-of-emotions techniques, this helped Helms come on at the end as a strong contrast, or resolution to the dilemmas raised by the ads. The impact was reinforced because Helms's positive moral image stood out in a generally negative North Carolina advertising environment. This is because a number of competitive races occurred from the congressional to the gubernatorial levels and, as we shall see in Chapter 9, greater use of negative advertising not only occurs in such races but is sometimes used successfully to make a race "competitive." [51]

THE CONTENT ANALYSIS: HUNT-HELMS IN ITS
STATEWIDE CONTEXT

Overall, the North Carolina nonpresidential affective appeal codings during the last ten days were positive, with 90.5 positive to 74.5 negative minutes of 30-second ads. If the 30-minute Hunt documentary commercial is added, however, the balance is tipped heavily in the negative direction. As in the other states included in the 1984 ad sample, the greatest levels of positive ad appeal codings occurred on the lower levels, particularly in the ads for local candidates. Significant amounts of negative advertising occurred in the races of losing candidates for governor and lieutenant governor, Rufus Edmisten and John Carrington—but not in that of the winners, Jim Martin and Robert Jordan.[52]

Although there was less negative advertising in congressional races, the level was still high, at one-third of all codings, a figure that rises to one-half with the independent expenditure ads Jim Broyhill cut for all of North Carolina's Republican candidates removed from the sample. In addition to his pro-Helms ads, Broyhill provided assistance to his congressional colleagues, gaining visibility for his 1986 statewide race. He represented the leading positive force during the final days of the race. Overall, this was an extremely negative time for North Carolina voters, where in competitive races ads were even coded for fear strong enough to tap a sense of "impending doom," implying that the opponent's deceitfulness was so profound as to reach a threatening level of criminal intent.

Even in this context, the Hunt-Helms race richly deserved its reputation for heavy use of negative advertising. The 30-second commercial affect-level codings were 49.0 negative to 33.5 positive minutes of airtime, with the balance shifting even more heavily to the negative side if the 30-minute commercial is included. In the 30-second category, although Helms included more total positive adtime, the Helms ads were more heavily negative than Hunt's, with a total of 32.5 to 19.5 negative to positive compared to Hunt's 16.5 negative to 14.0 positive minutes.

In the 30-second spots the Helms ads were more heavily negative than the Hunt ads, with 32.5 to 19.5 minutes negative to positive compared to Hunt's 16.5 negative to 14.0 positive. The 30-minute Hunt commercial again tipped the balance.

The profound level of Hunt-Helms negativity is indicated by the high level of strong fear, uncertainty, and anger codings in the ads taken from the air during the final ten days of the election. Six of the Helms ads were coded for both. Five of these used either insinuating or threatening voices, horror movie (doomsday) music, or blowing wind. These sound effects underscore the theme of political duplicity, making the potential danger to the voter all the more sinister because it is a hidden one.

In the case of the Hunt ads the four that were coded for uncertainty were also coded for anger. All four also used doomsday music. Again, a viewer attitude that might be tapped is one of vulnerability in the face of a candidate who is linked by means of hidden cash, through Jefferson Marketing, with a right-wing network whose identity he has been hiding, but which is now made visible in the form of individuals—Jerry Falwell, Tom Ellis—all depicted in the ads. Visuals and heavy thumping sound effects pound away on the theme "What Is Jesse Hiding?" The implication is not only of Helms's duplicity, which would induce a reaction of anger. It is also that the opponent is involved with a group of ideologues whose single-minded villainy could cause harm to ordinary people.

From a tally, which reports on attempts to code the Hunt ads by more traditional "type" (as opposed to categories developed on the basis of sound and visuals), the conclusion also emerged that the ads of both candidates were heavily negative. There was a difference, however. The Helms ads focused on the personal attack, which took two forms: that Hunt was a "liar" and that he was "just a politician" who "serves his own interest." Three Helms "liar" ads ran more heavily than any other type of ad in the sample, with a total of 12 airings. Hunt ran fewer total ads. The centerpiece was three ads that linked Helms to the radical right.

This tally also confirms Helms's greater use of the positive-image ad with nine airings to four for similar Hunt ads. The centerpiece of these Helms ads was "Broyhill Testimonial," a talking head ad that, like similar advertising for Ronald Reagan, concluded with swelling music, Schwartz's route to "evoked recall."[53]

"Young Farmer," also a positive ad, pleaded that the undecided voter should support Helms for incumbency reasons: Helms was on the Agriculture Committee and could help North Carolina. Advertising theory suggests there is an advantage to coming on with a positive ad at the end to offer a reason to vote *for* your candidate. Helms's more positive image, wheel-of-emotions style, was indeed resolution to a lot of uncertainty raised in a negative campaign.

CONCLUSION

Hunt-Helms witnessed the full flowering of the negative attack, and it was effective so long as the attacker could keep *his* image positive and formulate issues in a fashion perceived to be fair by a general audience. Targeting was used. Symbolism that was racially oriented was used in a fashion that stressed "deniability." Another principle was that of never discussing strategy, so as to avoid the label *political,* not moral or mythic, leader. Further, a precept was to always stay on the offensive. Helms's imagery and Four Commandments of attack, including that of stressing visual imagery and maintaining deniability, would resonate in the discussion of the 1988 Bush campaign, which included the Willie Horton ad.

But the secondary effects of the advertising are significant as well. They emerge as feedback, or "lessons" that guide subsequent campaign efforts; and as examined in this chapter, these were significant. In 1986 heavy money would need to be spent early to define the character of one's own candidate in positive terms and, if threatened with a serious challenge, attack the opponent's credibility early. One corollary emerged: It is not wise to husband resources for the final period, when a candidate's credibility may be gone, the agenda set, and the airwaves cluttered. Another was that in the negative attack, it is better to focus on familiar bogeymen, with whom a referential link to the opponent will be perceived as fair, not unknown foreigners. One of the bogeymen is the "taxman"—and Democrats definitely learned a lesson in this regard. Further, Hunt's effort to "savage" Helms by linking him with right-wing ideologues and dictators would not be attempted again in the 1980s.

There were other lessons. One was the effectiveness of the full-frontal talking head ad used to respond to an attack ad. Used both in the case of the irate "ordinary citizen" responding to a Hunt Social Security attack and Mrs. Helms responding to a Hunt family planning attack ad, this format was generally used by Republicans in 1986 and 1988. In 1988, the Republican National Committee advised candidates that negative advertising indeed "works," and that the most effective response to it is a full-frontal of the candidate or a surrogate saying "shame on you." Thus, in the final stage of the close 1988 Washington state Senate race between Republican Slade Gorton and Democrat Mike Lowery, Gorton used this formula to respond to a key attack by Democrat Lowery. It was subsequently argued that his "shame on you" response was the move which finally turned the race in Gorton's direction.[54]

NOTES

1. For one example of a news story produced by the media blitz of the final ten days of the election, see Chuck Alston, "Hunt Seeks to Show Voters Where Helms Stands," *Greensboro News and Record,* February 14, 1984, p. B1.

2. For the significance of direct-mail appeals in producing funding for television advertising, see the taped lecture by Michael Murphy, "Integrating Polling and Media," *Campaigns and Elections* Conference, Washington, D.C., May 6, 1987.

3. Murphy, "Integrating Polling and Media." For an analysis of the new technologies as used in the Helms race, see Alan Ehrenhalt, "Technology, Strategy Bring New Campaign Era," *Congressional Quarterly* 43 (December 7, 1985): 2559-61, 2563-65 and "A New Breed of Consultants Joins the Fray" *Congressional Quarterly* 43 (December 7, 1985): 2562.

For analysis of the background and philosophy of Helms's consultants, including Michael Murphy and his partner Alex Castellanos, see also Chapter 2. For the figure on the number of people involved with the Helms campaign, see Murphy, "Integrating Polling and Media."

4. Timothy John Walker, "Hunt and Helms," unpublished manuscript circulating in New York Democratic political advertising circles, summer 1985.

5. Interview with Joseph Grimsley, Hunt campaign comanager, Raleigh, North Carolina, December 28, 1984.

6. See also Chapter 3.

7. Grimsley interview.

8. For a review of the experimental literature on negative advertising, see Susan A. Hellweg, "Political Candidate Campaign Advertising: A Selected Review of the Literature," paper presented at the International Communication Association Convention, New Orleans, May 1988; Doug Schoen, lecture at the *Campaigns and Elections* Conference. May 7, 1987. See also Chapter 2.

9. Grimsley interview; interview with campaign cochair Gary Pearce, Raleigh, North Carolina, December 28, 1984.

10. For academic literature that has confirmed the lasting significance of establishing an image early, see Donald Cundy, in *New Perspectives on Political Advertising* ed. Lynda Lee Kaid, Dan Nimmo, and Keith R. Sanders (Carbondale: Southern Illinois University Press, 1986). See also Michael Pfau and Michael Burgoon, "Inoculation in Political Campaign Communication," paper presented at the International Communication Association Convention, New Orleans, May 1988.

11. Interview with David Paletz, Duke University, Durham, North Carolina, December 29, 1984.

12. Mike McLister, taped speech presented at the Triangle Marketing Association, February 20, 1984. Alan Ehrenhalt, "A New Breed of Consultants Joins the Fray," *(Congressional Quarterly)* 43 (December 7, 1985):2562.

13. Ibid.

14. Richardson Preyer in William D. Snider, *Hunt and Helms, The North Carolina Senate Race, 1984.* (Chapel Hill, N.C.: University of North Carolina Press, 1985), p. 108.

15. For excellent journalistic analyses of direct mail, see Ann Cooper, "Middleman Mail," *National Journal,* September 14, 1985, pp. 2036–41. See also political pollster and consultant Roger Craver's view that Helms was "a marvelous devil to raise money against," in Bill Peterson, "In Victory, Helms Proves He Is an Innovator," *Greensboro News and Record,* November 22, 1984, p. B3.

16. Quoted in a review article by Bob Hall, "The Media Maven," *The Nation,* June 29, 1985, p. 806.

17. Interview with Gary Pearce, Hunt cocampaign manager, Raleigh, North Carolina, December 28, 1984.

18. Interview with Russell Walker, who until 1982 was North Carolina Democratic state chairman, Asheboro, North Carolina, December 17, 1984.

19. Interview with Wayne Boyles, office of Senator Jesse Helms, Washington, D.C., December 26, 1984. See also Timothy John Walker manuscript on Helms's deniability.

20. Appointment with Carter Wrenn, Raleigh, North Carolina, December 28, 1984.

21. For a discussion of Helms and the Martin Luther King Birthday issue, see Snider, in *Hunt-Helms,* op. cit. pp. 100–103.

22. Grimsley interview; Ehrenhalt, "Technology, Strategy." p. 2569.

23. "Who Is Bob Harris?" *60 Minutes,* Vol. XVIII, No. 1, as broadcast on CBS, September 15, 1985.

24. Ibid.

25. Grimsley and Pearce interviews. See also Chapter 9.

26. Grimsley interview.

27. Ibid.

28. See William D. Snider, on the real differences between Hunt and Helms on Social Security, in *Hunt-Helms,* op. cit., pp. 128–130.

29. Pearce and Grimsley interviews.

30. For a discussion of taboo language and visceral issues that eluded the pollsters in the 1986 election, see Timothy Noah, "10 Political Words That Dare Not Speak Their Name," *New York Times,* November 19, 1986.

31. One of the consultants who created antecedents in this area is Ken Swope, as noted in Chapter 2.

32. See also Chapter 2 for the strategic use of words in relation to the "Crying Farmer" ad series.

33. For quick-response theory, see Murphy, C&E Conference. "Integrating Polling and Media." See also Chapter 2.

34. Murphy, "Integrating Polling and Media."

35. Pearce interview.

36. Grimsley interview.

37. Pearce interview.

38. Ibid.

39. Ibid.

40. Grimsley interview.

41. Sawyer is quoted in Peterson, "Helms Is Innovator."

42. Pearce interview.

43. Ibid.

44. Ibid.

45. Ibid.

46. Ibid. For the reaction of Hunt supporters, see Snider, *Hunt-Helms,* p. 194.

47. According to Pearce, the campaign, which had been behind since Labor Day, pulled to even the Saturday before the election. He does not believe any last-minute shifts were caused by the advertising: "We were four points behind on Labor Day, and four points behind on election day."

48. Grimsley interview.

49. Lisa DeMaio Brewer, "PACs on the Warpath: How Independent Efforts Re-Elected Jesse Helms," *Campaigns and Elections,* (Summer 1985): 5–11. Brewer describes efforts of the Fund for a Conservative Majority to assist Helms by coming on at the end with a positive independent expenditure campaign featuring Jim Broyhill ads supporting Jesse Helms.

Brewer favorably quotes the *Charlotte Observer's* chief political correspondent, Ken Eudy, to the effect that the FCM television spots helped bridge the gap between the conservative and moderate Republicans, a split he has seen since 1972. "If there were any doubt, particularly among the western, mountain Republicans, who to vote for, I think Broyhill helped them stay with Helms," he observes, adding that voter groups targeted by the National Rifle Association and Christian organizations were "pretty well staked out beforehand." Brewer argues that this effort was crucial to the Helms victory in 1984.

See also the discussion of changes in talking head ads in Chapter 4.

50. Brewer, "PACs on the Warpath," p. 6.

51. See also Chapter 9.

52. For the coding totals and method, see Chapter 4, pp. 74–76.

53. See also Chapter 4.

54. Republican National Committee Campaign School, Washington, D.C., February 1988. Interview with Dan Payne, Boston, January 2, 1989.

8

Theory and House Practice: Ad Campaigns in the Heartland

Political advertising theory suggests that ads are not heavily used in major metropolitan areas because the lack of overlap between district and television market boundaries makes other forms of communication more cost-effective. This benefits congressional incumbents, since they have other means of communication as well as greater access to campaign funds to help them advertise, even in expensive market situations, if necessary. In addition, theory maintains that advertising is used in more competitive than noncompetitive races because challengers can raise money to pay for television advertising in such races.[1]

Theory also holds that challengers use more negative and issues-related advertising than do incumbents because their task is to give reasons to vote against an incumbent. Incumbents, by contrast, tend to stay positive because of the danger that negative advertising can backfire against them, making them appear "mean."[2]

Finally, theory suggests that there are four stages of communication in a challenger's campaign against an entrenched incumbent. The first focuses on the development of *name identification,* without which voters will not pull the lever for a candidate. The second stage *positions the candidate* as an individual and on the issues. After polls indicate that a positive image has been developed, the third *attack* phase begins. Failure to focus on developing a positive image before attacking may lead to the candidate becoming known negatively. A return to *positive* advertising comes at the end.[3]

Ed Blakely, a skilled veteran strategist who in 1984 was with the National Republican Congressional Committee (NRCC) explains that, according to this theory, the attack stage begins after "you have made your candidate trusted and likeable. Then, in the last six weeks launch a negative wave of attacks on your opponent as not the right person for the job." The intention at this stage is to move voters who say they favor the incumbent into the ranks of the undecided by giving them reasons to vote against him. Democratic party officials agreed with their counterparts on the NRCC that the most effective issues on the congressional level are less those related to national policy, than to performance, what the candidate has done for the district—or as Blakely expressed it, "the potholes on Route 1." There have been years in which public policy issues were quite important—Ed Blakely cited 1980—but in 1984 "it was our first and foremost job to show that these politicians [the incumbents] weren't doing the job we voters want."[4]

According to Blakely, if there is no way the voter could be moved into the positive column, for example, one could hope the attack advertising would at least get the voters angry enough to say "a plague on both your houses" and stay home on election day.[5]

Returning to the high road, in the fourth and final phase of the race, the campaign would ideally provide positive reasons to vote for the challenger. This might involve rerunning the candidate's early ads, perhaps modified to include new information. This, as consultant Tony Schwartz noted, evokes "people's full experience of the early commercials by using bits and pieces of them, properly designed. This makes use of a principle of perception, that people most readily understand things they have seen and heard before."[6]

Priorities vary, of course, as all races involve different problems. In Blakely's opinion, roughly 20 percent of expenditures of both time and money by an unknown challenger should be devoted to name identification. Greater amounts should be devoted to the message component of the campaign, 35 percent to developing the message about one's own character and issues, and 35 percent to developing the message about the opponent. If money is tight, combining the name identification and ad message components is possible.

Despite the great deal of emphasis in this strategy on building up one's own candidate, Blakely added, speaking after the 1984 election, it is important to anticipate that a race can turn heavily negative. Thus, 10 percent of a campaign's resources should be reserved for what Blakely calls "preemptive" spots scheduled either in anticipation of or in response to an incumbent's attack. Others might call such spots inoculation ads that attempt to deal with one's own area of weakness.[7]

Overall, the 1984 ad sample confirmed many of these theories, but it also produced some surprises.

There was substantially less House than Senate or presidential advertising, with a total House figure of 27 minutes, which represented 8.7 percent of the adtime in the 1984 sample. This adtime was still considerably greater than the House race newstime, which totaled 17 minutes.[8]

There was, as expected, little use of congressional advertising in the largest areas in the sample, Los Angeles and Atlanta, where congressional districts and market areas did not overlap. Paid advertising appeared on the air in the 1984 sample taken from the final ten days of the campaign in only 3 of the over 20 congressional races in these two urban areas, although in Atlanta it contributed significantly to the defeat of Democratic incumbent Elliott Levitas. The greatest amount of congressional race advertising occurred in the North

Carolina market area, which included two competitive districts, in both of which televised advertising played a significant role. This was followed by the Indiana markets, where it played a major role in one competitive district, had little significance in a second marginally competitive district, and was used in one "safe incumbent" district.[9]

In this and the following chapter, the focus is on the significance of political advertising in all of the races in which it played a role, in Indiana and the central Piedmont, as well as in one race in Atlanta, Georgia. These case studies illustrate the difficulty of positioning a challenger by means of issues-oriented television advertising. They also demonstrate that advertising on the visual media is more effective if the character and issue messages dovetail. This applies as much to the dovetailing of messages as between congressional and presidential races as to individual races. Classic theory to the contrary, at least one challenger found that an incumbent cannot be counted on to stay positive if he or she begins to slip in the polls.

These contests also shed fresh light on the potential for and limitations of a national party effort to offer assistance to a challenger. Given the fact that, as we saw in Chapter 3, the generic Republican party advertising was such a significant factor in the overall message environment during the final period of the election, the question of developing ways to understand it becomes doubly important and remains a fruitful subject for future research.[10]

APPLYING CLASSIC THEORY IN A COMPETITIVE INDIANA DISTRICT

If, as theory suggests, positioning is best directed to incumbent vulnerabilities in the area of character and performance, what is a challenger to do if the candidate is well liked and perceived to be doing a good job for the district? The well-funded challenge by Ken MacKenzie to Phil Sharp in Indiana's Second District illustrates some of the difficulties. He attempted to follow classic theory, but like other challengers whose views are examined in this and the next chapter, he concluded in retrospect that sharper-edged approaches would be more successful in future campaigns. His challenging campaign, MacKenzie believed, should have launched an early soft-sell negative attack to break the incumbent's credibility. As it was, at some point during the campaign each candidate sought to achieve this objective through negative advertising, but unlike North Carolina senatorial candidate Jim Hunt, Phil Sharp never lost his credibility and so survived all his challenges.

The Second District has little internal cohesion. It ranges from the suburbs of Indianapolis south and eastward through rural heartland to the blue-collar industrial towns of Columbus, Richmond, and Muncie. A former congressional aide and college professor, Sharp came to Congress with the Watergate class of 1974 after two previous attempts. Except for a 60 percent margin in 1976, he had since won reelection in the 53 to 56 percent range, offering Republicans the continuing prospect of recapturing the congressional seat. In Washington Sharp was the fifth-ranking Democrat on the powerful Energy and Commerce Committee and chairman of its important Subcommittee on Fossil and Synthetic Fuels. He enjoyed wide respect as a fair and effective member of Congress.

Redistricting in 1981 by the Republican state legislature deprived Sharp of half his old district, thereby driving a wedge in the "incumbency advantage" with territory not only in which he was unknown but which was heavily Republican. Still, the congressman won again in 1982, a good year for Democrats, with 56 percent of the vote. The election of 1984, which offered the prospect of presidential coattails in a district that favored Reagan 2 to 1, presented new hope for the Republicans, particularly since the incumbent was not yet deeply entrenched with all the constituents in his newly minted district.

A public relations executive with the Ball Corporation of Muncie and a former congressional aide, Ken MacKenzie was an able and articulate spokesman for Reaganomics. Conditions in the district clearly held promise in 1984. Energy PACs that opposed Sharp's positions on natural gas deregulation led the list of PAC contributors. MacKenzie's campaign was cited at the Republican National Convention for leading the Republican field in terms of Republican PAC contributors. Clearly, the resources would be there to mount a competitive race against Sharp.[11]

Following classic theory, MacKenzie's problem was to first develop name identification and then draw a positive contrast on issues and character between himself and an incumbent who, according to his polls, was viewed as hardworking, intelligent, doing a good job for the district, and keeping in touch.

Next Time, Attack Early

MacKenzie said that for him the lesson of 1984 was that this positioning should have been attempted in the area of performance, quite apart from how Sharp was perceived in the district. Next time around, if he could raise the money to afford a Roger Ailes, he would utilize the approach developed in Ailes's successful 1984 "Hound Dog" advertising campaign against Dee Huddleston in Kentucky.[12]

The "Hound Dog" strategy was one that used a highly entertaining but hard-hitting soft-sell negative ad early in the race. It followed a different strategy, less geared to policy issues and trying to develop a positive image of one's candidate. Although some attention was paid by Republican Senate nominee Mitch McConnell to the first stages of the traditional challenging campaign, name recognition and candidate positioning on issues, much greater attention was devoted to an early, not a late, attack on the incumbent. Indeed, a heavily repeated ad featured a roving hound dog searching endlessly for an "absentee" senator who is elsewhere when rollcall votes occur.

The verbal message concerned the missed votes, but the ad also relates to the breaking of bonds of empathy—and identity—breaking bonds of trust, in short, between the incumbent and his constituents through visually and aurally linking the opponent with the pleasure spots of a Las Vegas or Acapulco. The impact of such advertising is to focus early on not only performance but also underlying character. Some of the assumptions, examined in Chapter 2, apply—for example, the assumption that a negative message is more persuasive and more readily recalled by voters.[13]

MacKenzie's focus in 1984, however, was more that of applying classic theory: attempting to build up the challenger, perhaps necessitated by the fact that Sharp was so highly regarded in the parts of the district he knew and had served for some years. According to David Iles, MacKenzie's campaign manager, the idea was to "raise MacKenzie to the level of a Sharp, as a 'Mr. Smith goes to Washington.' " A major initial concern of the campaign was also how Sharp and MacKenzie differed on policy issues. The campaign, MacKenzie said, decided to "create Ken MacKenzie as the same type of person [as Sharp] but with the district on the issues." Thus, the case was made, according to David Iles, that "in voting for MacKenzie one would buy a Sharp, along with a pro-Reagan vote." Brian Francisco, political reporter for the *Muncie Star,* raffishly described the approach as a "two-for-one deal—buy Ken MacKenzie and get Ronald Reagan thrown in free. Or vice versa."[14]

Classic Positioning

Economic issues were the most promising ones. The district supported Reaganomics and was happy with the decline in inflation and interest rates. The polls indicated that young urban professionals (yuppies) were particularly supportive of the "economic opportunity dimensions of Reagan's performance." The campaign believed it could make the case that Sharp was anti-Reagan because he had voted for Reagan's programs only 38 percent of the time. When they were developed, MacKenzie's ads were targeted, according to a MacKenzie campaign worker interviewed in the *Muncie Star,* at independent voters and big-city Republicans, which the official called Ruppies, a term said to have been coined at the Republican National Convention.[15]

These were not "new" issues, that is, ones that were unfamiliar to the public. MacKenzie considered the idea of raising one such issue, natural gas deregulation, which would in fact have comprised a major difference between the two if he scored an upset. In his position as chairman of the Energy Subcommittee of the House Energy and Commerce Committee, Sharp was a leading proponent of regulation. MacKenzie believed that by limiting price hikes, regulation discourages exploration, the best assurance of ultimate low prices. He thought of developing "hard-hitting commercials explaining how much per-vote gas prices had gone up during Sharp's tenure," but he was advised against it by his consultants, who said that raising new issues in political ads, in short, trying to "educate voters," is like "trying to move a boulder up a hill."[16]

Ineffective Issues Ads

Although not opting to educate the public to a "new" (and presumably unpopular) issue, MacKenzie sought to position himself differently from Sharp on some of Ronald Reagan's economic issues in a fashion that was more conservative, more "in keeping" with the attitude of the pro-Reagan district. The problem, as stated by MacKenzie and Steve Nix, the Republican Congressional Campaign Committee Midwest advisor with whom he met regularly, was one of creating effective issues-oriented ads. The ads prepared by Arthur Finkelstein of New York, the campaign's conservative media advisor, represent a test of a traditionally highly political, as opposed to a more commercially oriented, style. They were purposeful issues-based talking head ads.[17]

The result? While they may have represented the candidate's views on the issues, they were ineffective because they failed to take into account two other components of televised political advertising in the 1980s: personality and entertainment values.

Unlike the conservative president with whose policies he sought to link his candidacy, MacKenzie attempted to position himself on the basis of commitment to ideas without the benefit of the warm smiles, the parables, and the music that added up to the character side of the Reagan advertising effort. "The House" linked MacKenzie with Reaganomics in general, and in particular with yuppies who could buy houses because of low interest rates attributed to it. In the ad, MacKenzie stood within the wooden framework of a house under construction speaking of his and the president's common interest in cutting federal spending and keeping interest rates low. In "Budget," which was said to be directed at a broader segment of the population, MacKenzie slammed a "budget" on the table to emphasize his commitment to a presidential line-item veto. In "I Believe," standing in front of a picture of Ronald Reagan, he decried excessive government spending and said that "Democrats like Walter Mondale and Phil Sharp think the solution is more taxes and more government. They're wrong." He concluded, "I will not vote to raise taxes and *I* mean it." According to his campaign manager, "I Believe" got "limited play."[18]

The ads began to run during the Republican National Convention in August and later during breaks in state and local newscasts. The NRCC conducted a study and concluded that the ads did not work. The effect of these ads was compared through polls with those of a direct-mail piece that was sent out at the same time. The letter provided information about the MacKenzie family, detailed his public policy positions, and was, MacKenzie recalled, "tougher" on Sharp because it was mailed only to registered Republicans. The NRCC study indicated that it was more effective than the "shotgun" televised issues advertising approach, however. Equal percentages of the electorate—25 percent—could recall having seen a television ad, or receiving a mailing. The startling difference, according to MacKenzie, was in the greater persuasiveness of the letter:

Of course, the people who received the letter were Republicans. Still, Sharp was leading me by a big margin. If you go to just those who had seen the television ads, he was leading me by only 2 or 3 points less than that huge margin. So there was hardly any movement at all for having seen the ad. Among the people who received the letter, however, vroom, there was a shift of 15 to 20 percentage points in my direction.[19]

The NRCC's midwestern representative, Steve Nix, who advised the Mac-Kenzie campaign, believed the television ads were "bad, too heavy." The emphatic commitment by a candidate standing in front of the cameras dropping a book to underscore his stand on the issues espoused by a popular president, without the benefit of the intimate character side presented by that president, did not work in the context of that campaign with a general television audience. As a result of the study, the NRCC decided to direct its money allocated to the campaign entirely to direct mail, taking advantage of the fact that the Indiana Republican party had developed some of the best mailing lists in the country. Developing a positive image utilizing classic theory was not an easy task.[20]

Problems in Coordinating Local and National Efforts

David Iles, the MacKenzie campaign manager, viewed the challenger's major problem as one of failure to stick with what he described as the Reagan-MacKenzie linkage theme. He also viewed the Reagan-Bush campaign as being insufficiently committed in this area. It came through only at the last minute with a televised ad linking Reagan and MacKenzie. The spot had been filmed in August at the Republican National Convention. It was only on November 1, however, that a press conference was held to announce that MacKenzie had gained Reagan's endorsement and that a Reagan-MacKenzie ad was available "for preview."[21]

"If people really wanted to elect a Republican House," Iles said later, "they would have helped us much earlier. 'We need Reagan,' Ken had been saying in 1983." The campaign would meet at least every other week with Finkelstein and an NRCC representative in Indianapolis and would make this point, but Iles believed it "boiled down to the fact that the NRCC doesn't have the clout to get Reagan or Bush." It came down to when the White House said yes. The NRCC's Blakely asserted afterward, however, that Reagan had helped GOP congressional aspirants more than any previous president.[22]

The road to alignment of the presidential and congressional campaign constellations is clearly fraught with perils. This story of one endorsement ad indicates that there were limits to the Reagan-Bush presidential campaign's assistance to its party's presidential challengers, even in this race that many believed the Republicans could win. The problem is not as simple as that of one ad, of course. As we have seen, although MacKenzie's advertising dovetailed with the *policies* of the president, it did not present the same *character* side of the combined message of an ad.

Nor was MacKenzie's advertising synchronized with the single-issue tax focus of the national Republican advertising effort. In this, his efforts illustrate a major difficulty encountered by the Republican party's House candidates in its effort to take advantage of what, as the 1984 ad sample indicated, was clearly a successful Republican effort to inundate the airwaves with its message.[23]

It could well be argued that although the Republicans won only 14 net additional House seats overall and lost 2 Senate seats in November 1984, this effort was not in vain. In 1986 no national party advertising theme was developed and the GOP lost 5 seats in the House and 8 in the Senate. William Greener, director of communications at the Republican National Committee, suggested one reason why their 1984 congressional effort, although effective in using presidential coattails to change some votes, did not translate into more widescale victories. In addition to incumbent communications advantages, examined next, the Republican challengers' failed overall to tie together the two sides of their message in a fashion that dovetailed with the national effort. "Say, the candidate was running as 'Mr. Studious.' The image was not connected with opposition to the tax hike," he argued.[24]

As the MacKenzie case study illustrates, this was indeed a problem. MacKenzie focused on a *variety* of Reaganomic issues, not just taxes. It was actually Sharp who managed to dovetail *his* character message with opposition to higher taxes, the Republican theme that so dominated the airwaves. Phil Sharp was personally frugal, the character side of the tax message. This was well known, and it was stressed during the campaign along with the incumbent's opposition to higher taxes. MacKenzie did try to attack Sharp on the issue in a referential ad, trying to tie him to Democrats who favored higher taxes and were negatively perceived. But an ad that he ran linking Sharp with Mondale's "tax plan," which the incumbent had publicly said he did not support, played only briefly. It was apparently not effective.[25]

Sharp's campaign had a further advantage in turning this issue back on MacKenzie. Unlike Jim Hunt of North Carolina, against whom the tax issue was used effectively, there had been no previous credible attack on a Sharp's character or consistency.[26]

Theory developed by William Greener of the Republican National Committee concerning the failure of Republican generic advertising to elect more candidates also suggested the difficulty for incumbents of developing "local" issues. The MacKenzie advertising that appeared in the 1984 ad sample confirmed this difficulty. It was the incumbent, Phil Sharp, rather than the challenger, Ken MacKenzie, who was able to raise a local issue successfully. This occurred at the end of the race, when the Sharp campaign was under heavy challenge by MacKenzie's direct-mail pieces, which ran increasingly heavily during the final days of the race in the 2 to 1 Republican district. This tied MacKenzie to Ronald Reagan's increasingly strong coattails, and Sharp experienced a mid-October dip in his support comparable to that of Democratic incumbents in a number of other districts, such as Tim Wirth's in Colorado, which were heavily Republican and pro-Reagan and which had fully funded challengers.[27]

Incumbents Do Not Stay Above the Fray

Contrary to the theory that suggests that incumbents should "stay positive," Sharp instead returned fire at the end with an ad that focused the television agenda on an issue of direct pocketbook relevance to the voter. It was also one that carried an implied character message about the challenger: His fortune is linked with that of big oil companies, not the people of Indiana. Although he mailed out three last-minute direct-mail attack pieces signed by prominent Indiana Republicans, MacKenzie made no response on the airwaves to Sharp's late television advertising.[28]

Sharp's campaigns were normally positive. The congressman had even been joined by his old friend Robert Redford in one campaign appearance—a near-perfect marriage of campaign advertising and news. MacKenzie had not prepared for such return fire as now came from Sharp's direction. It was a hard-sell negative attack ad that used black-and-white visuals and heavy sound effects and raised the populist specter of "outside forces." It was an ad that also helped the Democratic incumbent rather than the Republican challenger focus the race on a local issue, but in a fashion similar to that developed elsewhere across the country by candidates of all political persuasions. At issue was whose interests would be served by a challenger who had raised $40,000 from oil PACs. The news side of the effort was carried by Democratic state chairman John Livengood, who called a press conference to charge:

Never in the history of elections in Indiana have high rollers from Texas and Oklahoma moved into our state in such a concentrated effort to defeat one of our Congressmen. There is no mystery as to why they are here. Phil Sharp is leading the fight in Congress to hold down natural gas prices, and the result may cut into big oil companies.[29]

The challenger was caught in a bind. The route he had selected to make his race competitive, accepting PAC money from oil companies, had, as he said, "involved getting funding from anywhere I can find it." Now spread over the airwaves, in a race that was coming down to the wire in a photo finish, with only a few points' difference between the candidates, was an example of how a local issue could well have contributed to the challenger's failure to ride the Reagan coattails to victory. The conservative PAC funding that enabled him to launch a high-tech media campaign was a double-edged sword.[30]

The Value of Early Ads to Inoculate

Although MacKenzie had been warned against the risk of taking oil PAC money, he did not inoculate himself against it. Speaking generally on challenger strategy after the 1984 election, the NRCC's Blakely argued that 10 percent of total television campaign budget should be used to either defend oneself against or launch a preemptive attack on the opponent in relation to a thorny issue. *Inoculation* theory, thus confirmed by recent academic research, suggests that early ads should be run in relation to one's potential area of vulnerability.[31]

Both candidates had received large amounts of PAC money. As of September 30 each had received close to $270,000 in campaign contributions, with Sharp by that point receiving $155,000 and MacKenzie $90,000 from PACs. Ultimately, Sharp and MacKenzie raised and spent almost identical amounts of money, with Sharp collecting $429,340 from various sources: $161,027 of it from individuals, $16,654 from the national party, and $242,902, or 57 percent, from PACs. Of this PAC money over 40 percent came from organized labor. Sharp's campaign expenditures totaled $409,117. MacKenzie raised $404,512, 43 percent of it from PACs. He spent $399,755. MacKenzie made such points in the press, but not in his television advertising, where his remaining resources were paying for Reagan linkage ads during the final days of the election.[32]

Sharp replied that any inference that he had been swayed by PAC money was "an insult to my personal integrity and pride." Contributing to Sharp's believability was the fact that in no way had his credibility been touched during the course of the campaign. Further, he had a long-held reputation in Indiana as a consumer advocate in the matter of natural gas regulation, a reputation bolstered by the fact that other Indiana representatives from both sides of the aisle supported him on the issue. Sharp had never lost credibility, and MacKenzie was an unproven entity espousing deregulation, whose theoretical merits were not readily apparent to the public. Sharp won reelection with 53 percent of the vote.[33]

The overarching lesson was that with every possible break from the challenger's point of view—redistricting, a district heavily of one's own party, and a popular president—it is still difficult for a nonincumbent to use traditional advertising methods and win, even in a year of heavy coattails. The postelection assessment from the Republican candidate was that the next time around, he would not focus so much effort on developing his own image and issues. Instead, early attack ads would focus around the opponent's performance.

THE CHALLENGER WHO MUST RELY ON
NEWS COVERAGE

For the unknown challenger facing an incumbent in most noncompetitive congressional districts, the problem of positioning was no less difficult than MacKenzie's race against a vulnerable but highly respected incumbent. The two other such races, in the Indiana sample, including one in which the challenger served as his own campaign manager during the final days of the race, demonstrate the frustration of trying to break an incumbent's ability to obtain press coverage.[34]

One challenger was Joe Watkins, an attractive young black Republican minister who challenged Andy Jacobs, the popular long-term Democratic incumbent from the Tenth Congressional District, which covers some 70 percent of Indianapolis and which I have termed marginally competitive because the incumbent won by 59 percent of the vote in 1984. Watkins focused much of his media effort on generating favorable press coverage, eschewing paid television ads, except for one positive appeal in which he did not attack the incumbent. His campaign manager, Joe Smith, concluded at the end of the 1984 race that "there are two major ways to communicate to large numbers of voters. They are paid media and an organization of volunteers, principally on election day. [To run again in 1986] $35,000 during the primary and $110,000 during the general election would be needed for electronic media." Together, election day organization, and electronic media

make up 99.9 percent of all efforts that will actually influence the vote totals in November—this includes earned media [the press]. They must be priorities at all times! Time and money should be devoted to almost nothing else.[35]

Negative Personality Ads Next Time

He also concluded that anti-Jacobs television advertising focusing on *personality* would be necessary to defeat the popular incumbent because in his view the district voted for Jacobs on the basis of personality. Without "anti-Jacobs" ads it would be impossible to "recapture" Jacobs's Republican supporters, normally 20 percent of all Republicans. Relying on Reagan coattails, without attack advertising, Watkins was able to reduce this figure only by 7 percent. Of Jacobs's Republican supporters, 13 percent voted for him again in 1984 irregardless of how they felt about his 80 percent Americans for Democratic Action, 71 percent American Federation of Labor-Congress of Industrial Organizations, and 38 percent Americans for Conservative Action ratings; and Jacobs won reelection with 59 percent of the vote. A winning coalition would require such Republican Jacobs supporters, as well as significant support from the black community in Indianapolis, concluded Watkins's 1984 campaign manager, Joe Smith.[36]

On June 23, 1985, Smith presented the candidate with this analysis as part of the process of deciding whether to run again in 1986. This television-based focus, including negative advertising, would represent a shift of strategy, for as part of his 1984 campaign Watkins had concentrated on publicizing his development of model self-help efforts in black communities. These models made a point that he believed was important and that did receive extensive coverage in the news media, resulting in extraordinarily high name recognition, 85 percent in the black community and 70 percent in the white community. Despite all the publicity in the news media, without a significant amount of televised political advertising providing voters with a reason not to vote for the incumbent, on election day Watkins gathered only a disappointing 5.5 percent of the black vote. Following Smith's presentation of his plan for 1986, with its focus on fund-raising to pay for expensive television ads in the Indianapolis market that would emphasize differences with the incumbent, Watkins decided not to run again in 1986. This was a blow to the Republicans, given the advantage his high level of name recognition would represent in a second campaign.[37]

If the need for an expanded television-based second effort, including negative advertising, contributed to Watkins's decision not to run again, the same was true for Democrat Art Smith, the underfunded 29-year-old real estate agent and former congressional aide who challenged nine-term Republican incumbent John Myers in 1984 in Indiana's Seventh Congressional District. This is a rich farming district lying along the western state line, traversed by the Wabash River, and having in Terre Haute and Lafayette two major population centers of consequence.

The Seventh District was considered so safe for the Republicans that Smith did not even receive the support of elected local Democratic officials. His race demonstrated not only how a safe and well-funded incumbent can scare off experienced challengers, but also how an underfunded and inexperienced candidate, operating largely on his own in an effort that combined into one the first three phases of classic four-stage communications theory—name recognition, positioning, and attack—can identify himself in the press primarily as a lost cause. The congressman would neither debate nor respond to questions raised by reporters about the challenger's campaign issues and was accordingly able to control the press agenda, even in a sophisticated media market.[38]

Given his failure to make a case in the press, an objective that represented his one possibility to raise enough money to make the race competitive, Smith was unable to launch what was planned as a much broader advertising effort in the fall. The greater part of his advertising expenditure went to pay the fees of his commercially oriented media consultant, Joe Cerrel of Los Angeles, whose associate, Steve Powell, made "Bouncing Ball," a flip-flop soft-sell negative ad that had been produced at the Harriman Communications Center and won a Clio award from the International Association for Political Consultants. After paying the consulting bills, however, Smith had only $7,000 to put his ads on the air. He is a classic example of what can happen when a candidate has high hopes for what televised political advertising can do for a candidate but does not have the resources or the experience to run a press-based effort, much less one that combines press and advertising efforts that must be run out of two media centers in the district. Smith won only 31.5 percent of the vote, the lowest percentage any Democrat had ever received against the long-term incumbent.[39]

In reassessing the race after the 1984 election, Smith said that with a limited budget he did not believe you could "nice-guy" an incumbent out of office.

"If you don't have enough money, go negative." Following advice he had received to this effect, he developed an ad modeled on one employed in the 1982 race of Richard J. Durbin, an Illinois Democrat who had defeated veteran GOP congressman Paul Findley. The Durbin ad focused on the names of oil companies that had contributed to Findley's campaign. Smith said he developed but did not air one just like it although Durbin, also a former congressional aide, had said it was the "clincher" in his race against Findley. According to Smith, the idea was to

find the ugliest picture of [the incumbent] that could be found, place it on the screen, and then roll every big name oil PAC you could find over it. . . . He was a major oil PAC recipient. And then you say, "Now you understand why we need to change." It didn't take a genius to figure out who was supporting him. And that he wasn't going to help the people of the district when it came to oil bills.[40]

STRATEGY FOR INCUMBENTS

While spot advertising can become desperately important to challengers, incumbents have other means of communicating with constituents. Two alternative methods of advertising are illustrated by incumbents who were challenged by Watkins and Smith.

Andy Jacobs came to Congress in 1964 and has there remained except for one term (1973–74), when Republican redistricting caused him to lose his seat temporarily. Remapping after the 1980 census forced him into a primary against a neighboring Democratic congressman and good friend, but he won handily and now has a predominantly urban, Democratic district. Jacobs eschews all PAC money and spent very little on his 1984 reelection effort, which included no televised political ads. He is highly popular in his urban district, which has a centralized communications system. He returns once a month to Indianapolis for no-holds-barred press conferences that often focus on his experience as the sixth-ranking Democrat on the House Ways and Means Committee, which handles all tax legislation.

His ideas are expressed in simple, graphic language, which is replete with visual imagery readily understood by all. He exemplifies what is maximally possible for an incumbent in the area of "free media." According to James Beatty, he is "on television an average of once a week year in and out, as often as the stars of the biggest television shows. And on radio, and in the newspapers." In 1984 he was outspent 4 to 1 by challenger Joe Watkins.[41]

Safe incumbent John Myers did advertise on television during the final days of the 1984 election, but with "traditional" style, low-tech ads designed primarily to alert viewers to the fact that there was an election and that it was time to go out and vote for him. Voters had already made up their minds, according to the campaign's polls, in the summer. Myers's low-budget ads were made at Channel 10 in Terre Haute. Ron Hardman, his campaign manager, says that

> this was because he didn't perceive the urgency of it all. If we really felt the heat of an opponent, we might be tempted to go elsewhere. But the only time we had sophisticated, slick advertising was 18 years ago [when Myers first ran for office].[42]

He spent \$165,693 on his reelection effort and had an unspent surplus of over \$100,000 at the end of 1984. His opponent, Arthur E. Smith, whose frustration has been detailed, spent \$89,222. Myers enjoys great popularity for his close attention to constituent services, and he has high name recognition throughout the district. According to the NRCC Midwest representative, Steve Nix, this, combined with the Myers war chest and the need to advertise in two distinct market areas, usually wards off serious challengers.

ODDS ON INCUMBENTS

The different meaning of advertising for safe incumbents and challengers are readily apparent. For challengers, an increasingly sophisticated and costly communications structure can be a daunting obstacle, but incumbents can pick and choose according to their strengths. In 1984, while Ronald Reagan was carrying every state except Walter Mondale's own Minnesota, the voters in the presidential campaign also sent back to Washington over 96 percent of all incumbent congressmen seeking reelection. In absolute numbers, 390 incumbent members were returned for the 99th Congress, just one short of the all-time record set in 1968. Specifically, 16 incumbents lost in primaries or the general election and there were 29 open seats without an incumbent candidate. Only 22 House seats shifted to the opposition party. The Republicans had a net gain of just 14 seats.[43]

The reasons for this are numerous. Most House district boundaries drawn by state legislatures, of course, enclose a solid Democratic or Republican party constituency. The number of true swing districts has been variously estimated, but it would appear to be under 75. It is at its minimum, of course, early in the decade immediately after the redistricting required by the decennial census, but it should increase year by year thereafter as demographic changes occur.[44]

In addition to politically sensitive boundaries, another factor helping to entrench incumbents in office has been the distribution of PAC money, which totaled \$105.3 million for House and Senate primary election candidates in the 1983–84 election cycle. According to a Federal Election Commission (FEC) study, incumbents received 72 percent of all PAC contributions made during that period. Only 16 percent was given to their opponents; the remainder went to candidates contesting open seats. Democrats received 57 percent, Republicans 43 percent. PAC spending rose to an estimated \$140 million in 1985–86.[45]

INSTITUTIONAL ADVANTAGES OF INCUMBENTS

The institutional advantages of incumbency include ample congressional staff to respond to constituent concerns and reinforce the member's legislative performance, including the franking privilege, which covers not only the member's voluminous correspondence but also up to six newsletters a year sent to every "Resident" or "Postal Patron" in his district. Thanks to the demographic breakdown of population clusters by zip code, mailings can be even more precisely targeted to the interests of the recipient. The elective power of the incumbent's newsletters, a marriage of positive content and sometimes skillful graphics, is recognized in the statutory prohibition against their being mailed within 60 days of a primary or general election in which the member is a candidate. Over $200 million had to be appropriated to cover the cost of official House and Senate mail during the 98th Congress, which preceded the fall 1984 election.

Each House member was also entitled to an annual "clerk-hire" allowance of $336,384 for a staff not to exceed 22 employees and also from $88,850 to $279,470 for official expenses, a figure that varies according to transportation costs to the district, telecommunications costs, and the expense of office space. By one estimate, the average value of official "incumbent power" exceeds $1 million yearly.[46]

Most members employ a press secretary, whose principal responsibility is to keep the member's name and activities constantly and favorably before his or her constituents. That functionary's job is made easier because of the inherent news value of a congressional office, which deals constantly with legislation of concern to the people of the district.

Content analysis of print press coverage of congressional elections by Peter Clark and Susan Evans indicates that incumbents receive far more press coverage than challengers. Not surprisingly, the least coverage is accorded low-budget challengers without the funds to pay for the staff and television time required by a serious campaign. Long-term incumbents receive the greatest news advantage.[47]

Inexpensive video facilities that can be used to create clips to send to television stations and political ads have been added to the incumbent's list of advantages. In 1984 Democrats could use the newly established Democratic Media Center, now the Harriman Communications Center. According to John Franzen, its executive director, this saved about $400,000 from the cost of campaigning for those who used its facilities. Given the convenience of its location on Capitol Hill, and their greater resources, it was used by three times as many Democratic incumbents as challengers. The Republicans have had a sophisticated media operation since the early 1970s; the operation regularly prepares radio and TV advertising at minimal cost to the member. It, too, produces a continuous stream of radio "actualities," or 30-second takes by congressmen and congresswomen discussing a vote or commenting on a newsworthy event, which are immediately circulated to local stations for insertion into their news programs.[48]

When all these elements are coupled with the increasing cost of campaigning, which is driven by advertising and associated technology costs, it is clear that the communication structure—in both its news and advertising dimensions—highly favors incumbents. This translates into a large gap between their electoral prospects and those of their challengers. The question that will need to be examined in further research is whether the growing emphasis on more commercially based advertising, with greater sophistication and a growing price tag, will contribute to widening this gap further.

CONCLUSION

This analysis has focused on the different meaning that advertising has for incumbents and challengers. The prism has been the competitive, marginally competitive, and noncompetitive Indiana districts whose advertising appeared in the 1984 ad sample. The overall difficulty of using advertising to overcome such incumbent advantages as congressional communications, press coverage, and fund-raising is manifest, along with the incentive for increased levels of costly attack advertising in challenger campaigns.

Both of the unsuccessful Indiana challengers of the "safe" incumbents, Art Smith and Joe Watkins, were aware of their potential funding requirements and so decided not to run again in 1986. The third challenger, Ken MacKenzie, who came close to defeating an incumbent in a competitive district, made the same decision. He also followed classic political advertising theory, which involves successive stages in the use of political advertising beginning positively, focusing heavily on the issues that divide the candidates, and only later moving into negative advertising. From this race, the lesson could be drawn that more emotional and entertaining early negative advertising—that is, soft-sell negative advertising—would be used early in future campaigns.

Analysis of the 1984 ad sample indicates that there was greater use of negative advertising among challengers than incumbents; it also underscored the fact that attack advertising developed by the Republican party can be very significant. Still, for a variety of reasons including stylistic ones relating to such questions as dovetailing, incumbents could localize the race. And although most emerged considerably more bloodied in a "nationalized" year such as 1984 than in the "localized" year 1986, when all party efforts were put into such things as computer targeting, not television advertising, they could still win reelection in most cases.

This analysis indicates that part of what is happening is that classic theory has cracked. "Endangered" incumbents, even those little disposed to use negative advertising, "return fire with fire." Theory has been confirmed concerning the greater need by challengers for negative advertising, but the competitive race picked up in the 1984 ad sample indicates that an incumbent, if heavily challenged, will use heavy negative advertising. In short, this study has found that advertising is being used in new ways in the 1980s and has isolated some of the obstacles to its use in an issues-oriented fashion and in relation to efforts to use party advertising to nationalize elections. The analysis turns to other new ways that advertising is being used in the 1980s, moving from America's heartland to its southland.

NOTES

1. See Edie N. Goldenberg and Michael W. Traugott, "The Information Environment," *Campaigning for Congress* (Washington, D.C.: Congressional Quarterly Press, 1984), pp. 109–124. Their analysis is based on political advertising expenditures in competitive and noncompetitive 1978 congressional races.

2. For the presidential level see Anne Johnston Wadsworth and Lynda Lee Kaid, "Incumbent and Challenger Styles in Presidential Advertising," paper presented at the International Communication Association Convention, Montreal, May 1987.

3. See the theory of consecutive stages, outlined in Diamond and Bates and examined in Chapter 2, and Larry Sabato, "The Media Masters," in *The Rise of the Political Consultants: New Ways of Winning Elections* (New York: Basic Books, 1981).

4. Interview with Ed Blakely, director of broadcast services, National Republican Congressional Committee, Washington, D.C., February 8, 1985.

5. Blakely interview. Cf. Larry Sabato's conclusion that there is some evidence that the negative barrage of television commercials has helped to reduce voter turnout in a number of specific cases. Larry Sabato, "TV Politics: the Influence of Television in Political Campaigns," *Vital Issues* 32 (October 1982): pp. 1–4. See also Chapter 1.

6. Schwartz as quoted in Sabato, *Rise of the Political Consultants,* p. 140.

7. Blakely interview. Michael Pfau and Michael Burgoon, "Inoculation in Political Campaign Communication," *Human Communication Research* 15, no. 1 (Fall 1988): 91–111.

8. See Tables A.2 and A.3, Appendix B.

9. The 1984 races in which advertising figured, and whose ads were picked up in the sample, were the following: In the Piedmont, Fifth District incumbent Stephen Neal over Stuart Epperson, 54–46 percent; Sixth District challenger Howard Coble over Robin Britt, 51–49 percent. In Indiana, Second District incumbent Philip R. Sharp over Ken MacKenzie 54–46 percent; Seventh District incumbent John Myers over Art Smith, 67–32 percent; Tenth District incumbent Andy Jacobs over Joseph Watkins, 59–41 percent.

10. See Chapter 3.

11. Interview with David Iles, Ken MacKenzie's campaign manager, Lafayette, Indiana, July 24, 1985.

12. Interview with Ken MacKenzie, Muncie, Indiana, July 24, 1985.

13. "Hound Dog" is a soft-sell negative ad of the absentee variety described in Chapter 5. It combines a "record" dimension with a light-hearted but sharp attack on candidate integrity.

14. Iles interview; Interview with Brian Francisco, reporter, *Muncie Star,* July 24, 1985.

15. Francisco interview, West Lafayette, Indiana.

16. MacKenzie interview, Muncie, Indiana.

17. Ibid.; Interview with Steve Nix, Washington, D.C., August 5, 1985.

18. MacKenzie, Nix, and Iles interviews.

19. MacKenzie interview, Muncie, Indiana.

20. Nix interview; interview with Republican party chairman Gorden Durnil, July 19, 1985; interview with Democratic State Committee Chairman Larry McKee, July 21, Indianapolis.

21. Iles interview; MacKenzie for Congress Committee press release, November 1, 1986.

22. Blakely interview.

23. See Chapter 3.

24. Interview with William Greener, director of communications, Republican National Committee, Washington, D.C. July 17, 1985.

25. MacKenzie interview, Muncie, Indiana.

26. See Chapter 7.

27. Interview with John Franzen, Executive Director, Democratic Media Center (Harriman Communications Center), Washington, D.C., March 5, 1985; speech by Gary Nordlinger at the American University School of Communications, November, 1984. For an analysis of the comparable Stephen Neal race, see Chapter 9. Comparable incumbent difficulties occurred in races from California to Colorado and West Virginia.

28. MacKenzie interview.

29. Brian Francisco, "Sharp, MacKenzie Spar over PAC's," *Muncie Star,* October 3, 1984, pp. 1–3.

30. MacKenzie interview.

31. MacKenzie interview. Michael Pfau and Michael Burgoon, "Inoculation in Political Campaign Communication," *Human Communication Research* 15, no. 1 (Fall 1988): pp. 91–111.

32. Francisco, "Sharp, MacKenzie Spar."

33. Ibid.

34. Democratic challenger Gerald Johnson in Atlanta experienced similar difficulties. Interview with Gerald Johnson, Atlanta, Georgia, March 8, 1985.

35. Interview with Art Watkins's campaign manager, Joe Smith, Indianapolis, Indiana, July 23, 1985.

36. Interviews with Art Watkins on July 22, 1985 and Joe Smith, campaign manager for Art Watkins Congressional race, Indianapolis, Indiana, July 23, 1985. See also "Watkins' 84 Campaign: Post-Election Analysis" and "Campaign Plan 1986," unpublished documents.

37. Joe Smith interview, July 23, 1985, the day after he met with Watkins to discuss these reports.

38. Interviews with Jim Cox, *Lafayette Journal-Courier,* Lafayette, Indiana, July 26, 1985, and Jan Faker, Art Smith's press secretary, Monticello, Indiana, July 28, 1985.

39. Interview with Art Smith, West Lafayette, Indiana, July 26, 1985.

40. Ibid.

41. Interview with James W. Beatty, member, Andrew Jacobs Campaign Committee, Indianapolis, July 22, 1985. Interview with Andrew Jacobs, Washington, D.C., February 27, 1985.

42. Interview with Ron Hardman, campaign manager and administrative assistant for Congress John Myers, R-Indiana, Washington, D.C., March 4, 1985. Hardman said 80

percent of the voters, unassisted, knew Myers was their congressman in an early campaign poll. "Teeter was amazed," he said, "because this was one of the highest name recognition figures in the country."

43. At the time of the November 1984 election there was one vacant House seat caused by the death of a Republican member. The GOP held onto that seat. Thus their gain could variously be described as 14 or 15 members.

44. Quoted in *Congressional Quarterly,* November 17, 1984, p. 2979. David W. Brady of Stanford University has pointed out that the percentage of competitive House seats defined narrowly as those with elections resolved by margins of 5 percentage points or less fell from 39.2 percent in 1860 and 34.5 percent in 1896 to 15.7 percent or 64 seats in 1980. In his view, this sharp drop in the twentieth century has made it impossible for the Republicans to gain control without a shift in their support of well over 5 percent. "House Democrats Called Bar to Realignment," *Washington Post,* September 15, 1987, p. A13.

45. *Federal Election Commission Report on Financial Activity, 1983–84: Party and Non-Party Political Committees* (Washington, D.C., GPO, 1985).

46. For analysis of "incumbent power" see Gary Jacobson, "The Incumbency Factor," *The Politics of Congressional Elections* (New York, Little, Brown, 1983), pp. 25–37. See also Edie N. Goldenberg and Michael W. Traugott *Campaigning for Congress* (Washington, D.C., 1984). The $1 million figure was an estimate by Michael Malbin, *Wall Street Journal,* September 24, 1986.

47. Peter Clarke and Susan H. Evans *Covering Campaigns: Journalism in Congressional Elections* (Stanford, Calif., 1983).

48. Franzen interview.

9

To Make a House Race Competitive: Ads in Southern Political Cultures

What role is played by a congressional candidate's record in the electoral process? A recent study indicated that from 1974 to 1984 the greatest number of well-financed and therefore competitive challenges develop when an incumbent's voting record is either more liberal or more conservative than his or her district. Given that the Democrats control the House and that the fund-raising community that finances challenges against them is predominantly conservative, a Democratic congressman or congresswoman would appear to run the greatest risk of being seriously challenged when his or her voting record is more liberal than that of the district he or she represents. In the sample of 1984 ads that appeared on the air during the final days of the 1984 election, three southern Democrats had moved to the right while in office, but this was not enough to stave off well-funded challenges to them in 1984.[1]

The hypothesis explored in this chapter is this: Early televised advertising is being used by challengers in districts in which an incumbent is potentially vulnerable for the purpose of getting news coverage that contributes to the success of fund-raising efforts and thereby helps make the race competitive. The use of advertising in the three races closely examined in this chapter suggests that competitiveness may develop in ways that have less to do with actual voting records, particularly with regard to economic issues, than with the ability of a challenger to break an incumbent's communications advantage. In two very different types of districts and media markets, one in the Atlanta suburbs and the other in the North Carolina Piedmont, political advertising played an important role in this process.

In each instance, spot advertising began early in the campaign, before the challenger had the money necessary to finance the entire race. As the campaign manager for one successful challenger put it afterward, "We risked everything on those ads." The ads, however, did not follow the classic pattern of challenger advertising suggested in the last chapter, starting with name recognition built through spot advertising. Instead, they were designed to serve two major objectives.

The first, implemented early in the race, involved the use of attention-getting negative ads to attract news media attention. This involved an attack on the incumbent for a connection with an issue or personality that was "hot" in the local political marketplace because it echoed deeply felt aspects of the voter's cultural and personal experience.

Through this connection with a controversy that had local significance, the race emerged as a subject of news interest, creating what has been called a media permutation. This meant that a challenger whose race became a topic of discussion and whose name was accordingly recognized by substantially more people was transformed from a visible candidate to a competitive candidate, and thus successful fund-raising became possible. More money could then be spent on campaign organization, advertising, and other efforts to advance his candidacy. In the newly competitive environment, according to campaign polls reported in this chapter, as the result of attack advertising and press discussion of a real "race," "soft" supporters of the incumbent joined the ranks of the "undecided" and were ready to listen to reasons to vote either against the incumbent or for the challenger.[2]

At that point the second stage of major advertising could begin. For Republican challengers, blessed in 1984 with a popular national ticket, that second phase was spelled "coattails." This article of clothing was particularly important in the South, where increasing numbers were expected to vote a straight Republican ticket, and where, with favorable Republican or Reagan percentages running at over 65 percent, heavy use was made first of Reagan-Bush and then of generic Republican advertising.[3]

Republican congressional challengers in 1984 suffered from the fact that their message, which of necessity sought to get the voters to throw the rascals out, ran counter to the "good feeling" message of the presidential advertising. This was less true in the case of races included in the Southern portion of the 1984 ad sample, however. This included the presidential level. In the more competitive, southern portion of the ad sample fully 10 percent of the ads cut by incumbent president Reagan were negative and thus more closely attuned to a total southern media environment that was both more negative and competitive, with a greater number of seat turnovers, than other regions.[4]

MORE NEGATIVE ADS THAN EXPECTED

Over half of the Republican congressional challenger ads, in terms both of total numbers and time aired, were still coded as negative in the 1984 ad sample, despite theory suggesting that toward the end of a race the candidate should come on with positive advertising to give voters an affirmative reason to vote in his favor. Interestingly, also despite theory that negative advertising turns voters away, these areas of heavy negative advertising also drew a heavy turnout of voters, suggesting that such advertising in and of itself does not reduce voter participation. In both Georgia and North Carolina, intense grassroots activity also occurred during the campaign by religious groups to whom some of the early advertising was directed.[5]

This chapter examines how challengers used advertising in races in this competitive atmosphere in both medium and large media markets. These included incumbent North Carolina congressman Robin Britt from the Sixth District and Stephen Neal from the Fifth District as well as Elliott Levitas from the Fourth District of Georgia. Neal and Levitas not only had considerable seniority but were important subcommittee chairmen as well.

The Neal case illustrates what happened in the South and elsewhere where challengers used early media to make the race competitive and also where incumbents under such heavy fire employed their own negative response advertising.[6]

The situations in the Levitas and Britt cases were more complex. Both, however, are classic examples of the type of Democratic incumbent to which the minority Republican party has devoted considerable attention in recent years: the "dinosaur" and the "freshman." In both cases, the hope is that the incumbent will lose votes through the failure of some crucial part of the mix necessary to develop and nourish contact with his or her constituents. "Dinosaur," the almost affectionate term of the game-hunter for his prey, is the description Ed Blakely of the National Republican Congressional Committee applied to candidates with the appearance but not the reality of invulnerability. The "freshman," of course, is presumed to have relatively shallow electoral support. These races tell us that both "dinosaur" and "freshman" vulnerability must be assessed not solely in terms of voting records, constituent services, or trips back to the district, but in a campaign communications dimension as well.[7]

Levitas was certainly what Blakely would describe as a "dinosaur." By 1984 he had been in Washington for ten years, where he had developed a reputation as a prickly fighter and an effective legislator, a major force on both the House Government Operations Committee and the Committee on Public Works and Transportation. Levitas had recently uncovered evidence of political manipulation in the hazardous waste disposal grant program administered by the Environmental Protection Agency (EPA), a disclosure that led to a much-publicized contempt-of-Congress citation and forced resignation of administrator Anne Gorsuch. This and other examples of his national role, such as his contribution to airline deregulation and the legislative veto issue, were not mentioned in the 1984 ad sample. They focused instead on a side of the congressman that was in fact increasingly rare in the district: the incumbent finding time to "press the flesh" with constituents in an Atlanta shopping center and to stroll leisurely along the Chattahoochee River on land that he had helped acquire for a public park.

Robin Britt, the "freshman" incumbent from Greensboro, North Carolina, could hardly have been more different. He had been in office for only one term and, according to his campaign manager, had not yet found a way to become an effective congressional leader. Yet voters who received their information from their respective campaign advertising on local television would hardly have been able to distinguish between the two incumbents in terms of their seniority and accomplishments.[8]

The two men represented opposites, the large urban fringe district versus the mixed industrial and rural district, vast experience versus relative inexperience. Their televised message, however, was the same: caring for constituents as the benevolent leader. And the focus of the initial referential ads used against each of them to "make the race competitive" was similarly interchangeable, not dealing with experience but touching underlying feelings relating to gender and "real" southern folks whose lifestyles are clearly quite distinct from those of the liberal tax raisers "up North."

MEDIA AND COMPETITIVENESS IN A MAJOR MARKET AREA

In general, little advertising was used by congressional candidates in the major market areas in the study, because of the cost of paying for market saturation in districts other than one's own. Still, incumbents raise the money to pay for such advertising, if need arises. Generally, there was little advertising and little competitiveness in the major market areas in California and Georgia. One race was an exception, however. It was the 1984 race of Atlanta incumbent Elliot Levitas, which raised questions about the implications for incumbents of running for office in a costly media environment. It also raised questions about the as yet unexamined potentially differing perspectives about the role of televised news and advertising between a candidate and his pollster and media consultant.

Levitas was considered to be a "safe" incumbent because he had won his last three elections by over two-thirds of the vote, and because his spring polls registered comfortably above 60 percent favorable. As a result of the 1980 census he had lost a substantial part of his Democratic in-town Atlanta base, however, and acquired Republican territory in the suburbs to the east of the city. He generally did not begin his campaign, including his fund-raising activities, until September in an election year. In 1984, his first ads appeared in October after polls indicated that his support had declined to 59 percent immediately after Labor Day, in early September, and, most surprisingly, to around 51 percent by October 1. In the second poll, Levitas was perceived by a growing number of voters as "remote."[9]

Candidate Versus Consultant Views

Levitas's campaign manager, Tim Ryles, said after the election that the candidate had fallen victim to self-inflicted wounds because he was unwilling to raise money to buy ads that would "cocoon" him by starting in May-June, continuing with a round in August, and closing with a spurt during the last ten days before the election. With such early cocooning, according to Ryles, the challenger's attacks, when they came, would be considered desperate. Indeed, recent academic research has confirmed the value of such early advertising efforts.[10]

But, according to Ryles, speaking in early 1985,

If [in the Atlanta market] you don't have $400,000 or a candidate putting forth his own money, you can't do it. . . . Levitas's problem was that he wouldn't ask for money. The candidate is the principal fund-raiser. If a candidate wants the money, he'll get it. He's in a position to do favors, in a powerful position and people need access to him. With Levitas's voting record, he should have gotten millions. Look at liberal Wyche Fowler [from the adjacent Fifth District, who ran successfully for the Senate in 1986]. He's sitting on $300,000 after the election. Levitas had no finance chairman the whole time. That is extraordinary in the annals of American politics.[11]

Levitas failed the war chest test, which provided an incentive and an apparent opportunity for those considering funding a serious challenge to him. In April 1984, he had only $35,000 in the bank, and he did not start his fund-raising efforts until the fall.

From the candidate's perspective, however, the extensive coverage he received in Atlanta's newspapers for his legislative role in Washington and for the issues colloquia that he chaired in the district provided adequate evidence that he was "safe." Levitas's record did in fact conform with that of his increasingly conservative district. Although he had begun as a liberal "Watergate baby" in 1974, his voting record had become progressively more conservative. Yet in the end he lost, 53–47, to Patrick Swindall, a 34-year-old attorney and furniture store owner who had never held public office, but who ran on a Christian morality platform with the grassroots support of fundamentalist churches. Four years later Swindall lost his seat following news media exposure of his negotiations for a home loan reportedly funded with money from illegal drug and gambling activities.[12]

Levitas believed the main reason for his loss in 1984 was Ronald Reagan and the Republican ticket, as well as the unpopularity of the Democratic ticket with which he was successfully linked, "thanks to the half million which the Republicans put into the effort, which was too much for my $70,000 salary."[13]

Much of the $382,557 spent by Levitas and the $535,729 spent by Swindall went into television advertising as the battle for the Fourth District took to the airwaves. For Levitas, the advertising

played a major role. It established the idea that in certain types of media markets where TV plays a substantial role, the imagery became the relevant thing rather than the reading of the incumbent's record.

The campaign took on a momentum of its own. I was highly visible, through newspapers, television, town meetings, and newsletters. At some point, I began to think, overly visible. But the public's mind is short, and all of the things I had done became irrelevant, and what was important became the campaign.[14]

The effect of television's growing role in politics, Levitas further believed, is a separation between what you do in office and the campaign process.

This divorces people from what happens in Congress, as what you have to do to succeed in an election is irrelevant to the office. The public picks up not on the substance of the congressman's record, but on its portrayal.[15]

Levitas also believed that the news media did not perform responsibly. This was true, not of newspapers, which "no one reads," but of television. In his view, television should go beyond "here's one charge and here's the other" to provide analysis of the news, and it should report what is true about a candidate's record. Although this happened in the print media, it did not on television.

Overall, in the 1984 sample of ads and news, articulation of congressional issues took place largely in slogan ads, and in an Atlanta television news environment that did not focus on issue-related arguments. Such news stories may well have come earlier in the race, of course. But the political ads consumed more television time than the political news in the 1984 sample, an indication that ads rather than news set the image as well as the issues agenda during the final period of the race. Levitas argued that such an imbalance had existed for some time, since his entry into the campaign in the fall, and that local television news *should* examine the issues that are raised in ads, particularly those that purport to represent an incumbent's record. Local news, he felt, should take some responsibility for determining the accuracy of charges that appear in negative ads.[16]

This should, he argued, take place in relation to his voting record—specifically the charge that "I had voted like a liberal. I don't think my responses were adequately and fully reported." His campaign manager Tim Ryles believed, however, that Levitas's views, expressed strongly to television reporters during the latter part of the campaign, were evidence that he had grown accustomed to national press coverage while in Washington. His strong articulation to local reporters of how they should cover stories only alienated them. "The national press will undertake analysis of candidates' records," Ryles argued. "Local reporters, with whose routines he [Levitas] had lost touch, rarely do."[17]

Overall, Levitas believed that his voting record was distorted by the Pat Swindall campaign. His record was a conservative one, but he was, according to both sides, successfully linked with his party's liberal leaders, including Walter Mondale, Tip O'Neill, and the increasingly controversial vice-presidential candidate Geraldine Ferraro.

From the perspective of the Republicans, Levitas was a prime target. As a prominent Democratic member of the House who had opposed many administration initiatives and helped force out the EPA director, Anne Gorsuch, national Republicans could rally around the idea of toppling him. According to Swindall's final campaign manager, Rob Austin, there were also polls indicating that although people kept voting for him, Levitas in their opinion had gone "punchy." His district was thus targeted by the NRCC, and Swindall received the $42,000 available in such cases along with $39,497 in coordinated party expenditures and an assigned NRCC strategist who specialized in southern races and stopped in to advise the campaign every week to ten days. He also received the $10,000 maximum from the local Republican party, whose chairman, Robert Bell, said that Swindall was a "model candidate." Such funding enabled the Swindall campaign to secure the services of New York consultant Roger Ailes, the Republicans' hard-hitting media strategist. Ailes's entry into the race caused Levitas's Atlanta-based media consultant, William Pope, to remark that "I knew we were meeting the devil . . . That man carries a scalpel."[18]

In Pat Swindall, the Republicans had a candidate who was manifestly inexperienced, but, according to Pope, this may even have been an advantage in the video age. He had no record and was accordingly invulnerable to advertising attacks on his legislative consistency or past positions on public policy. Further, the challenger had worked and organized successfully at the grassroots level long before local or national Republicans gave him a dime. This contrasted sharply with the style of Levitas, who remained largely in Washington until Congress finished its work in early October, and whose reluctance that fall to "press the flesh" or show up at campaign headquarters caused Democratic party faithful and his own consultants to compare his style unfavorably with that of Swindall.[19]

The Significance of Advertising

Tim Ryles, who had worked for Levitas since he first won election in 1974, believed his defeat was "political euthanasia." He had "gotten tired. Something had happened to him between 1982 and 1984." As for fund-raising, Ryles said he raised the issue with Levitas in April, arguing that the congressman should immediately raise $350,000, at least a third of which should go into early "cocooning" ads. At that meeting, said Ryles, "people looked around and said no way did they want to raise that money and even one of Levitas's best friends said maybe it was best for Elliott to hang it up. The outcome was predictable and preventable."[20]

According to media consultant Pope, in the absence of an overall budget there was no indication of where the money was going to come from for the ads that were decided upon after the October poll. "I was in despair. It was a hurry-up, rush job," said Pope of "Chattahoochee," which was produced just before the last week of the campaign. "Thank God, the weather was good."[21]

After the election, Levitas's advisors agreed with the Republicans that he had indeed "gone Washington" and did not take the task of campaigning seriously. This was because he had rarely faced a significant challenge. The consequence of this was deplorable, and evident early on to Ryles, who after the 1982 campaign had delegated to Levitas's office the responsibility for maintaining a phone bank of 500 precinct volunteers who had put up yard signs and were to be "massaged" over the next two years. They were to be the "infantry" in 1984; but when Ryles came back to work with the campaign and asked for the list, he found that no one had been contacted. "When calls were made people said, 'Where have you been?' They were mad at being ignored and called on only every two years. At that point, some had already been contacted by Swindall. There was nothing to work with. You need connecting rods in a campaign." [22]

For their part, Democratic officials in the Fourth District felt no enthusiasm for Levitas, who had become more conservative than the local activists. They believed Levitas had taken them for granted because the more liberal elements of the party, who had originally helped elect him, had no place to go. They had protested his "devotion to the Reagan budget" and felt he had lost touch. According to Gary Leshaw, chairman of the Democratic Party of De Kalb, "when he called at the end of the campaign and said, 'I need some people to put up yard signs,' it was the first time in two years." Had they believed he would lose, however, they would have made an effort to find more volunteers. But the local Democrats did not believe Elliott Levitas would lose. The election outcome, however, proved to be 53–47 for Swindall, a catastrophic shift of 18 percent of the vote away from Levitas since his 1982 reelection with 65 percent of the vote. According to Bill Lewis, Democratic member of the county election board and a party statistician, "I thought it would have been that [close as the election came down to the wire], but the other way." He attributed 2 to 3 percent to "the Republican stuff" but the other 3 percent to Levitas's lack of personal charisma and organization. [23]

Yard signs are a tradition in Atlanta, and, said Ryles, Swindall had them on every street in the district. Although electronic media are important, Ryles was convinced that "a campaign requires targeted direct mail, yard signs, billboards, telephones, door-to-door and person-to-person contact, which creates an image of a person. Direct mail is critically important. Levitas didn't do much. But Swindall did." [24]

It thus was not just the electronic advertising that was perceived to be important in the race. But when Levitas did get around to desperate home-stretch fund-raising, which brought in one-half of his total campaign budget of $382,000 in the month of October, many of the funds were spent on the electronic media, beginning with radio and then going to his television ads, which ran twice as heavily in the 1984 sample as those of Swindall. Ideally, despite the view that the television advertising dollar is wasted in a large market area, according to Pope, in an area such as Atlanta half of one's budget would go for television, 20 percent for direct mail, and 30 percent for radio. By this point the mix was becoming irrelevant, however, for Levitas had been brought to what Ryles called a state of collapse.[25]

In enumerating the reasons for his candidate's success, the successful Swindall campaign manager, Rob Austin, listed Levitas's "punchiness" and his challenger's early grassroots efforts, along with "the fact that [Swindall] was young, energetic, a success, and a born-again Christian. This was very much in tune with his district."[26]

Nonetheless, Austin believed that the television advertising was crucial. Indeed, the candidate would have lost without it. This is because even though voters had not paid much attention to the incumbent for some time, they would nevertheless have voted for him. According to Austin:

Our job was to make a race of it. . . . People don't naturally think about congressional races. Their minds are on whether they're going to get their grandmother to the doctor, or their trip to the grocery store or the kids. We had to get them to talk about the race. It had to be the 'in thing' to be aware of.[27]

How did one bring the race to the consciousness of voters who are otherwise so preoccupied with their personal concerns?

Stage One: Raising Money and Voter Consciousness

Quite specifically, according to Austin, this was done by means of a television ad that compared Levitas with Geraldine Ferraro. "She was new and interesting." It was an ad that ran from September 25 to October 8, an attack spot, which linked Levitas's voting record with Ferraro's and followed a "powerful" 30-second radio ad, appropriate to the large market area, which ran heavily throughout September at less cost. It said the race

in the Fourth Congressional District is about the issue of taxes. You can vote for Mondale, who is for higher taxes, or you can vote for Swindall, who is for lower taxes. You can vote for Mondale, who opposes the balanced budget amendment, or you can vote for Swindall, who supports the balanced budget amendment. Levitas supports Mondale. Swindall supports Reagan.[28]

Levitas charged at the time, and again in a later interview, that neither this radio ad nor the Ferraro-linkage spot "were within the legitimate range of campaign exaggeration. . . . These types of things, said about anyone to their detriment would otherwise be actionable." Concerning the relationship between his record and that of Ferraro, Levitas said:

We took Gerry Ferraro's ratings by four of the interest groups—two conservative and two liberal. It was ADA 90 percent for Ferraro, I was 25 percent. COPE 100, I was 45. ACU I was high and she was not on the scale. . . . By the interest group standard our records were miles apart.

The correlation was based on the fact that there are a number of noncontroversial votes. If there was a 70 percent correlation with Ferraro in my case, Ferraro correlated with Jack Kemp and Newt Gingrich in 60-plus percent of the cases.[29]

Concerning the linkage with Mondale's tax position, Levitas declared, ''I went to San Francisco to be there and disavow it.''

Levitas saw a cultural undertone to the Ferraro linkage ad. She was a New York liberal, and

it was called to my attention that ''New York liberal'' means Jewish. New York is a Jewish city, its mayor is Jewish, and it has an active, visible Jewish population. When I had voted against the congressional bailout for New York City, people said they liked this.[30]

Supporting this, in Levitas's view, was the Swindall campaign's use of the slogan He Is One of Us. Further, there was the kind of woman Ferraro was, associated not only with the feminist movement but with unpopular national Democrats. She was viewed as an ''abrasive woman, flip, testy and very liberal. The connection which the advertising made with her was not just the Equal Rights Amendment and abortion.'' Ed Blakely of the NRCC believed the linkage with Ferraro was not a matter of gender but with a ''liberal from New York.''[31]

There were also ads that linked Levitas directly with Tip O'Neill, ''just a politician'' ads charging that the congressman talked one way in the district and voted differently in Congress.

According to Swindall's campaign manager, Rob Austin:

When [Levitas] said we were lying, we saw no need to respond. He was supporting Mondale. He had a difficult choice: not to do so, but he didn't take this. He also did vote for higher taxes in 1983—a $40 billion tax package. We never said ''personal taxes.'' We said ''higher taxes.'' There were also 30 balanced-budget amendments that he didn't vote for.[32]

Austin said it didn't matter what Levitas said because people did not read the newspaper stories that reported his response and, in the case of editorials, supported Levitas's view that his record had been distorted because a number of ''balanced-budget votes had been contrived'' and conservatives, including Ronald Reagan, had voted for or signed the bills favoring the ''higher taxes'' that served as the basis for the charge that he was a liberal.

To counter the impact [of the ads] he would have had to use a similar response on television. . . . With our communication structure, it didn't matter what [Levitas] said. People didn't see a liar, a right-wing nut. [In Swindall] they saw a hard-working, attractive candidate in tune with the district.[33]

The Swindall communication structure was one of reinforcement of the advertising. "Everything we did on TV or radio was reinforced through direct mail. . . . We were trying to reach through direct mail everyone we couldn't reach through personal appearances on the part of the candidate."[34]

By the time of Levitas's October 1 poll, which came at midpoint in Swindall's Levitas-Ferraro referential advertising effort, and followed equally tough September radio ads, Levitas had plummeted from around 59 percent favorable just before Labor Day to 51 percent to Swindall's 36 percent. Further, of the 51 percent who still favored Levitas, according to Ryles, 42 percent indicated that their support of the incumbent was "soft." The consultants' polls indicated a large movement of voters from Levitas's column into the ranks of the soft and undecided.[35]

This movement illustrated the role that early negative advertising, reinforced by other means of communication, can play in making a race competitive in terms of opinion polls that play a major role not only in relation to voter consciousness but in the area of campaign fund-raising efforts as well.

On the question of the ethics of Swindall's ads, the views of his pollster, Claiburn Darden, differed from those of the candidate. Youthful and photogenic, Darden is a successful commercial pollster, whose "Poll of the South" made the 1984 national news during the blitz. Darden said he concentrates on commercial clients because they pay their bills, but he works for a few political campaigns "willing to pay my rate of $250 per hour." In his view, the Swindall's referential negative ads "might've been cheap shots, but who says there aren't those in politics." In campaigns

there are only three things: emotion, emotion, and emotion. What's in fourth place doesn't count. And that's how we start off a candidate. Use facts to create emotion. Everything we deal with is emotion, aimed at that middle class.

In an ad you want to say things that make sense, and you can make things up about an opponent through inference. Every piece is correct, but the average person says, "There's something wrong here."[36]

The purpose of ads, including those used by Swindall, is not, in Darden's view, that of defining serious differences between the candidates. "The whole thing is strategy—getting your opponent on the defensive. Once that is done, you can defeat him." Most significantly, Darden believed, Swindall's radio ads took *crucial segments of the voting population not only into a state of increased awareness, but they also prompted a change of attitude.*

The person who makes $12,000 or under and drives around with a gun in a pick-up truck makes the difference. This voter will not be aware of quite a few details of policy. According to a poll taken a year and a half ago, one-half the adult southern population didn't know who the vice-president was.[37]

The Swindall ads were directed to voters, focusing on the attitudinal area of identification or empathy. They

isolated the vote that might believe that Levitas didn't represent the people of his district, and if you tell them that enough, they'll start to believe it—until it's combated. It's like the "big lie." Repetition is the key. Why do people believe the Bible? Because it's repeated again and again.[38]

Empathy and Allegory—Not Issues

Tim Ryles, Levitas's campaign manager, also believed the issue was in the area of empathy or identification, not how Levitas voted on the issues. Unlike the congressman who believed that a vote on the Hill *should* make a difference in a campaign, Ryles asked who cares about a vote. "When does a vote make that much difference, anyway?" What was projected by the Ferraro linkage ad was an *image of a lifestyle* that conflicted with that of the district's voters. "Levitas's problem was that he tried to analyze it [in issues terms]. That doesn't work. People see the linkage, and they say Levitas-Ferraro. And Ferraro was not well liked."[39]

The congressman and his consultants agreed, however, that images about which voters held strong feelings—whether of "pushy" women or "New York liberals"—were significant, whether or not that should be the case in an ideal world.

According to FEC reports, Swindall raised $26,725 in personal contributions and $19,900 in PAC contributions during the July 26 to August 26 period before he began his radio and television ads. After he began stage one—fundraising and consciousness raising—his receipts increased to a total of $318,374 reported in the forms filed for the three reporting periods that ran for the entire July 23 to November 26 period. His expenditures from July 26 to August 26 were $4,000 to Roger Ailes, with $4,115 for postage (spent from July 26 to September 14). He paid Ailes $8,000 on September 19. On September 25 he paid $25,266 for radio and TV time, and again $17,368 in radio time for a three-week run for the September 26–October 17 period. His expenditures for all forms of communication rose greatly after that time.

Stage Two: Swaying "Soft" Voters

By October voters were believed to be ready for the second stage of the advertising campaign. It involved giving "undecideds" and "soft" Levitas supporters reasons to vote against the incumbent and for Swindall. In 1984 such an effort would involve primarily "coattails," which was effective in the campaign's view because the preceding stage had given voters the idea that there was a choice. Consciousness had been raised to the effect that there were two candidates. "So when people came to focus on it, during the last days,"

Austin said, "they were ready for the message which we repeated again and again: Swindall-Reagan, Levitas-Mondale, Taxes–No Taxes. That's what the last few days were all about."[40]

In driving this message home, according to Austin, the Swindall forces were aided by a variety of factors, including Vice-President George Bush's personal campaign efforts. But linkage with the overall Reagan-Bush and Republican-dominated television-message environment was critically important. This included the generic congressional ads, "all the talk of a [presidential] landslide in the [news] media," and "the feelings associated with Reagan's advertising."[41]

Further, the campaign's referential Reagan endorsement ad was allegorical and translated the national effort into recognizable local symbols. In "The Touch," a positive intergenerational bonding ad focusing on hope which ran heavily in the 1984 ad sample, the youthful Pat Swindall was linked with Reagan through a ritual, the laying on of hands. This ritual was as old as religious faith and as new as a South that values continuity and interpersonal relations. On that afternoon in Washington when a group of challengers filed through the White House to pose with Ronald Reagan, the Swindall strategists asked the president to touch the challenger's arm. He agreed, and so raised the character side of the Swindall message to a new symbolic level.[42]

Levitas received no help from the Democratic party, however. Ironically, Tip O'Neill, with whom Levitas was successfully linked in Swindall's negative advertising, refused the Democratic incumbent's desperate last-minute fund-raising request because, according to the candidate, "the campaign had not been labeled 'doubtful.' "[43]

The period of the 1984 ad sample saw Levitas enact consultant Claiburn Darden's rule: *If you can throw a campaign on the defensive with the help of an ad campaign, you can beat it.* With the campaign's October 1 polls favoring Levitas by only 51 percent and with 42 percent of those "soft," a reassessment was necessary. Because of redistricting resulting from the 1980 census, in 1984 there were more Republicans in Levitas's district and fewer blacks than in previous years who had regularly voted Democratic. To win, Levitas would thus have to bring 14,000 *new voters* into his column, and the floating voters were there, 30,000 of them, in De Kalb county, the heart of the district. In pollster Darden's view, they were "ready to be swayed by personality."[44]

NEGATIVE VERSUS POSITIVE ADVERTISING

What does one do under the circumstances? Should the incumbent attack the challenger, or should he run a positive ad such as "Chattahoochee"—a trust-building reassurance ad that would connect Levitas with feelings associated with a local scenic landmark—to compensate the image of "remoteness" that was turning up in the polls following the opponent's negative advertising. It was an image that would dovetail with strength, for he had in fact saved the river for ordinary citizens and been a major force behind its preservation. On the other hand, Darden argued that Swindall must be pushed to the radical right using negative advertising. This would be

hard to do. But Elliott told me Swindall said God told him to run for office. I told Elliott we ought to let a lot of folks know God told him to run. He should be wrapped around the religious right, which can be an albatross. A question was asked in the polls about how people felt about an endorsement by Jerry Falwell. Twenty to 25 percent of the people were opposed. It was bad—worse than an endorsement by Jesse Jackson.

But, instead, "there was Levitas [in the final advertising that appeared in the 1984 ad sample] picking up beer cans from the river and riding around in a Winnebago in a shopping center."[45]

Further, in Darden's view, damaging personal documents obtained from within the Swindall campaign should also have been released to "crack his born-again Christian stance. All you need is a little crack." When things go wrong, "there's only one way to bail out—break the integrity of your opponent. You can do this at the last minute, at the last second."[46]

William Pope, Levitas's media consultant, believed such information had already been shown to some individuals in the press, who were not interested, and that carrying such efforts further would be "perceived as a low blow. I've slung mud, but if you come out with it late, as Jimmy Carter did in 1980, you'll be perceived as a mudslinger. Mud has to be early and consistent." Pope added that by this time Swindall was perceived by voters as an attractive young man. An attack might seem unfair by Levitas, an older man. Further, he had no public record one *could* attack. "It's easy to recommend negative, when you don't have to stay around and face the consequences," said Pope. "Further," he said, "the money wasn't there. To respond to all of these charges, one by one, in 30 seconds, would cost a lot of money."[47]

Swindall instead charged that *Levitas* had traded a vote, his support for an administration bill to refinance the Kennedy Center, for a decision by the under secretary of the treasury to reverse his decision to attend a Swindall fund-raiser. After the undersecretary cancelled, Swindall called him, and the conversation, which was taped, seemed to confirm the charge. The Levitas campaign was already in trouble at this point, but Swindall's subsequent highly publicized charge that this example of "power brokering" constituted a "felony" delivered a further blow.

It was the challenger who attacked. The incumbent had no advertising response. He tried to turn the issue with a press conference alone. According to Ryles, its purpose was to go on the attack, to make an issue of Swindall's failure to pay income taxes. It produced two lengthy stories that appeared on Atlanta's Channel 5 and were covered in the 1984 sample. One focused on mudslinging but included nothing of the substance of Levitas's view concerning Swindall's interpretation of his record, and it made only passing reference to the Swindall income tax issue. This came out as Levitas saying he would release his tax return "if Swindall will." The reporter's analytical focus was on the horserace issue, which reflected poorly on the consistency of the Levitas image. The reporter stated that "he might say he expects to win by a comfortable margin, but he's campaigning and talking as if the race were a whole lot closer." [48]

The second story reran Swindall's tape, which provided "evidence" of the incumbent's vote swapping along with Levitas's "Goebbels-tactics" reply and the reporter's view that the campaign had shifted from issues to personalities when Swindall accused Levitas of vote swapping. The overall effect was to further circulate the vote-swapping charge. Ryles gave up on the campaign when Levitas withdrew a strong version of his nonpayment-of-taxes charge against Swindall, which was to be passed out at the press conference. Ryles believed this charge failed to shape the news media agenda in the news conference because he made his counterattack on Swindall, which supposedly related to the leadership quality of a man who failed to pay taxes, as "When I go to Washington, I'll make sure everyone pays their taxes." Perhaps equally problematical was that the charge was not made in a coordinated advertising and news attack, and thus according to the new theory of media usage. [49]

In any case, the final television news story about the race picked up in the 1984 sample indicated that it was Swindall who also defined the issues of the race covered in televised news as well as in advertising as questions such as taxes and abortion.

Alan Ehrenhalt, the *Congressional Quarterly* columnist, said in an interview that his biggest criticism of the current campaign process is that commitments on many important public policies are not enough a part of it. Elliot Levitas expressed this in his own way when he observed that a campaign can take on a life of its own that has little to do with the substance of a candidate's voting record. The 1984 campaign in the Fourth Congressional District of Georgia offered ample support for this point of view. Further, it demonstrates how a coordinated radio and television advertising strategy can be used to contribute to district competitiveness even in a major urban market. [50]

HARDBALL IN THE "AFFORDABLE" PIEDMONT

In 1984 the political guns volleyed and thundered all across North Carolina from Cherokee County to Albemarle Sound. When the smoke cleared from the battlefield in November, Jesse Helms had kept his Senate seat, the Republicans had captured the statehouse for the second time in this century, and the GOP had increased their House delegation from two to five. In no less than 6 of the 11 congressional districts the winner's margin was 51 percent or less, and 3 of those 6 were seats the GOP wrested from the Democratic incumbents.

Two of these competitive districts were in our ad sample, and televised advertising was heavy. One was that of Sixth District Democratic freshman incumbent Robin Britt, a 42-year-old from Greensboro, who was not a sequoia. His fall did not create nearly as great a crash in the political forest as did the defeat of Elliott Levitas. Nevertheless, his race raised many of the same questions: how to respond to challenger advertising that included a regional dimension and that sought to split the Democrats, rally conservatives from both parties, and in its first stage create news media coverage that would make the race competitive by building the challenger's name recognition and consequent fundraising potential?

The Sixth District is centered on Greensboro, a textile, manufacturing and banking center and the second-largest city in the state. It also includes the furniture manufacturing towns of High Point and Thomasville as well as diversified farming areas. Given Britt's inexperience, and Reagan's 62 percent landslide in the state, the incumbent congressman's heavy television expenditure could be perceived as almost snatching victory from inevitable defeat. As in the Levitas race, however, "winnability" as much as the substance of Britt's record (which was conservative) fueled the Republican challenge by Howard Coble, a state senator and lawyer. Britt's deficits included a "fuzzy" image, which taken together with the inherent possibilities of a "coattails year," helped inspire maximum Republican efforts.

Britt's "fuzziness" was caused by several factors, including his shift to the right during his own term in office. The congressman had decided, according to Doug Tanner, his local campaign manager, "to go for the white male business vote. We got it and raised a lot of money." But his original, more liberal supporters were alienated in the process, and his campaign "lost ground with senior citizens, women, and blue collar workers." Whether or not working-class Democrats were impressed by an ad that appeared in the 1984 sample showing the hard-hatted incumbent demonstrating his commitment to textile workers, many of his former foot-soldiers were not. It was, further, a candidate-centered appeal based on identity with an economic group and as such stood out in a year characterized by a decline in positive group-related appeals.[51]

CULTURAL CONNOTATIONS

Britt had also failed to use the communications advantages available to the congressional incumbent. He had even failed to get out a newsletter because, Tanner said, "things kept coming up and we wanted to include them." Furthermore, despite other candidate-related ads included in the 1984 sample ("My Decisions" and "Seen not Heard") that emphasized his independence and a leadership role which was unusual for a "freshman," he had not in fact developed such a role. Further, national exposure had muddied his image. The *New York Times* had run a picture of him asleep at a Harvard foreign policy seminar, and this was reprinted in the local papers. Challenger attack advertising using this image achieved additional resonance because it was based on the familiarity of a news story. There was also the implicit suggestion of North-South differences used to break the trust connection based on bonds of identity and empathy. What was Britt doing in Cambridge, Massachusetts, when he could have been in Washington working on behalf of his constituents? The overt message was, "When he isn't asleep, Congressman Britt is spending your tax money."[52]

The *New York Times* did not allow the challenger to use the actual photo from Harvard, but an actor playing Britt appeared asleep in a congressional committee hearing room. The truth was that Britt might have slept in Cambridge, but he worked hard in Washington. Gary Jacobsen has suggested that charges of absenteeism and neglect can normally be expected from necessarily opportunistic challengers, but that their appearance would be occasional because of the relative rarity of the behavior to which they refer. In 1984, there was ample indication that such charges could find new and creative visual expression and, if unanswered, take on a life of their own. This lesson would resonate for the remainder of the decade.[53]

Creative response did not characterize Britt's reelection effort. A consultant attuned to the unspoken North-South and Middle American message of the sleeping congressman ad might well have responded that Harvard was an *excellent* place to snooze, given the candidate's need to conserve energy for his work "minding the store." A Republican such as George Bush in 1988, who was advised by Roger Ailes, was quick to appeal to the very sort of cultural attitudes that make North Carolina's Sixth District so competitive; he termed his opponent's foreign policy as "bred in a Harvard Yard boutique." There, too, was almost certainly a humorous response that could be exploited to dispel the negative charge.

But the Britt campaign did not develop a humorous response to the Harvard seminar ad, nor any response at all to the "coattails" attack ads that followed as the campaign moved into its second stage. Particularly serious, according to Tanner, was Britt's failure to respond to his opponent's "$157 per month is what you save in taxes if you vote for Coble because Britt is linked with the Mondale tax plan" ad. Doug Tanner believed the problem was faulty polling data in the volatile district, a problem that had similarly afflicted the reelection campaign of Gene Johnston, the man Britt defeated in 1982.[54]

Tanner said they had a response to "$157 per month" in the can but "we didn't run it because our data said we didn't need to. In our polls he [Coble] never came over 40 percent. . . . The sample was skewed." The flaw lay in the fact that in 1984 the base of "likely voters" who were polled were those registered in 1980 and 1982. Not included in Britt's polling sample were white voters in Britt's largely white district who were activated in 1984 by conservative, Republican, and fundamentalist registration efforts. According to Lou Kitchen, Republican challenger Howard Coble's media consultant, 8 percent of the Sixth District opposed abortion. Such a polarizing television spot that focused on this issue early in the race could well be credited with assisting this new registration effort during stage one, as well as contributing to the campaign's fund-raising effort.[55]

AN AD FOR FUND- AND CONSCIOUSNESS RAISING

It was ironic that Coble, a bachelor in his 50s, emerged as a spokesman on the abortion issue. At the outset of the campaign, he was best known in the Greensboro newspapers for fiscal parsimony and his preference for weekends back home "squiring the ladies" far from the bright lights of Raleigh. His reputation as a budget-cutter had helped him win in a difficult Republican primary race against an ultraconservative Congressional Club candidate, and he was known for the "sharp pencil" he vowed to apply to the budget process in Washington.[56]

According to his campaign manager, Patrick Murphy, it was necessary to lead him kicking and screaming into the world of fund-raising. And money was desperately needed in the early summer. Coble's most urgent requirement was to reach Republicans through direct mail, since only 51 percent of them had supported him in the divisive GOP primary, and those who had voted for his erstwhile opponents were not coming home. According to Murphy, the campaign had to reach them by "wrapping itself in Ronald Reagan, who was getting 90 percent of the vote in the polls." Republicans, he said, should receive a letter from Reagan to make them "feel guilty for not voting for you [Coble] if Ronald Reagan wants you to."[57]

Although there was heavy GOP registration in Britt's district, there were not enough Republicans to win the election. Conservative Democrats with a potential for ticket splitting also must be reached—but through televised appeals, which are more broad gauged than those included in direct mail. Coble's communications objectives could not be achieved without money. Further, fund-raising was perceived to be a major problem in 1984, with well over $20 million going into the Hunt-Helms Senate races and $7 million into a spirited gubernatorial race. A June-July campaign poll indicating that Coble was low on districtwide name recognition and running 31 percent to Britt's 57 percent created further fund-raising difficulties. The incumbent was "the big gun. It was a hard fight for us because he hadn't done that badly, or at least many businesses thought he would win and argued, 'We can work to improve him.' "[58]

In short, the campaign was having difficulty with the fund-raising community.

Under these circumstances, Coble's media consultant, Lou Kitchen, who was also southern regional chairman for Reagan-Bush, recommended an abortion ad. The idea was to produce an ad opposing federal funding of abortion, which was heavily opposed in the district, contrasting Coble's position with that of Britt. The woman who appeared in the ad, and whose motherhood was allegedly threatened by Britt's views on abortion, looked as if the baby might be born right then and there. "Here's one person who's going to vote for Coble," she said, but then patted her protruding abdomen and added, "no, two." If Coble's vote was not thus exponentially doubled following its airing, his name recognition was. According to Kitchen, "it got the campaign underway."[59]

Personally, however, Kitchen said he found the ad objectionable, and Murphy later argued that such an ad should not be run again. Kitchen said he was traveling with President Reagan when it was cut, took one look at "that woman's big tummy" and called for it to be pulled, concluding that there were differences in taste between Atlanta, his homebase, and Greensboro, North Carolina. News stories offered heavy coverage of the airing of the ad, increasing viewer awareness of the race, making a race of it, however. Britt's protest that Coble had voted *for* abortion in the state legislature and so had no right to criticize the incumbent was not translated into response advertising and did not make it into the ongoing news coverage, which focused on the airing of the ad in stories that established the uniqueness of such an event in the life of a now more interesting bachelor legislator. The abortion ad ran only briefly, but it lived on in the news coverage.[60]

NEGATIVE ADVERTISING IS THUS EFFECTIVE

Money was raised—in the end Coble spent $372,231 to Britt's $472,199— and heavy advertising followed in August. According to campaign manager Patrick Murphy, Coble spent nearly half of his total television budget in the first two and a half weeks of August. One August ad linked Britt with tax raisers. A second was the Harvard ad, and a third was a soft-sell negative ad that incorporated the catchy tune "Downhill Racer," suggesting that Britt was part of a spending process that was out of control. Demonstrating the effectiveness of negative advertising, into which the campaign put much of its resources, Murphy believed that by the end of August the incumbent was "defending himself on our issues." Britt's 26-point lead in July disappeared as his supporters joined the undecided, and Coble advanced to within a competitive 10 points.[61]

The Britt campaign attempted to counterattack with a Social Security spot, but Coble had run a preemptive "inoculation" spot on the issue of the type researchers have proven effective, before the Britt campaign got to it. It was a downhome trust spot featuring the candidate's family—following in the tradition of Massachusetts Democratic congressman Barney Frank's 1982 ad that featured his mother carrying the attack message on Social Security. In this 1984 version of the family trust spot Mom and Pop "inoculated" their son against such attacks, in the unique language of the North Carolina Piedmont. Indeed, should the Republican candidate even *think* of tampering with Social Security, they would "take a switch to him." The ad ran heavily on the programs that the elderly watched and on the Sunday religious programming.[62]

Murphy believed that this ad, together with a presidential Social Security "rescue" plan, which had received heavy news coverage, mitigated the effects of the subsequent combined news and advertising attack that Britt launched on the issue: "They brought in Claude Pepper, but a lot of people had gotten the idea by that point that this was demogoguery." Britt's Tanner agreed: "Social Security didn't cut for us. The Republicans did a good job of . . . reassuring people that the issue had been taken care of, so that it appeared that we were 'demagoguing,' which we were."[63]

In short, like Levitas, assisted by a major presidential-level media consultant, the Coble campaign simply ran a more effective campaign. This involves early negative advertising and controlling the message agenda on television in both news and advertising in relation to one's own as well as the opponent's issues. Coble won a 51 to 49 percent victory, by 2,662 votes, and was narrowly able to withstand a rematch in 1986 in a year of Democratic gains.

A DIFFERENT STRATEGY FOR AN INCUMBENT IN TROUBLE

Next door to Britt, in North Carolina's tobacco-and-textiles Fifth District, long-term Democratic incumbent Steve Neal was in trouble in 1984. The district is dominated by Neal's home town of Winston-Salem and surrounding Forsyth County, which together cast just under half the total vote. In the hill counties to the north and west there is a strong Republican tradition among the small farms and fruit orchards.

A former mortgage banker and publisher, Neal had arrived in Congress with the Watergate class of 1974 after a narrow 52 percent victory over a popular four-term Republican congressman, Wilmer D. "Vinegar Ben" Mizell, a former National League pitcher. He beat Mizell by 54 percent in a rematch two years later, but he never exceeded that percentage until 1982, when he received 60 percent. Now in 1984 the Republican tide was running strong in North Carolina, thanks to Reagan's name at the top of the ballot and a trend toward voting a straight GOP ticket during presidential election years.

Neal had risen swiftly in seniority on the House Banking Committee, where he ranked fifth among 28 Democrats. Because of a fluke number of retirements and election defeats, he had chaired its Subcommittee on International Trade, Investment and Monetary Policy since his first term in Congress and also had considerable seniority on the House Government Operations Committee. Early in his career a major legislative accomplishment had been blocking the construction of a dam on the New River, which flows from North Carolina into Virginia, preserving the considerable scenic beauty of one of the oldest rivers on earth. Neal generally voted with the Democratic leadership in the House and in 1984 gave only 51 percent support to the Republican-southern "conservative coalition." He usually registered in the midrange of support for both the ADA and the ACA positions on legislation.

Neal's narrow 51 percent victory in 1980, the first time Reagan had headed the ticket, put him on the vulnerable lists of the national PAC's, and his district, like those of Britt and Levitas, was targeted for a high level of national

Republican party involvement. His fundamentalist opponent was Christian broadcast station owner Stuart Epperson, who did not respond to requests for an interview about advertising strategies. Epperson began his campaign by using media to attack from a "Christian" perspective, stressing the need for a congressman who represented the district on such religious and cultural issues as prayer in the schools. He also toured the district's media markets with a lantern, inquiring whether anyone had seen the congressman.

In 1984 Neal was perhaps less visible than in previous years in the district and his House committee assignments were clearly "Washington" ones. In previous elections a constituent mailing of his entire voting record had been followed with generally positive television advertising. In the 1984 ad sample, however, by contrast with Levitas and Britt, who followed classic advice to stay positive, Neal's advertising reflected a desire to target both his advertising and news messages to the character of his opponent.

In a hard-sell negative ad that ran frequently, he described his opponent as a man with a "record." The ad fit into the harsh advertising menu of the 1984 North Carolina ad sample, as a knife-edged voice intoned that Stuart Epperson may not have had a record "before," but "now he does." It's a "record of deception and deceit." He may never have been elected to any public office, but he has nevertheless compiled a record—one of distortion of Neal's record on such issues as taxes and protection of the local textile industry. In an interview with television reporters that ran at the same time, Neal described Epperson as having "no record of accomplishment, service, or understanding."

The "Man with a Record" ad was a response to Epperson's hard-sell negative advertising barrage accusing Neal of misusing his leadership role on the House Banking Committee to vote for U.S. contributions to the International Monetary Fund (IMF), thereby encouraging that very foreign competition which was costing North Carolina's textile workers their jobs. Local mill employment was declining and such an attack had considerable potential.

The Epperson attack further illustrates how issues and character messages can commingle in an advertising appeal. The ads were theoretically about votes, but on the character side they implied that the incumbent was *hiding* his vote for the IMF, an inference extended to "higher taxes" as the campaign moved on to connect a local attention-getting charge with the broader current of national Republican advertising. These hard-sell negative spots included harsh sound effects, which underscored not only their point about Neal's alleged character flaw—deceitfulness in hiding his votes—but his unwillingness to debate the challenger as the ad campaign moved into a new phase, an unwillingness that comprised "proof" of the deceitfulness charge.

WHY UNANSWERED NEGATIVE ADVERTISING WORKS

William Taylor, Neal's campaign manager, spoke of the reason for Neal's sharp reply to Epperson's ads. It was necessary to fight fire with fire because "negative advertising works." There will always be a small percentage of the population who believe what they see on television, thinking, mistakenly, that political ads, like product advertising, may exaggerate but they don't actually *lie*. "Lying," he said, "is the more accurate term. The people who believe an ad on television may be a small percentage of the voting population—5 to 10 percent," Taylor said, "but elections are decided by small percentages."

On all levels [the IMF ad] was a lie, and Epperson was confronted. He was appealing to the emotion of fear that people would lose their jobs under Neal. The ad created fear and was designed to show that if Neal didn't care about textile jobs, he didn't care about any jobs.

On the decision not to debate: Like all incumbents, Taylor said, Neal made this decision early because there was no reason to help the challenger obtain media exposure.[64]

Although Epperson's IMF charge was mentioned in the one television news story that referred to congressional issues, it was the televised ads that carried the issue for the viewing television public during this period of the 1984 ad and news sample. Taylor believed Epperson's ads were responsible for a "glitch" that appeared in the October polls. The campaign's media consultant, William Morgan of New York, whose work could be classified as of the traditional school less oriented to the more high tech ads of the 1980s, also reached this conclusion and recommended a strong response ad. Neal's hard-sell negative ad, "Man with a Record," which played on the double entendre of the word *record*, which could have a (possibly criminal?) character as well as an issues connotation, premiered in mid-October.[65]

Like many Democratic response ads in 1984, "Man with a Record" also cited the popular Republican president Ronald Reagan's support for the incumbent, seeking to blunt Epperson's ads by emphasizing his own support for Reagan's policies. "Record" said the president agreed that Epperson had distorted Neal's record on the IMF. Reagan had in fact publicly declared his support for the bill, after a protest by the House leadership following similar ads used against Democrats in several congressional races. Neal ran his response ad heavily, as evidenced by the fact that it ran eight times in the 1984 ad sample to five for his positive ads.

The contrast with the restraint of incumbents Levitas and Britt, who did not "fight fire with fire," that is, respond in kind to negative advertising, was notable. So were the differences in election results. Unlike Levitas and Britt, Neal won his close election. In the end, although outspent by Epperson $317,773 to $256,685, Neal won a narrow 3,232-vote victory; 51–49 percent, to retain his congressional seat. The campaign community did not fail to learn his "lesson" from a highly competitive district.

CONCLUSION

These three southern campaigns discussed in this chapter illustrate how early negative advertising can be used by challengers in nontraditional ways to break an incumbent's communications advantage, in both medium-sized ("affordable") and major ("expensive") media markets. Such ads are being used early by challengers for two reasons.

The first reason, in stage one of a race, is to gain the attention of the press in a fashion that will greatly amplify the effect of a small amount of money actually spent on the ads. Such advertising can contribute to "competitiveness" in the sense of facilitating fund-raising efforts, which previous literature has more generally associated with questions relating to a candidate's voting record. Also, such early advertising can make a race competitive by raising viewer consciousness of the fact that there is a contest that presents a clear electoral choice. Further, if unanswered—and this research clearly indicates that a candidate cannot rely on local television news to examine his or her record in relation to charges made in ads in a fashion that can combat an opponent's media blitz—it can take on a life of its own. For one thing, ads on the House of Representatives level, during the final stage of an election, quite simply represent a greater percentage of campaign information than television news.[66]

These case studies from the 1984 ad sample have also illustrated the use of the categories of positive and negative ads examined in previous chapters. Negative and positive referential (or theoretically affect-laden) ads, which also dovetail issues and character messages are in common use. Ads also relate to the complex attitudes of individuals in a specific political culture. Thus in the South, highly personal issues such as abortion, religion, "pushy women," and "northern liberals" all made their appearance in ads focusing on character as well as on issues. On the positive side, the "coattails" of a popular president was an important part of strategy.

Did advertising make any difference in the outcome of any of the elections? The answer must be yes. Early on it helped make two races competitive. Later it helped Republicans grasp the presidential coattails, which could be important in close races such as those examined in this chapter.

Strategy also assumes new importance. The Neal race was effectively managed and followed a strategy that would resonate into the later part of the decade. It ran counter to the expected view that the incumbent should "stay positive." The lesson was like that of a similar competitive race, in Indiana: An incumbent who is slipping in the polls will respond in a negative fashion. The result of such races is increased belief in the effectiveness of negative advertising and need to raise money for early advertising, which has been proven effective to "inoculate" the incumbent against it.

NOTES

1. For a discussion of factors that contribute to a congressional challenge, see Gary Jacobsen, *The Politics of Congressional Elections* (Boston, Toronto, 1984). For a close analysis of voting records and contributions to congressional challengers, which led to the view that voting records are the factor that contributes most heavily to well-funded

challenges, see John C. McAdams and John R. Johannes, paper for delivery at the 1986 Annual Meeting of the American Political Science Association, Washington, D.C., August 28–31, 1986.

2. For an overview of the concept of media permutation, see Sidney Blumenthal, "Does Visibility Ensure Credibility in Democrats' Quest for Senate?" *Washington Post*, July 19, 1986, p. 8. He cites a then forthcoming article by William Schneider for the *New Republic* that predicted that on the basis of this "permutation" factor, Democrats would regain the Senate in 1986. It is argued by election analysts such as Jacobsen that this is a factor in Senate, but not in House, races that receive less news media coverage.

3. Interview with Lou Kitchen, southern regional director, Reagan-Bush 1984, Atlanta, March 20, 1985.

4. Ten ads for Ronald Reagan were picked up in the 1984 sample. One was a 30-minute, one a 5-minute, two were 1-minute, and six were 30-second ads. The 5-minute and two of the 30-second ads were coded for both positive and negative affect. Overall, Reagan's ads consumed three hours and 3.5 minutes in the ad sample. Of the 15 minutes of airtime coded for both positive and negative affect, 14 minutes were aired in the North Carolina and Georgia segments of the ad sample.

Overall, 9.2 percent of the airtime devoted to Reagan's advertising was coded for both positive and negative affect.

5. For a discussion of the issues in congressional ads, see Figure 2.2. For an analysis of coding for affect in the 1984 ad sample, see Chapter 4 and 5.

Voter turnout in North Carolina is examined in Mark McDonald, "1984 Voter Turnout Reverses 20-year Slide in Participation," *Greensboro News and Record*, November 8, 1984, p. 4.

6. See also Chapter 8.

7. Interview with Ed Blakely, February 8, 1985.

8. Interview with Douglass Tanner, Robin Britt's local campaign manager, Greensboro, North Carolina, December 27, 1984.

9. Interview with Tim Ryles, Elliott Levitas's campaign manager, Atlanta, Georgia, March 19, 1985.

10. Donald T. Cundy, "Political Commercials and Candidate Image: The Effect Can Be Substantial," in *New Perspectives on Political Advertising*, ed. Lynda Lee Kaid, Dan Nimmo, and Keith R. Sanders (Carbondale: Southern Illinois University Press, 1986), pp. 210–235. Michael Pfau and Michael Burgoon, "Inoculation in Political Campaign Communication," *Human Communication Research* 15, no. 1 (Fall 1988: pp. 91–111. See Chapter 1.

11. Ryles interview.

12. Interview with Elliott Levitas, Washington, D.C., February 1985.

13. Ibid.

14. Ibid.

15. Ibid.

16. Ibid.

17. Levitas and Ryles interviews.

18. Interview with Rob Austin, Patrick Swindall's final campaign manager, Washington, D.C., February 11, 1985. Interview with William Pope, Levitas's media consultant, Atlanta, Georgia, March 18, 1985. Robert Bell, chairman, Republican party Georgia, March 19, 1985.

19. Interview with Gary Leshaw, chairman, Democratic party of De Kalb, Atlanta,

Georgia, March 18, 1985. For "homestyle" see Richard Fenno, *Home Style* (Boston: Little, Brown, 1978).

20. Ryles interview.

21. Pope interview.

22. Ryles interview.

23. Leshaw interview. Interview with Bill Lewis, Democratic member, De Kalb County Election Board, Atlanta, Georgia, March 18, 1985.

24. Ryles interview.

25. Pope interview.

26. Austin interview.

27. Ibid.

28. Ibid.

29. Levitas interview.

30. Ibid.

31. Blakely interview.

32. Austin interview.

33. Ibid.

34. Ibid.

35. Ryles interview.

36. Interview with Levitas pollster Claiburn Darden, Atlanta, Georgia, March 19, 1985.

37. Darden interview.

38. Ibid.

39. Ryles interview.

40. Austin interview.

41. Ibid.

42. Ibid.

43. Levitas interview.

44. Darden interview.

45. Ibid.

46. Ibid.

47. Pope interview.

48. Ryles interview.

49. Ibid.

50. Interview with Alan Ehrenhalt, Washington, D.C., April 16, 1986.

51. Interview with Doug Tanner, Robin Britt's local campaign manager, Greensboro, North Carolina, December 27, 1984.

52. Ibid.

53. Gary Jacobson, *The Politics of Congressional Elections* (New York: Little, Brown, 1987). Jacobson's view was that the genre would be little used because "few incumbents are open to serious public criticism on these grounds," p. 52.

54. Tanner interview.

55. Tanner and Kitchen interviews. Interview with Gene Johnston, Washington, D.C., August 8, 1985.

56. Jim Schlosser, "When Coble Got Gusto, It Paid Off: He's Country and Frugal; Finds Niche in Politics," *Greensboro News and Record,* November 8, 1984.

57. Interview with Patrick Murphy, Howard Coble's campaign manager, Washington, D.C., January 14, 1985.

58. Ibid.

59. Kitchen interview.

60. These conclusions are based on an analysis of the news coverage of the Coble-Britt race in the *Greensboro News and Record* for the months of June and July, 1984.

61. Murphy interview.

62. Murphy and Tanner interviews.

63. Tanner interview.

64. Interview with Jim Taylor, Stephen Neal's campaign manager, Washington, D.C., January 1, 1985.

65. For how negative ads dealing with a "record" can implictly or explicitly add a character dimension, see Chapter 5.

66. See Chapters 3 and 8 for comparative figures on congressional ads and news.

10

Conclusion: The New Mass Media Election

Political advertising is playing an important role in U.S. elections on all levels. It is also highly influenced by commercial advertising theory and freighted with entertainment values and what are described as emotional appeals. It is quite different from the advertising of the early 1970s, which was more heavily influenced by documentary news styles and by the fact that longer time slots were readily affordable and available for political advertising, which moved into commercial advertising time slots during election campaigns.

The purpose of political advertising has also changed. Today it is increasingly part of a broad approach to campaign communication that must take account of the growing electronic media role in U.S. politics—a role that has increased as Americans read fewer newspapers and attend fewer political party functions. Given these changes, and the fact that the electronic media is commercially driven, campaign strategists have moved to develop the "new" mass media election. The relevant metaphor for today's mass media campaign is the commercial message—that of "touching someone"—which influences not only candidate political advertising, but candidate and political party media strategy as well.

Today's consultants do not simply create an ad and launch it onto the airwaves. They must not only develop a campaign message according to styles that can compete with entertaining and affect-laden commercial ones; but in many cases they must also help focus news media strategies as well. The role of creating and promoting messages on television has become such an important one that the consultant may even be, as was Roger Ailes, media advisor to 1988 Republican presidential candidate George Bush, with Robert Teeter, the campaign's pollster, one of the few individuals involved in the selection of a vice-presidential candidate. Consultants professionally responsible for developing a campaign's televised messages are also playing a key role in determining who the nation's top leadership will be.[1]

Campaigning in the advertising era requires the development of a limited number of readily comprehensible messages, suitable for the short "take," messages in which candidate character and issues blend, or dovetail for maximum impact. At least during the final stages of a campaign the issues that appear on the air reflect single-issue or common-thread theory. They relate to a successful role for campaigns, rather than to thousand-flower theory, which suggests that ads generally reflect a broad range of issues discussed in a society as a whole and its news media. The prevalence of single-issue advertising is a further reflection of the commercial advertising principles of repetition and remaining on the offensive with one's own message. Given all the dovetailing or visual, aural, and issue messages, and the repetition of simple issues, it is hardly surprising that recent research continues to find that political ads quite effectively convey their messages.[2]

Commercial advertising values that seek to draw the viewer into an "experience" have also heavily influenced the political advertising community. The content coders in this research developed a set of theoretically affect-laden categories of appeal to help in understanding the experience of both the feel-good advertising and the less generally understood feel-bad messages.

In 1972 there were two major political advertising philosophies, the emotional and the informational schools. By the mid-1980s a distinction was still discernible between the advertising of the emotional school and the greater issues emphasis of a new informational school. The difference was that the emotional school was using ever more elegaic video techniques to create a misty-eyed effect. But both the emotional school and the new informational school of the 1980s used a commercial advertising technique known as referential advertising, which seeks to transfer affect-laden meaning to the candidate from a symbol that already has meaning to the viewer.

So, too, did a third school of media consulting, which had made its appearance by the end of 1984 and had a heavy impact on the entire media-consulting community. This was the quick-response school. It drew inspiration from the short quick "takes" of television news as much as from advertising, and it was more concerned with when an ad is aired and its message than with high-quality sound and visuals. No less than the two other major schools of advertising, however, it used referential advertising techniques. Wheel-of-emotions-style ideas—a variant of the old "get 'em sick, then get 'em well" formula, which is as old as commercial advertising itself—were also in use, by all schools, by 1986. In the 1980s, therefore, by contrast with 1972, commercial advertising principles were routinely used in high-budget, competitive campaigns.

By 1986 negative advertising, which focuses on the opponent rather than on the candidate in terms of both issues and character, was also considered to be a necessary evil by representatives of all the schools, a regrettable but indispensable part of the well-funded candidate's campaign arsenal. It was used in most competitive 1986 senatorial races. There were major differences of philosophy concerning appropriate themes of negative advertising and its frequency of use. But the fact was that its effective use on various levels in the

1984 races examined in this research would engender augmented future use. Thus it was used in most competitive 1986 senatorial and gubernatorial races, as this analysis indicates. It was therefore not surprising to find negative advertising used heavily on the presidential level in both the 1988 primaries and general election. It was credited by network and candidate polls with giving a major advantage in 1988 to Richard Gephardt in the Iowa caucuses, to George Bush in the New Hampshire primary, and, most significantly, to George Bush again during the late-August to mid-September period of the general election.

Given the prevalence of its use, it is important to break the concept of negative advertising down into its component parts. Categories have been developed for this research based on aural and visual devices. These may involve the development of a theoretically affect-laden and values message, even when the ad is described as "comparative" or issues oriented. Issues are now personified through the use of visual and aural effects. For example, the crime issue *becomes* Willie Horton, and it is with this personified entity that a candidate is linked. More research should be conducted on the interaction between issues and visual and aural effects in ads—dovetailing, in short.

But from this research a few points are clear. Two overarching approaches apply on the negative side of the advertising spectrum. These approaches are the substance of hard-sell and soft-sell ads. Hard-sell ads might be likened to a bludgeon. They use strong, dark colors, "scary" music, thumping sounds, insinuating voices, and negatively perceived human or group symbols of alienation to amplify the reaction that the ad—like all advertising—is designed to provoke. In 1986 a variation emerged. It might be termed subtle-shock advertising because, like soft-sell negative ads, it uses bright colors and the sounds and symbols of "life," all of which fit into a commercial entertainment environment. But a shock comes when all this is interrupted by a catastrophe, such as a crime.

By contrast with the "lighter" soft-sell negative ads, hard-sell ads have greater potential for backfiring against one's own client, particularly in the press. This study demonstrates, however, that both soft-sell and hard-sell negative advertising were used by both incumbents and challengers in a manner that campaign polls indicated was effective in competitive races in a variety of statewide and congressional levels in 1984 and 1986. Further, they were used on the presidential primary election and general election level in 1984 and again in 1988.

That early negative advertising will be used in the future on all levels is clear. The lessons drawn from the Democratic primary and general election in 1984, however, reinforced the significance of drawing a distinction between soft-sell and hard-sell negative ads. The negative ads used by both Gary Hart and Walter Mondale in the 1984 primary were hard-sell advertising, associating the opponent with negative forces in a highly threatening fashion. Most of the 1988 Democratic presidential primary contenders, by contrast, sought to avoid a threatening negative association. They did go negative, but they did so using the milder, more entertaining form of soft-sell negative advertising. Dick

Gephardt, by contrast, used hard-sell negative advertising in the crucial Iowa caucus, focusing on all the scary things that would happen if a trade bill were not passed. It "worked" in Iowa, after Christmas, and under conditions of limited national press scrutiny.

However, positive imagery is still more broadly acceptable, and as indicated by the chapters in this book on the 1984 Jim Hunt senatorial race in North Carolina, the Elliot Levitas congressional race in Atlanta, Georgia, and Walter Mondale's presidential race, divisions concerning its use exist, particularly on the Democratic side, where the consulting community is much less unified than is the case with the GOP. Among Republicans Roger Ailes leads the field after his continuing success on the presidential level, dating from the 1972 election of Richard Nixon, to the 1988 election of George Bush.

It is clear from this research that negative advertising *and* what may be termed Ronald Reagan's brand of emotional advertising have become nearly indispensable in competitive races. Few can argue with the success of Roger Ailes's effort in these areas on behalf of George Bush on the presidential level. On lower levels, challengers who fail to raise money to pay for negative advertising, such as Art Smith in western Indiana and Art Watkins in Indianapolis in 1984, may be doomed to defeat.

An analysis of the North Carolina races indicates that negative advertising can also be used to spiral the competitiveness of races upward—and public repugnance as well. Hunt-Helms was not an anomaly in the U.S. political system. That race redefined how negative advertising can be used in a fashion that is perceived to be "fair," and how wheel-of emotions, mythic, positive advertising, and media blitz strategies can be used effectively in a negative campaign.

A further lesson from all levels supported by an increasing body of academic research is that early image-making efforts are important on all levels. The same lessons were learned on the congressional, senatorial, and presidential levels in 1984. The early battle is therefore on to define not only one's own but one's opponent's imagery.

Nothing in this research, however, in which few serious challengers emerged in the largest media market areas, Los Angeles and Atlanta, suggests that the growing significance of televised advertising does anything but reinforce entrenched incumbents, whose fund-raising abilities and other communications advantages are legend. Still, in Atlanta, Georgia, a successful challenge to Elliot Levitas was launched using early negative advertising, ironically by a successful challenger, Patrick Swindall, who ran unsuccessfully for a third term in 1988 while under federal indictment for perjury in a drug money investigation. In other races, as well, early negative advertising was used to create a media permutation, that is, news coverage, which dramatically increases a candidate's visibility and therefore his or her fund-raising potential. This may be the basis for "shaking patterns of belief" in an incumbent.

Whether it comes early or late, negative advertising is an intergral part of advertising in the 1980s. This is because it "works" according to campaign polls. It may come in a variety of genres, but most are designed not only to present a case relating to issues but also to break or prevent the development of bonds of trust between the opposing candidate and the voter.

On the positive advertising side, the question may be asked whether heroic myths, fables, the candidate as family man—musical and visual devices to lighten, entertain, and build the "ties that bind," and, in the case of myths, to offer a moral lesson—are replacing the "purposeful" candidate, the "benevolent leader" of yore, the Bobby Kennedy, for example, who campaigned with his jacket slung over his back and his platform in full view.

Two principles from commercial advertising characterize the contemporary political advertising that drives the "new" mass media election. The first, which had emerged clearly by the end of the 1984 campaign, is that the ads are individually oriented. This is because political information must fit within a commercial environment. Party symbols, which had disappeared in political advertising a decade earlier as new communications technologies produced a professional political consultancy, were joined in oblivion in the 1984 ad sample by a fadeout of interest groups in all but negative advertising. The second principle is that the media blitz concept, which combines news and advertising efforts according to advertising principles, is now the prevalent concept. The Reagan campaign presented an archetypal example of the effectiveness of such an approach, but the same approach was used on other levels, in 1984, including those of the successful Helms candidacy, which overwhelmed the news coverage with its advertising.

What, then, of television news? Is it still an "unseeing eye," the baleful antihero of the mass media election? Coverage of the issues of campaigns is extremely important, to an informed electorate, but this research indicated that during the final period of a campaign, network and local news still focuses on horserace coverage, and on a category of noncandidate coverage relating to the election process in general, to such questions as turnout and voting patterns. Research during other periods of an election should be conducted before major generalizations can be drawn. It is striking, however, that in one highly educated congressional district a local station competed quite successfully with larger, more entertainment-oriented nearby stations by using highly issues-directed campaign coverage.

A further fact has emerged: Advertising can overwhelm news coverage— whether on the senatorial level in North Carolina over a long period of time or at the last minute in a negative advertising campaign whose impact was doubled by means of follow-up news coverage on a station in a major market area. If such challenges to the press are not possible in all news media environments, future research should focus on reasons for such variation.

Future research should focus on how local and national news, as well as cable, will cope with the challenge of campaigning in an era in which political advertising is playing an increasingly important role. By what standard should news efforts be evaluated in such an era? Should the news effort, like that of campaign communication in the commercial era, be judged by the ratings, or by how many people can be induced to watch? Further, how does the news media report or analyze the candidate's chosen "message of the week?" If it supports any one conclusion, this research reinforces the need for good investigative reporting on all levels.

On one level, advertising has not changed. Ads have always been "catchy" and sloganistic. The difference is that whereas in the past such slogans were intended to draw people to the meeting where they could hear a candidate or his or her surrogate speak about the issues and how they will deal with them, the ads alone, or news staged according to advertising principles, are becoming the campaign for many increasingly uninvolved voters. The ultimate question is what this will mean for democracy. Can one's civic responsibility be adequately nurtured while alone viewing 30-second political messages on the flickering screen? Will Americans be satisfied with a video-oriented political culture, in which, as Tony Schwartz commented, Americans don't learn to read, or study geography, because they don't need to?

The debate concerning the responsibility for creating a "serious" electorate will increasingly be joined. From the campaign perspective, if the U.S. public will not watch more serious issues-oriented campaign efforts or further discussions, why should campaigns be expected to develop such messages, which will only play to an empty house?

There are other ethical questions that should be raised Ads may tell the truth, but it is frequently not the whole truth. The danger of giving half-truth more than its due is quite real, particularly in a video world in which truth, fiction, and fabrication already commingle. This is a problem that all—candidates, consultants, press, educators, and certainly most of all voters—must confront squarely.

One final conclusion relates to the fact that political advertising, like its commercial counterpart, now appeals to the individual in his or her own right, not as a member of an economic or social class, a political party, or other institution above the family level. While a party may target southern whites, or blue-collar voters, or western independents, the advertising appeal will employ qualities that are universal and yet deeply felt by the individual, such as patriotism, regional pride, or family values.

The commercial world will continue to influence televised political appeals as long as politics is conducted on a commercial medium. Whatever direction they may take, future mass media elections will respond to the merger of politics and commercial advertising principles.

NOTES

1. "CBS Evening News," August 17, 1988.

2. Marion Just, "30 Seconds or 30 Minutes?" Paper delivered at the Midwestern Political Science Association Conference, Chicago, Illinois, April 14–16, 1988.

APPENDIXES

APPENDIX A
CAMPAIGN CONSULTANTS WITH RESPONSIBILITY FOR THE MEDIA

The following consultants were either interviewed by the author or their methodological statements, delivered at various conferences in Washington, D.C., between 1984 and 1988, were examined. Their conference appearances were frequently accompanied by illustrations of their work. Many of their 1986 campaign ads were viewed in the course of the author's preparation of the film *Political Advertising Classics 1986,* for which a total of over 2,000 ads were reviewed.

Jill Buckley
Steve Sandler
Deno Seder
Betsy & Ian Weinschel
Michael Murphy   polling
Doug Schoen   polling
Paul Maslin   polling
Richard Wirthlin   polling
Gary Nordlinger
Stanley Greenberg   focus groups
Jeff Browne
Robert Goodman
Adam Goodman
Roger Stone
John Franzen
Scott Swensen (Moore, Hoch & Hughes)
Ed Blakely
Frank Greer
Don Ringe
Ben Goddard
Peter Fenn
Tom Edmonds
Judy Vaughn Fraser
Chris Mottola
Michael Fenenbock
Richard Leone
Dan Payne
Mike Fernandez
David Sawyer

Robert Squier

Roger Ailes

Dick Dresner & Dick Sykes

Robert Beckel

Lou Kitchen

Raymond Strother

Joel Bradshaw

Frank Tobe

Robert Shrum

Frank Luntz   polling

Paul Sipple

Karl Struble

The following media consultants and other individuals were interviewed by the author with particular reference to strategic considerations in a sample of 110 ads broadcast in Georgia, California, North Carolina, and Indiana during the final eight days of the 1984 campaign. If not a consultant, other identification is provided.

Party officials connected with political advertising, interviewed in Washington, D.C.:

Mark Johnson and Tom Ryder, Democratic Congressional Campaign Committee

Will Marshall, Democratic Leadership Council (press secretary with Hunt Senate campaign in North Carolina)

Randy Moorehead and Steve Nix, Republican National Congressional Committee

Paul Curcio, Republican Campaign Committee, liaison with media consultants

Atlanta, Georgia

Pat McKemie

Bill Pope

Tim Ryles

Claiburn Darden

Gerald Johnson, candidate

Lansing Lee, chair, Democratic party

Bob Bell, chair, Republican party

Elliot Levitas, Democratic congressman defeated in 1984

Rob Austin, campaign manager

California

William Zimmerman

Stuart Mollrich

Peter Broderick

Michael Berman

Mike Gage

Jules Radcliff

Carlos Moorhead, Republican congressman

North Carolina

Russell Walker, former Democratic party official

Dick Carlton, campaign manager

Mike McLister (on tape given by campaign manager)

Chris Shields, press secretary

Gene Johnston, former Republican congressman

Doug Tanner, campaign manager

Patrick Murphy, campaign manager

Gary Pearce

Joe Grimsley (Hunt campaign manager)

Jim Taylor, campaign manager

Television station managers in Winston-Salem, Greensboro, and High Point

Indiana

Wayne Townsend, gubernatorial candidate

William Schrieber, Democratic caucus

Larry McKee, Democratic State Committee

Larry Conrad, former gubernatorial candidate

Andy Jacobs, Democratic congressman

Ken McKenzie, congressional candidate

Ron Hardman, campaign manager, consultant

James W. Beatty, campaign manager

Gordon Durnil, chairman, Indiana Republican Party

Ed Mahern, campaign manager

Ray Scheelie, statewide candidate and consultant

Greg Fleetwood, Democratic consultant

Dick Dresner & Dick Sykes

Television station owners, advertising manager, and local newspaper reporter in West Lafayette-Lafayette

APPENDIX B
DATA FOR THE 1984 AD AND NEWS SAMPLE

Table B.1
The 1984 Ad Sample by Type: Number, Total Time, and Percentage

	All Ads (315 minutes)		California (19.5 min)		Georgia (57 min)		Indiana (63 min 40 sec)		North Carolina (174 min 50 sec)	
10 sec	3 30 sec	0.002%					1 10 sec	0.003%		
30 sec	289 144.5 min	45.9%	39 19.5 min	100%	34 17 min	29.8%	57 28.5 min	44.8%	2 20 sec	0.002%
5 min	4 20 min	6.3%			2 10 min	17.5%	1 5 min	7.9%	159 79.5 min	45.4%
30 min	5 150 min	47.6%			1 30 min	52.6%	1 30 min	47.2%	1 5 min	2.9%
									3 90 min	51.4%

Table B.2
The 1984 Ad Sample by Subject: Total Time and Percentage

	All Ads (315 minutes)		California (19.5 min)		Georgia (57 min)		Indiana (63 min 49 sec)		North Carolina (174 min 50 sec)	
President	166.5 min	52.9%	10 min	51.3%	45 min	78.9%	39.5 min	62%	72 min	41.1%
U.S. Senate	63 min	20%			5 min	8.8%			58 min	33..1%
U.S. House	27.5 min	8.7%	0.5 min	2.6%	3.5 min	6.1%	5.5 min	8.6%	18 min	10.3%
State-wide	22 min	7%					7.5 min	11.8%	18 min	10.3%
Local	9.5 min	3%					8.5 min	13.3%	1 min	0.4%
Proposition	8.5 min	2.7%	8.5 min	43.6%						
Generic	14.5 min	4.6%	0.5 min	2.6%	3.5 min	6.1%	1.5 min	2.3%	9 min	5.1%
Vote	3.5 min	1.1%					1 min 10 s	1.8%	2 min 20 s	1.5%

Table B.3

Comparison of Total Time Devoted to Ads and News: President, U.S. Senate, U.S. House, and Overall

	All States		California		Georgia		Indiana		NorthCarolina	
	Ad Time	News Time	Ad Time	News Time	Ad Time	News Time	Ad Time	News Time	Ad Time	News Time
President	166.5 min	40 min 4 sec	10 min	24 min 39 sec	45 min	9 min 46 sec	39 .5 min	5 min 4 sec	72 min	35 sec
U.S. Senate	63 min	11 min 32 sec			5 min				58 min	11 min 32 sec
U.S. House	27.5 min	17 min 5 sec	30 sec		3.5 min	8 min 52 sec	5.5 min		18 min	8 min 13 sec
Overall	315 min	174 min 21sec	19.5 min	47 min 53 sec	57 min	44 min 21 sec	63 min 40 sec	43 min 8 sec	174 min50 sec	38 min 59 sec

Table B.4
News in the 1984 Sample

	All States (174 min 21 sec)		California (47 min 53 sec)	Georgia (44 min 21 sec)	Indiana (43 min 8 sec)	North Carolina (38 min 59 sec)
President	40 min 4 sec	22.9%	24 min 39 sec	9 min 46 sec	5 min 4 sec	35 sec
U.S. Senate	11 min 32 sec	6.6%				11 min 32 sec
U.S. House	17 min 5 sec	9.8%		8 min 52 sec		8 min 13 sec
State-wide	33 min 41 sec	19.3%		1 min 11 sec	25 min 58 sec	6 min 32 sec
Local	9 min 39 sec	5.6%		7 min 4 sec	2 min 35 sec	
Proposition	1 min 51 sec	1.1%	1 min 51 sec			
Non-candidate	51 min 17 sec	29.4%	17 min 41 sec	13 min 41 sec	9 min 5 sec	10 min 50 sec
General	5 min 30 sec	3.2%		3 min 47 sec	26 sec	1 min 17 sec
Editorial	2 min 3 sec	1.1%	2 min 3 sec			
Vice President	1 min 39 sec	1%	1 min 39 sec			

APPENDIX C
PROFILE OF THE 1986 AD SAMPLE*

Gubernatorial	146
Other statewide	25
U.S. Senate	210
Congressional	188
Total	569

GUBERNATORIAL RACES

This sample included 146 ads for the following candidates in 17 competitive races and 4 noncompetitive races:

Competitive

Alabama   Guy Hunt, R

Arizona   Carolyn Warner, D

Colorado   Roy Romer, D

Connecticut   Bill O'Neill, D, and Julie D. Belaga, R

Florida   Bob Martinez, R, and Steve Pajic, D

Kansas   Tom Docking, R

Maine   John McKernan, R

Minnesota   Rudy Perpich, DFL, and Cal R. Ludeman, R

Nebraska   Kay Orr, R

New Hampshire   John H. Sununu, R

Oregon   Neal Goldschmidt, D, and Norma Paulus, R

Pennsylvania   Bob Casey, D

South Carolina   Carroll A. Campbell, Jr., R

Texas   Bill Clements, R, and Mark White, D

Vermont   Madeline M. Kunin, D

Wisconsin   Tommy G. Thompson, R

Wyoming   Mike Sullivan, D

Noncompetitive

California   George Deukmejian, R

Massachusetts   Mike Dukakis, D

Ohio   Richard F. Celeste, D

Rhode Island   Edward DiPrete, R

Six ads were included from gubernatorial primary candidates and 19 from races for lieutenant governor and state attorney general.

*Selected for analysis from over 2,000 ads reviewed.

U.S. SENATE RACES

This sample included 210 ads for the following candidates in 16 competitive races and 6 non-competitive races.

Competitive

Alabama   Jeremiah Denton, R

Alaska   Frank Murkowski, R

California   Alan Cranston, D, and Ed Zschau, R

Colorado   Tim Wirth, D

Florida   Paula Hawkins, R

Georgia   Wyche Fowler, D, and Mac Mattingly, R

Idaho   Steve Symms, R, and John V. Evans, D

Louisiana   John Breaux, D, and W. Henson Moore, R

Maryland   Barbara Mikulski, D, and Linda Chavez, R

Missouri   Kit Bond, R, and Harriett Woods, D

New York   Alfonse D'Amato, R

North Dakota   Kent Conrad, D

Oklahoma   James R. Jones, D

Pennsylvania   Bob Edgar, D

South Dakota   Tom Daschle, D, and Jim Abdnor, R

Washington   Brock Adams, D

Noncompetitive

Arizona   John McCain, R

Arkansas   Asa Hutchinson, R

New Hampshire   Warren Rudman, R

Ohio   John Glenn, D

South Carolina   Ernest F. Hollings, D, and Henry D. Mc-Master, R

Vermont   Patrick Leahy, D

Bibliography

Aden, Roger C. "Televised Political Advertising: A Review of the Literature on 'Spots.' " Paper presented at the International Communication Association Convention, New Orleans, 1988.

Armstrong, Richard. *The Next Hurrah: The Communications Revolution in American Politics.* New York: William Morrow, 1988.

Arterton, Christopher. *Financing the Presidential Campaigns: An Examination of FECA on the Conduct of Presidential Campaigns.* Cambridge, Mass.: John F. Kennedy School of Government, Harvard University, 1982.

Beiler, David. *Political Advertising Classics,* Campaigns and Elections Handbook. Washington, D.C., 1987.

Clarke, Peter, and Susan H. Evans. *Covering Campaigns: Journalism in Congressional Elections,* Stanford, Calif.: Stanford University Press, 1983.

Cundy, Donald T. "Political Commercials and Candidate Image: The Effect Can Be Substantial." In *New Perspectives on Political Advertising,* edited by Lynda Lee Kaid, Dan Nimmo, and Keith R. Sanders. Carbondale: Southern Illinois University Press, 1986.

Davidson, Dorothy K. "Toward a Theory of Videostyle: Three Hurdles to Election." Paper presented at the meeting of the Southwestern Social Science Association, Dallas, 1981.

Devlin, L. Patrick. "Contrasts in Presidential Campaign Commercials in 1980." *Political Communication Review* 7 (1982): 1–38.

Devlin, L. Patrick. "An Analysis of Presidential Television Commercials, 1952–1984." In *New Perspectives on Political Advertising,* edited by Lynda Lee Kaid, Dan Nimmo, and Keith R. Sanders. Carbondale: Southern Illinois University Press, 1986.

Devlin, L. Patrick. "Reagan's and Carter's Ad Men Review the 1980 Television Campaigns." *Communication Quarterly* 30 (1981): 3–12.

Diamond, Edwin, and Stephen Bates. *The Spot: The Rise of Political Advertising on Television.* Second edition. Cambridge, Mass.: MIT Press, 1988.

Edelman, Murray. *The Symbolic Uses of Politics.* Urbana: University of Illinois Press, 1964.

Ehrenhalt, Alan. "Technology, Strategy, Bring a New Campaign Era, and A New Breed of Consultants Joins the Fray." *Congressional Quarterly* 43 (December 7, 1985): 2559–65.

Elder, Charles D., and Roger W. Cobb. *The Political Uses of Symbols*. New York: Longman, 1983.

Fenno, Richard. *Homestyle: House Members in Their Districts*. Boston: Little, Brown, 1978.

Garramone, Gina M. "Voter Response to Negative Political Ads." *Journalism Quarterly* 61 (1984): 250–59.

Graber, Doris A. *Mass Media and American Politics*. Third Edition. Washington, D.C.: Congressional Quarterly Press, 1988.

Graber, Doris A. "Kind Pictures and Harsh Words: How Television Presents the Candidates," in *Elections in America*, edited by Kay Lehman Schlozman. Boston: Allen & Unwin, 1987.

Graber, Doris A. "Political Languages." In *The Handbook of Political Communication*, edited by Dan D. Nimmo. Beverly Hills and London: Sage, 1981.

Graber, Doris A. *Processing the News: How People Tame the Information Tide*. New York: Longman, 1984.

Gronbeck, B.E. "The Rhetoric of Negative Political Advertising: Thoughts on Senatorial Race Ads in 1984." Paper presented at the Speech Communication Association Convention, Denver, 1984.

Grossman, Michael Baruch, and Kumar, Martha Joynt. *Portraying the President: The White House and the News Media*. Baltimore: Johns Hopkins University Press, 1981.

Hellweg, Susan A. "Political Candidate Campaign Advertising: A Selected Review of the Literature." Paper presented at the International Communication Association Convention, New Orleans, 1988.

Hofstetter, C.R., and Buss, T.F. "Politics and Last-Minute Political Television." *Western Political Quarterly* 33 (1980): 23–37.

Jacobson, Gary. "The Impact of Broadcast Campaigning on Electoral Outcomes." *Journal of Politics* 37 (1975): 679–95.

Jacobson, Gary. *The Politics of Congressional Elections*. New York: Little, Brown, 1983.

Jamieson, Kathleen H. *Packaging the Presidency: A History and Criticism of Presidential Advertising*. New York: Oxford University Press, 1984.

Joslyn, Richard. *Mass Media and Elections*. Reading, Mass.: Addison-Wesley, 1984.

Kaid, Lynda Lee, Nimmo, Dan, and Sanders, Keith R. *New Perspectives on Political Advertising*. Carbondale: Southern Illinois University Press, 1986.

Kelly, Stanley, Jr. *Political Campaigning: Problems in Creating an Informed Electorate*. Washington, D.C.: The Brookings Institution, 1960.

Kern, Montague. "The Invasion of Afghanistan: Domestic vs. Foreign Stories." In *Television Coverage of the Middle East*, edited by William C. Adams. Norwood, N.J.: Ablex, 1981.

Kinder, Donald R. "Political Person Perception: The Asymmetrical Influence of Sentiment and Choice on Perceptions of Presidential Candidates." *Journal of Personality and Social Psychology* 36 (1978): 859–71.

Krosnick, Jon A., and Donald R. Kinder. "Priming and the Public's Presidential Evaluations: Reagan, Irangate and the Foundations of Popular Support." Paper delivered at the American Political Science Association Convention, Washington, D.C., 1988.

Krugman, Herbert E. "A Comparison of Physical and Verbal Responses to Television Commercials." *Public Opinion Quarterly* 19 (1965): 323–25.

Krugman, Herbert E. "The Impact of Television Advertising: Learning without Involvement." *Public Opinion Quarterly* 26 (1962): 323–25.

Lang, Kurt, and Lang, Gladys. *Politics and Television.* Chicago: Quadrangle Books, 1968.

Levy, Mark R., and Windahl, S. "Audience Activity and Gratifications: A Conceptual Clarification and Exploration." *Communication Research* 11 (1984): 51–78.

Lewis, William F. "Telling America's Story: Narrative Form and the Reagan Presidency." *Quarterly Journal of Speech* 73 (1987): 280–302.

Leymore, Varda Langholz. *Hidden Myth: Structure and Symbolism in Advertising.* London: Heineman, 1975.

Manheim, Jarol B. *The Politics Within: A Primer in Political Attitudes and Behavior,* 2nd ed. New York: Longman, 1982.

Manheim, Jarol B., and Albritton, Robert B. "Changing National Images: International Public Relations and Media Agenda Setting." *American Political Science Review* 78, no. 3 (1984): 641–56.

Mansfield, Michael, and Katherine Hale. "Uses and Perceptions of Political Television: An Application of Q-Technique." In *New Perspectives on Political Advertising,* edited by Lynda Lee Kaid, Dan Nimmo, and Keith R. Sanders. Carbondale: Southern Illinois University Press, 1986.

Merelman, Richard M. *Making Something of Ourselves: On Culture and Politics in the United States.* Berkeley: University of California Press, 1984.

Napolitan, Joseph. "Media Costs and Effects in Political Campaigns." *Annals, American Academy of Political and Social Science* 427 (September 1976): 119.

Nimmo, Dan. *Subliminal Politics: Myths and Mythmakers in America.* Englewood Cliffs, N.J. Prentice-Hall, 1980.

Nimmo, D., Mansfield, M., and Curry, J. "Persistence in Change in Candidate Images." In *The Presidential Debates,* edited by G.F. Bishop, Robert Meadow, and M. Jackson-Beeck. New York: Praeger, 1978.

Ogilvy, James. "The Experience Industry." *American Demographics,* 8, no. 12 (December 12, 1986): 27–29, 59.

Patterson, Thomas E., and McClure, Robert D. *Political Advertising: Voter Reaction to Televised Political Commercials.* Princeton, N.J.: Citizen's Research Foundation, 1983.

Patterson, Thomas E. *The Mass Media Election: How Americans Change Their President.* New York, Praeger, 1980.

Patterson, Thomas E., and McClure, Robert E. *The Unseeing Eye.* New York: Putnam's, 1976.

Pfau, Michael, and Burgoon, Michael. "Inoculation in Political Campaign Communication." Paper presented at the International Communication Association Convention, New Orleans, 1988.

Page, Benjamin I. *Choices and Echoes in Presidential Elections.* Chicago: University of Chicago Press, 1978.

Rudd, Robert. "Issues as Image in Political Campaign Commercials." *Western Journal of Speech Communication* 50, no. 2 (1986): 102–118.

Sabato, Larry. *The Rise of Political Consultants: New Ways of Winning Elections*. New York: Basic Books, 1981.

Schudson, Michael. *Advertising: The Uneasy Persuasion*. New York: Basic Books, 1984.

Shyles, Leonard. "Defining 'Images' of Presidential Candidates from Televised Political Spot advertisements." *Political Behavior* 6, no. 2 (1984): 171–181.

Shyles, Leonard. "Defining the Issues of a Presidential Election from Televised Political Spot Advertisements." *Journal of Broadcasting* 27 no. 4 (1983): 333–343.

Shyles, Leonard. "Political Spots: Images and Issues." *Video Systems* September (1984): 20–21.

Shyles, Leonard. "The Relationships of Images, Issues and Presentational Methods in Televised Spot Advertisements for 1980's American Presidential Primaries." *Journal of Broadcasting* 18, no. 4 (1984): 405–21.

Surlin, S.H., and Gordon, T.F. "How Values Affect Attitudes toward Direct Reference Political Advertising." *Journalism Quarterly* 56 (1977): 89–98.

Surlin, S.H., and Gordon, T.F. "Selective Exposure and Retention of Political Advertising." *Journal of Advertising Research* 5 (1976): 32–44.

Swanson, David L. "Political Information, Influence, and Judgment in the 1972 Presidential Campaign." *Quarterly Journal of Speech* 59 (1973): 130–43.

Tiemens, R.K. "Television's Portrayal of the 1976 Presidential Debates: An Analysis of Visual Content." *Communication Monographs* 45 (1978): 362–70.

Traugott, Michael W., and Edie N. Goldenberg. *Campaigning for Congress*. Washington, D.C.: Congressional Quarterly Press, 1984.

Trent, Judith S., and Friedenberg, Robert V. *Political Campaign Communication: Principles and Practices*. New York: Praeger, 1983.

Wadsworth, Anne Johnston, and Kaid, Lynda Lee. "Incumbent and Challenger Styles in Presidential Advertising." Paper presented at the International Communication Association Convention, Montreal, 1987.

Williamson, Judith. *Decoding Advertisements: Ideology and Meaning in Advertising*. New York: Marion Boyars, 1984.

Wolfson, Lewis W. *The Untapped Power of the Press: Explaining Government to the People*. New York: Praeger, 1985.

Zettl, Herbert. *Television Production Handbook*. Belmont, Calif.: Wadsworth, 1976.

Index

abortion: comparison of usage in Atlanta, Georgia and North Carolina, 198–99; reasons for selection of as an issue in advertising, 123–24; as theme in ads, 9; used for fundraising in North Carolina, 198. *See also* issues

Abzug, Bella, 109

advertising: absence of an overriding informational purpose, 56; classic versus single issue or "fanatic common thread" theory, 10, 48, 52–54; coding for issues, 51; documentary style, 4; effects, *see* effects of advertising; environment in America, 16; format, 4; issues in Congressional campaigns, 52; issues in National Republican Campaign Committee (NRCC), 52; issues in presidential compaigns, 52, 54–55; issues in Senatorial campaigns, 52; media market selection explained, 8, n. 17; negative, *see* negtive advertising; 1986 sample, 8, 223–25; personalization in the 1984 ad sample, 75–77; personification, 98, 110, *see also* dovetailing; positive, 7; predominance of Republicans in, 54, 56; predominance of single issue and slogan ads, 54; purpose of, 6; triad (entertain, inform, provoke a reaction), 142

advertising appeals, 13. *See also* emotional appeals

advertising categories (typologies): negative, 93–110; positive, 80–85

Agres, Stuart J., 30, 32

Ailes, Roger, 7, 24; eclectic style of, 42; "Hound Dog" ad, 164; 1986 furloughed criminal ad, 109; reputation among Republican Congressional candidates, 164; views on 1984 Democratic presidential campaign, 115, 123

Albritton, Robert B., 5

Andrews, Ike, 140

argument ads, 6

Aristotle, 13

Atlanta, Georgia, 8, n. 17; 18

atomic war, used in advertising, 33

attack ads, 6. *See also* negative advertising

attitudes, 13

Austen, Rob, 187, 189

Bailey-Deardourf, 24, 42, 148

bandwagon theory, in Republican party advertising, 102

Bates, Stephen, 13

Bayh, Evan, 108

Beckel, Robert, 117, 122–23, 125

Beiler, David, 33, 49

benevolent leader, 6

Bennett, W. Lance, 48

biological-psychological arousal, in relation to commercial advertising, 31

Black, Manafort, Stone, and Atwater, 138

Blakely, Ed, 85, 161–62, 183

Boschwitz, Rudy, 38

About the Author

Montague Kern earned her doctoral degree at the Johns Hopkins University. She is an assistant professor at the American University School of International Service and is co-author of *The Kennedy Crises: The Press, the Presidency and Foreign Policy.*